DAVID HARE

Recent Titles in
Contributions in Drama and Theatre Studies

DAVID HARE

Moral and Historical Perspectives

Finlay Donesky

Contributions in Drama and Theatre Studies,
Number 75

GREENWOOD PRESS
Westport, Connecticut • London

Library of Congress Cataloging-in-Publication Data

Donesky, Finlay.
    David Hare : moral and historical perspectives / Finlay Donesky.
       p.   cm. — (Contributions in drama and theatre studies, ISSN
  0163–3821 ; no. 75)
    Includes bibliographical references and index.
    ISBN 0–313–29734–7 (alk. paper)
    1. Hare, David, 1947–   —Criticism and interpretation.
  2. Historical drama, English—History and criticism.   3. Didactic
  drama, English—History and criticism.   I. Series.
  PR6058.A678Z66   1996
  822′.914—dc20   96–5803

British Library Cataloguing in Publication Data is available.

Library of Congress Catalog Card Number: 96–5803
ISBN: 0–313–29734–7
ISSN: 0163–3821

First published in 1996

Greenwood Press, 88 Post Road West, Westport, CT 06881
An imprint of Greenwood Publishing Group, Inc.

Printed in the United States of America

The paper used in this book complies with the
Permanent Paper Standard issued by the National
Information Standards Organization (Z39.48–1984).

10 9 8 7 6 5 4 3 2 1

Copyright Acknowledgments

The author and publisher gratefully acknowledge permission to reprint the following previously
published material: Selected passages from Simon Trussler, ed., *New Theatre Voices of the Seventies*
(London: Methuen, 1981); Chapter 3, which originally appeared in Hersh Zeifman, ed., *David Hare:
A Casebook* (New York: Garland, 1994); selected passages from *The Secret Rapture*, with permission
from Grove Press; selected passages from *The Bay at Nice, Murmuring Judges, Racing Demon, Teeth
'n' Smiles,* and *Paris by Night* with permission from Casarotto Ramsay Limited [All rights whatsoever in these plays are strictly reserved and application for performance etc., must be made before
rehearsal to Casarotto Ramsay Ltd., National House, 60–66 Wardour Street, London W1V 4ND. No
performance may be given unless a license has been obtained.]; selected passages from all other
works by David Hare cited herein with permission from Faber & Faber Ltd., publisher.

To my parents, Don and Jean Donesky, for sparking my interest in the relationship between moral values and history. And to Tracey, my wife and best friend.

CONTENTS

ACKNOWLEDGMENTS

In the years spent working on this book, I have been blessed with fine friends, students, and colleagues who have offered assistance and encouragement. I am particularly grateful for valuable advice from Benedict Nightingale and Enoch Brater at early stages, and from Hersh Zeifman and Stanton B. Garner Jr. at recent stages.

DAVID HARE

1

INTRODUCTION

When Peggy Ramsay became David Hare's literary agent in 1973 because of her high opinion of *Knuckle*, he recalls the following exchange with her:

Ramsay: This is an incredibly important play.

Hare: Oh, you mean it will be very successful?

Ramsay: Good Lord, no. Everybody's going to hate it. But that doesn't mean it isn't an important play. You're on a twenty-year burn.[1]

She was proven right on both counts. *Knuckle* closed after a short run at the Comedy Theatre. And after more than 20 years, Hare continues to burn with rare staying power.

Hare says the failure of *Knuckle* "winded me very badly," yet to be produced in a West End commercial theatre at all at that early stage of his career gave him enough confidence to continue writing.[2] Since then he has written twelve stage plays, four screenplays for television, three film screenplays, and one opera—roughly a new work every year. Few of the many playwrights who flourished in the 1970s have remained as productive in the less hospitable 1980s and 1990s. And even fewer have had their works produced as regularly and lavishly as Hare who appears to have a lock-hold on the National Theatre, which has produced every play of his since *Knuckle* except *Teeth'n'Smiles* (1976). However, it is not only sheer volume and regular exposure in the leading theatre in Britain that has established Hare's reputation as one of the major playwrights of his generation.

In *New British Political Dramatists* (1983)—which remains one of the more perceptive studies on Hare and his contemporaries—John Bull draws attention to the distinctive quality of Hare's work with the chapter title "David Hare: The State of the Nation."[3] Although chronicling the postwar decline of Britain is one of the central preoccupations of British writers, none have done so as consistently and deliberately as Hare. In three recent stage plays (the trilogy about British institutions: the Church of England in *Racing Demon*, 1990, the legal system in *Murmuring Judges*, 1991, and Parliament and the electoral process in *The Absence of War*, 1993) he continues to fulfill the mandate he set for himself as a playwright in a speech given at King's College, Cambridge in 1978: "I feel exactly as Tom Wolfe does in a marvelous account of his opportunism as a writer, 'About the time I came to New York the most serious novelists had abandoned the richest terrain of the novel: namely, society, the social tableau, manners and morals, the whole business of the way we live now.'"[4]

Hare's ability to write about the rich social and moral terrain of postwar England rarely goes unrecognized in critical responses to his work. Robert Brustein thinks *Plenty* offers "a comprehensive X ray of England's soul following World War II."[5] Mel Gussow begins his review of *A Map of the World* by saying: "As a playwright, David Hare is a surgeon who operates on the body politic."[6] The reviewer for the *The Sunday Times* called *The Secret Rapture* "a moral masterpiece for our time."[7]

I became interested in British drama after reading *Plenty* and *Licking Hitler* in 1981. Subsequent study of British drama and postwar history has deepened my sense that there are not many surer guides into contemporary British society than Hare's penetrating X rays of England's soul. The X ray image is apt because Hare is a highly intuitive writer whose sense of history has more to do with deeply rooted and characteristic ways of feeling than with government policies, formal ideology, or the careers of public leaders. Hare could be talking of his own work when he says, in the Introduction to his collection of prose pieces in *Writing Left-Handed*: "If you want to understand the social history of Britain since the war, then your time will be better spent studying the plays of the period—from *The Entertainer* and *Separate Tables* through to the present day—than by looking at any comparable documentary source."[8] Hare recommends reading plays by John Osborne and Terence Rattigan with whom he has been compared more frequently than any other playwrights. None of the work of these three playwrights is notably innovative technically (variations on the well-made play and comedy of manners). What sets them apart is how they register the spirit of their time in the emotional and psychological states of their central characters.

I suggest that Hare's sensitivity to the personal dimension is the source of his enduring appeal to mainstream audiences at the National Theatre, one of the few theatres still heavily subsidized by the government. Hare is as disturbed and angry about what he calls "the deep problems of reaction"[9] in Britain as other leftist playwrights, yet his work remains free of didacticism. This can't always be said of Edward Bond, John McGrath, Trevor Griffiths, and Howard Brenton, which is one reason why these highly accomplished playwrights are more often produced at the fringes rather than the center of the theatre establishment. Trevor Griffiths is the only playwright I know of capable of conveying learned ideological viewpoints in a witty, engaging, personalized way.

I'm certainly not out on a limb with my claim about the reason for Hare's enduring appeal. The widespread perception is that his ability to balance and integrate the public and private sets him apart from his contemporaries and is applauded so frequently that it has become the critical commonplace regarding the distinctive quality of his work. In his review of *Wetherby* Jim Hiley says "he is best known for placing private lives in a public historical setting."[10] Michael Billington of the *Guardian* begins his review of *The Secret Rapture* with "David Hare's great gift as a dramatist is for relating private despair to the public world."[11] Sheridan Morley says much the same in his review of *The Secret Rapture* in which he claims that Hare's importance as a playwright "lies in the way that he seems uniquely prepared to write of the human cost of current British politics. Among his contemporaries . . . Hare alone relates public to private morality."[12]

As these same critics remind us, none of this business about despair and private and public morality would be very palatable to mainstream audiences without the elegance and wit of his writing. Apparently Hare's personal behavior also oscillates between the light and the somber. In public he is very charming and articulate, while in private friends say that he becomes depressed easily and sometimes assumes "an air of luminous exhaustion like a Dominican monk lost in Gomorrah" when contemplating things like the spiritual health of his country.[13] In any case, he writes plays and films with a rare blend: the moral earnestness of a roundhead and the style of a cavalier.

While there is near total agreement among critics and reviewers about where Hare's special talent lies—the ability to relate private to public morality—there is virtual silence about what this actually means. While it's clear to everyone that Hare has a distinctive moral voice, no one is prepared to say what his moral vision is about in specific terms and how it relates to the society in which he writes. What moral values and political assumptions inform his powerful and moving parables of Britain in decline? How does he "relate" public morality to private morality? And what is the content of this private morality and public morality?

The analysis of otherwise articulate critics tends to trail off into vague generalities whenever they try to answer these questions. For instance, in his fine chapter on Hare, John Bull says there is "something else" to be learned from Susan's idealism in *Plenty* "from the sub-text of the play," yet in the end he doesn't say what this something is:

It looks as though, on a narrative level, there is only a choice between the cynical manipulation of the establishment and romantic idealism. The more subversive suggestion can be drawn from the sub-text of the play, that interaction between play and audience that Hare talks of, that there was a possibility of something else happening; that the presentation of English history, is not only that of a pessimistic procession towards decline, but also there to be learned from.[14]

Bull then moves on to discuss *Licking Hitler* without identifying that "something else happening" "to be learned from" in addition to the pessimism noted in Hare's presentation of history. At a later point, Bull claims Hare's work places more challenging demands on audiences than "neat theatre of political idealism" without identifying what audiences might be challenged to think or feel: "Hare's English plays offer not a program for change, but rather a gauntlet thrown down, demanding an analysis that must be made before any thought of change is possible. Their dramatic effectiveness must be judged by the extent to which they succeed in making an audience question the premises of the institutions to which, all radical and alternative politics notwithstanding, it still clings desperately."[15] This is a typical observation about Hare's work. What Hare does not offer (programs for change, etc.) is clearly established; what he does offer isn't. Bull doesn't press on and define the further "analysis" Hare's work demands, the "premises" of the institutions that audiences are provoked to question, or what such questions might be.

The difficulty of talking about Hare's moral vision in positive and specific terms is also evident in several passages from C.W.E. Bigsby's introduction to a volume of essays *Contemporary English Drama* (1981). Notice how Bigsby is impressed with the presence of a "clear-eyed analysis" of the moral health of England in Hare's work, yet he describes this "analysis" in only negative terms, as an absence of "simple" solutions presumably found in the drama of other leftist playwrights:

The England whose alternative history David Hare has been writing, from *Brassneck* to *Plenty*, is a country whose energy is spasmodic, nervous, artificial. It is a country in which private despair is the constant. There are no models of an alternative system, no calls for working-class solidarity, only a clear-eyed analysis of moral entropy, the failure of public myths and private values. And as such, I suspect, he is responding more directly to a national sense of failed purpose and moral attrition than those writers for whom a simple shift in the distribution of wealth and power constitutes a clear solution to problems which are perceived as primarily a product of late capitalism. He does insist that moral collapse is related to public values, and that the individual cannot sustain a moral self in such a context.[16]

The difficulty critics have discussing Hare's moral vision in positive and rational terms is nowhere more apparent than in Bigsby's suggestion several paragraphs later, that Hare's "clear-eyed analysis" and capacity to respond "more clearly" to the moral condition of his society is a function of his ability to evoke the "truth," considered true because it strikes people as true. Bigsby writes: "Hare's real power is, indeed, as a writer concerned with pressing towards this sense of truth, with elaborating painful images of decline rather than with mobilizing a revolt against a class and economic system which may itself be a symptom rather than the cause of disease."[17] The "truth" Bigsby refers to in the phrase "this sense of truth" is a word he employs uncritically from this statement Hare makes about the intimate focus of his TV film *Dreams of Leaving* (1980), a statement that Bigsby quotes just before he tries to define

Hare's "real power": "In *Dreams of Leaving* there are no big speeches or bursts of rhetoric . . . it's not a didactic work. At the end I'll be happy if people think to themselves 'It may not say anything but its true.'"[18] When Bigsby at last identifies what Hare is doing or saying, as opposed to what he is not doing ("mobilizing a revolt against a class and economic system," and calling for a "simple shift in the distribution of wealth and power"), his analysis shuts down around the mystical obfuscation of "truth."

The most obvious reason Bull and Bigsby have trouble discussing the "moral things"[19] (Hare's term for what his work is about) in concrete specific terms is that it's difficult to do, especially in a 35-page chapter (Bull's format) or a 6-page portion of an introduction to a book (Bigsby's format). It is simply impossible to align Hare's moral perspective with a particular movement, political party, or any systematic form of political thought. Nothing so specific as the influence of situationist theory, Leon Trotsky, Antonio Gramsci, or Labour Party policy can be detected in his work as it can in various works of his leftist contemporaries. Speaking of his duty to audiences in the Kings College speech of 1978, Hare said it was "not to give them easy handles with which to pigeonhole you."[20] He has remained faithful to this conception of writing.

In every Hare work there is one or two characters who clearly carry a powerful moral charge, yet he or she remains politically inarticulate and free of any affiliation that would allow their moral passion to be placed in a conventional way. Susan in *Plenty*, Archie in *Licking Hitler*, Jenny in *Knuckle*, Maggie in *Teeth'n'Smiles*, and William in *Dreams of Leaving* cannot be pigeonholed. We are told very little about where they grew up, where they were educated, what social class they came from, or (with the exception of Susan and Archie) about any social experience that could have forged their convictions. Thus it appears that Hare laments the loss of spiritual health in Britain from a moral vantage point parachuted in from a historical and social void.

The central purpose of this study is to render ideologically eloquent what appears to be an inarticulate moral void at the heart of Hare's work. I began to see how the moral "truth" animating Hare's main characters could begin to speak and identify itself when I realized that only in a society in which there were widely held and deeply rooted unconscious ways of thinking and feeling could a playwright hope an audience's instinctive response would be, as Hare says, "it may not say anything, but its true."[21] Recall that Hare said this of *Dreams of Leaving*, written in 1979 when, on the verge of Thatcher's election, England was more politically polarized than at any time since before the Second World War. To invoke "truth" at this juncture clearly suggests an appeal to a nonpartisan subterranean system of attitudes and beliefs.

My effort to render Hare's moral "truth" eloquent is much like Tom Nairn's probing of the concept of "Life" that underwrites F. R. Leavis's critical method. Both Hare and Leavis criticize a spiritually debased present civilization from an ethical position they refuse to or cannot define. For Leavis, the spiritual medicine for his age could be found in the idea of "Life" as expressed in the novels of D. H. Lawrence. Yet when trying to define "Life" in his discussion of Lawrence's *The Daughters of the Vicar,* Leavis falls back on a mystical empiricism—one simply recognizes it in the tale: "The phrase gets its force in the tale, the movement and sum of which define 'life' in the only way in which it can be defined for the purposes of the critic: he has the tale—its developing significance and the concrete particulars of its organization—to point to."[22] In other words, as Nairn says, Leavis wants us to believe that "one can only point at Life, not define it in arid categories."[23]

Treating the ineffable category of "Life" as the starting point rather than the terminus of inquiry, Nairn presses on in a way that parallels my approach to the basis of Hare's moral vision. I agree with Nairn's argument (my alternative vis-à-vis the "moral things" in Hare's work is reverent silence) that Leavis's ineffable concept of "Life" is not symptomatic of a vacuum or void at the heart of English society, but rather it could only make sense within a stable and cohesive "organic culture." As Nairn says: "Though Leavis's guiding notion was that the ideal organic community of England had perished and was due for reconstitution by such spiritual means, he could only preach that idea at all to an actually (if tacitly) existing organic culture—an intellectual class whose pulse would respond to the exaltations of Life and Community."[24]

The question remains, how does one identify and analyze the content of a moral vision that taps into deeply rooted unspoken subterranean ways of thinking and feeling? It seems inevitable that I have come to recognize Raymond Williams, the pioneer of cultural studies in Britain, as one of the chief influences on the way I think about Hare's work specifically and British society generally. I find his methods and critical language useful because he asks similar critical questions of the same cultural terrain: that is, how does one study the complex relationship between culture and society in a country whose sense of unity and identity is more instinctual, emotional and totemic than rational and systematic? Faced with the occluded mysteries of the British political and cultural identity, Williams developed a critical approach that can be likened to aerial reconnaissance followed by excavation. Much like tracing signs of ancient ruins that can still be seen from the air in certain parts of England, he brings the entire culture of an era into view in order to see more clearly the underlying patterns of feeling and thinking.

"Structure of Feeling" is his famous term for such patterns which he says in *The Long Revolution* is the first task of cultural analysis to discover:

I would then define the theory of culture as the study of relationships between elements in a whole way of life. Analysis of particular works or institutions is, in this context, analysis of their essential kind of organization, the relationships which works or institutions embody as parts of the organization as a whole. A key word, in such analysis, is pattern: it is with the discovery of patterns of a characteristic kind that any useful cultural analysis begins.[25]

Sixteen years later in *Marxism and Literature*, Williams offers a more nuanced definition of "structure of feeling" in which he places more stress on the insolution, prerational, lived nature of the patterns he looks for: "The term is difficult but 'feeling' is chosen to emphasize a distinction from more formal concepts of 'world view' or ideology. It is not only that we must go beyond formally held and systematic beliefs, though of course we have always to include them. It is that we are concerned with meanings and values as they are actively lived and felt."[26]

In short, the primary task of Williams' cultural analysis of literature can be defined as the effort to precipitate out and compare homologous forms and patterns of lived experience in society and a particular work. It is a method appropriate for Hare's work because he is an intuitive writer who obsessively reworks motifs and concerns so that clear patterns emerge, giving his work as a whole an unusual degree of cohesion and unity.

The weakness of this approach is that by attending primarily to the essential patterns I may arrive at a reading with the starkness of an X ray: bare bones without the interstitial tissue—the passion, wit, and polished verbal textures that initially attracted me to his work. In trying to identify the strengths of my study, I am reminded of John Osborne's famous statement in his essay "They Call it Cricket": "I want to make people feel, to give them lessons in feeling. They can think afterwards."[27] This book is my thinking about the underpinnings and implications of the moral convictions of Hare's central characters after being moved by their desperate attempts to keep faith with them.

The experience of the central characters who occupy the moral high ground is structured in ways that lead me to believe the basis of Hare's moral perspective is profoundly individual and universal at the same time. The universality of moral value is asserted in three ways: with hostility to any less-than-national basis of solidarity, with the assumption of being very widely possessed at a repressed level, and by being treated as if total and fixed, especially if located in the past.

The central preoccupation of Hare's early work is to expose the bankruptcy of diversionary would-be moral contenders: the BBC and other media institutions eager to support what are presented as fashionable and pseudo-revolutionary movements in the 1960s in *How Brophy Made Good* (1971); movements such as feminism presented as bureaucratically ingrown and sealed off from the rest of society in *Slag* (1971); the Labour Party characterized as full of self-indulgent ideological flashers in *The Great Exhibition* (1972); the countercultural movement of the late 1960s presented as supremely irrelevant to the task of political and social reform of England in *Teeth'n'Smiles* (1976).

In his first attempt to present morality in positive terms in *Knuckle* (1974), Hare universalizes the existence of moral opposition to capitalism with the assumption that Patrick Delafield can succeed as a banker in London because he is able to repress what he really knows: that capitalism is wrong. This capitalist-as-liar equation implies that the moral battle against capitalism has been conclusively won and that everybody would admit this if they were truly honest.

Five years later in his TV film *Licking Hitler* (1978) the universalizing impulse is more explicit as Patrick Delafield's lie is reworked and amplified into a "thirty-year-old deep corrosive national habit of lying."[28] During the Second World War the central character Archie Maclean represses his ideals to survive. Some 30 years later his wartime lover gradually came to understand the national decline as his lie writ large. Again the assumption is that deep down everybody really knows what is right. Morality is a national possession.

In *Plenty* (1978) Susan Traherne moves from a state of radiant happiness as a special agent during the war in France to 20 years of despair in the moral wasteland of postwar England. The abruptness of the shift from full presence to total absence reveals a conception of moral value as something monolithic and fixed rather than hegemonic and a matter of constant struggle. This fall-from-paradise narrative pattern is embedded in less obvious ways in most of his work of the 1970s and early 1980s.

Since the companion pieces *The Bay at Nice* and *Wrecked Eggs* in 1986, the soul has operated as the source of moral authority in Hare's work, most notably in *The Secret Rapture* (1988). The soul achieves universal currency as the emotional equipment we all possess deep down. In *The Secret Rapture* the conservative views of Marion Glass, a junior minister in the Tory government are shown to be a function of her blunted emotional faculties, just as Patrick Delafield's capitalist views are a function of his lying to himself. Both really know the truth deep down.

As for the profoundly personal dimension of Hare's moral vision: passionate, solitary, misunderstood, and passive describe the characters given the responsibility to carry it. In *Knuckle* (the first play with positive moral value) Max Dupree could be describing most of Hare's good characters when he says "Jenny soars above us all. Just—beautiful."[29] Along with her friend Sarah Delafield, Jenny clearly occupies the moral center, yet there is little evidence of how these young women acquired their soaring convictions. The play is set in Guildford in 1973, yet there is no indication of how growing up in the culturally and politically volatile 1960s might have influenced them. And during the course of the play neither woman says or does anything that illuminates the source or content of their moral authority. They are ascribed considerable moral power while remaining passive, ideologically inarticulate, and in isolation from any affiliation. The same could be said of Maggie in *Teeth'n'Smiles* and Isobel in *The Secret Rapture*. Archie in *Licking Hitler* and Susan in *Plenty* depart from the pattern in one way: we know the origin of their values—growing up in the Red Clyde region of Glasgow, and the Second World War, respectively.

The question remains, what then sets these characters apart? What gives them special access to moral values whether they be located in the public sphere or the soul? The consistent answer is their passion and emotional sensitivity. This makes sense if moral values have already been established and if everybody deep down knows what they are. One need only plug into them directly. Emotional impulse translates immediately into universal value.

How could British society give rise to moral experience structured in this way? I suggest that David Hare is arguably the most characteristic playwright of his generation in the sense that his simultaneously personal and universal moral perspective plays out the central paradox of postwar British politics and culture.

The social-democratic consensus, firmly in place from 1945 to about the mid-1970s, was only the latest manifestation of a more enduring paradox that became more apparent under Margaret Thatcher, who strengthened and further centralized state authority while at the same time celebrating the values of individualism and a free market. After the Labour Party lost to the Conservatives in 1979, there was a lot of intense head scratching among leftist intellectuals as to the reasons why. Most agree that the root cause is the undemocratic and unsocialist way the consensus was actually experienced by the average person. Socialist values never took root very deeply because they were never allowed to become a lived practice at a local level. The progressive spirit of the consensus, born from a mass desire for greater social equality and justice during the war, became a set of vague exalted ideals that both major political parties used to underwrite their authority to administer various social welfare programs on behalf of the masses. For politicians and administrators the consensus worked smoothly as long as the masses remained an aggregate of passive and solitary individuals. The history of the left in postwar Britain is largely an account of how the Labour Party resisted decentralization and marginalized individuals and groups that tried to influence party policies. Hence the paradox of liberal or Tory socialism: flourishing individualism under the auspices of soaring national socialist ideals.

Yet this paradox is more deeply embedded in English society than an analysis of only the consensus or the Labour Party could indicate. For three centuries British political culture has been shaped by two powerful and somewhat contradictory traditions: a commitment to market liberalism (more rooted in England than in any other European culture David Marquand contends[30]), and a commitment to institutions and structures of government that place the levers of real power in the hands of a very few at the top. The result, according to Marquand, is a widespread conception of power and authority as something absolute, unsharable, and finite, as opposed to federal and genuinely consensual: "The whole notion of federalism—the notion that state power should be divided between different tiers of government, each supreme in its own sphere—is alien. So is the central European view of democratic government as a process of consensus-building, based on power sharing between different social and political interests."[31]

The more trenchant critics of the undemocratic forces in British society contend that there will never be real power sharing on many levels between individuals and the government until fundamental changes transform Britain into a democratic Republic.[32] This would entail creating a written constitution with a Bill of Rights, reforming the educational system, reforming the first-past-the-post electoral system that produces stability at the expense of being unrepresentative, and abolishing the monarchy and with it the House of Lords and the entire honors system that perhaps more than anything perpetuate the class system. Until these changes occur, it is fair to say that British socialism and even British social-democracy will remain a contradiction in terms. Lack of reform on this scale explains why the ground-swell of radical feelings during the Second World War was so quickly and easily channeled into the old pattern of passive individuals versus power-hogging cultural and political institutions. Fresh new ideas had simply been grafted onto traditional forms.

In *The Break-up of Britain* (1977) Tom Nairn claims this grafting actually gave the old forms a much-needed mandate to continue unchanged. The credibility of the old Liberal Party was exhausted when fortunately the socialist ideas of the consensus came along to renew the hope of working people that they would be integrated more fully into the political life of the nation, which was precisely what was needed to divert them from pressing for more fundamental changes. As Nairn says: "In the guise of socialist novelty, tradition established a new lease of life and the integration of the proletariat into the British state assumed a new level of expression. By then, it was only in that guise that the system could perpetuate itself. Liberalism developed better without the vestment of the old Liberal Party."[33] Just as "liberalism developed better without the vestment of the old Liberal Party," the state at the top found it easier to strengthen its position without the elitist vestment of prewar Fabian and Tory paternalism. Top-heavy, power-hogging methods of governing became re-sanctified under the compelling mandate of serving national socialist ideals. By stopping well short of transforming or abolishing the aforementioned institutions, the postwar settlement ended up reinforcing the twin legacy of three hundred years of history: individualism (with individuals as subjects of a sovereign authority rather than as citizens constituting the sovereign authority), and a centralized and absolute conception of power.

There is no question that Hare's work presents a full-throated passionate indictment of British society, yet in the final analysis he calls for reform rather than transformation. He is a liberal with a tender heart who wants British institutions to be more caring and just. Which is to say, he is a socialist in the only way possible within the contradictory framework of the social-democratic consensus. His characters remain solitary and misunderstood because there are in fact very few ways of collectively protesting the way things are in Britain. His characters desperately keep faith with a moral power that exists as a fixed totality somewhere else, that doesn't need to be created or sustained in the here and now, and that retains its potency as long as it remains free of anything that might fracture it. In other words, they keep faith with a moral power that behaves just as power and authority have traditionally behaved in Britain.

In an interview that Peter Ansorge conducted with Trevor Griffiths and David Hare in July 1974, there is a revealing exchange in which Hare's consensual moral assumptions are contrasted with Griffiths' more radical ones. Hare has just been lamenting the absence of a theatre more hospitable to writers such as himself who want to write large epic plays about current British political scene:

Hare: They really have no home. I regret it. I believe that the public would rally round that home as soon as they recognized it. I think the decisive moment may have been missed. I feel socially that it may be too late. The culture has become so fractured after the political experience of the past few years.

Griffiths: I don't see that the culture is so fragmented. In many ways it's congealed into a number of fairly plastic blobs. It's like lasagna that's gone wrong—great strands of it all congealed together and completely inedible.[34]

How could one socialist playwright believe "culture has become so fractured after the political experience of the past few years" while another socialist playwright believes culture is "congealed into a number of fairly plastic blobs"? The answer, I suggest, is that Hare (although it's unlikely he believes in anything so specific as the consensus) works from a centered common moral ground within consensual parameters and wishes to protect this ground against centrifugal forces such as the prolonged national coal strike in February 1974, or the many single-issue movements that sprang up in the early 1970s; whereas Griffiths embraces a moral position outside the consensus which he therefore views as a congealed glob resistant to much-needed fracturing and real change. In his play *The Party* (1974), the central character Joe Shawcross, a TV producer for the BBC, is paralyzed with guilt and self-loathing for his complicity with the system. His star TV writer, Malcolm Sloman, is even more cynical about working within establishment institutions: "Wednesday Plays? It's the Liberal heartland, Joe. Every half-grown, second rate, soft-bowelled pupa in grub street is in there fighting with you. It's the consensus. It's the condition of our time. Impetigo. Pink Itchy. Mildly catching."[35]

Hare's proclivity to write from the center of the dominant gestalt of the time is perfectly illustrated when in *Dreams of Leaving* he began to move the foundation of his moral authority from the public ideals sustaining the consensus to the soul in the same year that Margaret Thatcher swept to power with a neo-liberal, free market ideology openly hostile to the consensus. One of her most notorious assertions was that there was no such thing as society, only individuals making moral choices on their own. In Chapter 9 I trace (in transitional works such as *A Map of the World* [1983] and *The Bay at Nice/Wrecked Eggs* [1986]) the somewhat labored process Hare went through in the early 1980s trying to work out and test the hypothesis that character and emotional sensitivity are more important than ideas and principles. One of the constants in Hare's work is that he lays claim to the most enlightened position within the prevailing assumptions. Hence in *The Secret Rapture* (1988), Isobel Glass's personal goodness versus her sister Marion's emotional insensitivity played out on the common ground of individualism in the decade of individualism. Twelve years earlier in *Plenty,* Susan Traherne's Second World War experience gives her a critical perspective on the public values of a society that still believed—at least nominally—in the national consensual ideals forged during the war.

In a *Plays and Players* article about Howard Barker, it's telling that when Barker accuses the National Theatre of being a "liberal humanist propaganda ministry" the author Lindesay Irvine immediately mentions David Hare. In the following passage Irvine clearly believes Hare's mainstream brand of radicalism accounts for his secure tenure at Britain's flagship theater:

Even at the Royal National Theatre which Barker ridicules as a "liberal humanist propaganda ministry," there has been little room for plays which resist our populist orthodoxy. It champions instead playwrights like David Hare who, despite massive government subsidy of his productions, is marketed as a radical voice of the left. Serious theatre in this country, much like the Church of England, has reached with increasing desperation for a broad appeal. This has led to a production style which lays the emphasis on entertainment and celebration and seeks to unite its audience in the cosy embrace of an easily understood message.[36]

I agree with Irvine that Hare's radical credentials are generally overrated, yet I also believe that what Ronald Bryden said in defense of Hare's flashiness in *Teeth'n'Smiles* in 1975 is even more valid today: "Rage as it may, the far theatrical Left has nothing to teach him until it has realized that, without success, political purity is as impotent as cheap music."[37] Which is to say, I believe Hare is as radical as it's possible to be and still remain heard on a regular basis in mainstream theatres.

Any radical artist in any country who wants to change the way things are will naturally be acutely aware of two unappealing options: self-censorship within the system, or political purity and marginalization outside the system. The comments of both Irvine and Bryden draw attention to the fact that for many leftist British playwrights it remains fairly tricky to negotiate successfully the contradictions of working within a system they oppose. First, because drama is a public art form and thus more liable to be marginalized and/or controlled if mainstream expectations are not fulfilled. And second, because while it's blindingly clear to many on the left that England remains locked in the powerful grip of "deep problems of reaction," relatively few are prepared to marginalize themselves politically or artistically by actually calling for the abolition or transformation of the deeply rooted institutions (the monarchy, the electoral system, and so forth) that sustain reaction. To do so still relegates one to the loony fringe of British cultural life, despite the rising chorus of discontent from members of Charter 88 (see Chapter 11) as well as journalists, politicians, and political commentators from across the political spectrum who are calling for radical constitutional/institutional reform. As is obvious to anyone who has spent a substantial amount of time in Britain, many people remain largely content with their institutions.

I suggest that the powerful taboo against actually articulating what most disturbs accounts for the perpetual innocence of the "angry" tradition of protest coming from leftist playwrights since John Osborne. Their vehement anger and disgust suggest that they have a mountainous problem in sight, yet their lack of analysis of causes or Band-Aid solutions—a little grassroots activism here, some Labour Party history there to rally the troops—keep them ambling about in the foothills. The "angry young men" phenomenon will remain one of the characteristic modes of protest in Britain as long as playwrights such as Hare continue to battle the political orthodoxy on the same ideological ground without contesting the parameters or foundations. That is, strong emotion will remain the currency of protest in the absence of genuine ideological conflict.

While many reviewers and critics justly praise Hare for the emotional power of his writing, only a few suspect an absence of alternative principles and values undergirding the emotion. In her review of *Racing Demon* Rhoda Koenig of *Punch* notes that what appears to be a genuine conflict in the Church of England turns out to be a clash of emotional styles: "In insisting that everyone should just be nice, Hare wrings his hands so hard that he dampens the entire proceedings with his sweaty earnestness. . . . Everything about *Racing Demon* is so mannered that the conflict between passion and wisdom comes down to a question of style. Lionel's temperateness and moderation is presented as preferable to Tony's pushiness and lack of skepticism and discrimination."[38] Similarly, Graham Hassell, in a *Plays and Players* article, claims that only attitude separates good and evil in *The Secret Rapture*: "'Evil' here is only an attitude, a denial of feeling. Sister Marion, a pushy junior minister (conjuring at the time an Edwina Currie figure), shuns emotion and thinks Isobel's mourning is a way of criticizing her."[39]

Hare's reputation as a radical has indeed been overplayed a bit, yet skepticism should be tempered with several realizations. Although Hare happily works within the expectations of mainstream audiences, the fact remains that if he were as politically uncompromising as John McGrath, John Arden, Edward Bond, or as scornful as Howard Barker of conventional dramatic forms and language, his voice of protest would not be heard to the remarkable extent it is.

It could be said that this book is really an exploration of the sentimentalism at the heart of Hare's work. That is, I demonstrate how his emotive mode of protest is a function of deeper agreement with what he protests against. Sentimentalism refers to the cultivation of the capacity to feel as a response to a social and political situation perceived as intolerable, inescapable, and highly resistant to change. To ascribe moral and spiritual power to feeling and feeling alone in such a context is usually a compensation for powerlessness and often masks complicity. To be skeptical of sentimental literature entails believing that the social context portrayed is not totally resistant to change, that action can have an impact, and that therefore feeling alone falls short of providing convincing opposition. I believe there is room for viable individual and collective action in England, yet the space is so small that any criticism of Hare for not seizing upon it and celebrating it should be mixed with sympathy. Furthermore, as Raymond Williams reminds us in *The Long Revolution*, sentimentalism is something that very few of us escape from: "In rebuking the sentimental comedy, as in both its early examples and its subsequent history it seems necessary to do, we should be prepared to recognize that in the point of moral assumptions, and of a whole consequent feeling about life, most of us are its blood relations."[40] Indeed, who can say their feeling and desires about their society are congruent with their actions and analysis?

2

THE EARLY PLAYS: WRITING OFF THE LEFT

> Mrs. Thatcher wanted "to put the Great back into Britain." A Churchillist, the Queen preferred to hold on to whatever greatness remained. Both worship Leviathan. Both assume and accept as natural as the day they were born, that power is singular and established, its source unified and known. This was the shared premise, the governing idea behind consensus as well as conviction politics.
>
> —Anthony Barnett, from "The Empire State" in
> *Power and the Throne*, 1994

According to Hare's three earliest published plays—*How Brophy Made Good* (1971), *Slag* (1971), and *The Great Exhibition* (1972)—the entire spectrum of political activity on the left had become completely bankrupt by the end of the 1960s. Asked to describe his feelings at this time, Hare said, "I was very pissed off with life while I was at University, and very disillusioned about the activities of the left."[1]

The anger and disillusion of these plays is typical of the dark mood that prevailed among leftist intellectuals and writers in the years from 1968 until about 1972 (when the miner's strike briefly revived hopes for working-class militancy and other forms of activism began to emerge). Although much has been said of Thatcher's demoralizing impact on leftist writers in the 1980s, those with leftist sympathies were angrier in the late 1960s because they faced betrayal and incompetence from the left rather than an aggressive and alienating right-wing government. In the early 1960s all the good ideas seemed to come from the left, yet by the end of the decade it was clear to many that their moral and intellectual ascendancy had been squandered. The relatively buoyant mood of leftists in the early 1960s—revived and sustained by regular injections of hope in the form of the CND (Campaign for Nuclear

Disarmament) movement, Labour Party victories in 1964 and 1966, and the countercultural movement—gave way to a sense of crisis and despair after 1968 when there appeared to be for the first time a complete shutdown of prospects for change on all fronts. The working classes showed no inclination to assume the historical revolutionary role assigned to them by Marxists and old left intellectuals. The Labour Party appeared less capable than ever of realizing the socialist aspirations of those who contributed to its landslide victory in 1966. And by 1969 the countercultural movement had demonstrated that it was incapable of creating radical and permanent change in society.

The events of May 1968 in Paris exhilarated countercultural forces everywhere and led Marxist intellectuals to reexamine and transform their theories about social change, yet the swift reassertion of the status quo in France demonstrated with demoralizing clarity that spontaneous student protests would have a negligible long-term impact. On May 30, two weeks after the massive violent demonstrations at the Sorbonne, Charles de Gaulle dissolved the National Assembly and called a general election. The Gaullists and their allies won 358 seats out of 485. "Repressive tolerance" clearly had its limits. In Britain a similar reaction against permissiveness and political chaos began to form at about the same time in ways that Robert Hewison discusses in *Too Much: Art and Society in the Sixties 1960-75.*[2]

In describing his reaction to the events of May 1968, Howard Brenton speaks for the generation of the left-wing playwrights (David Edgar, Trevor Griffiths, Howard Barker, David Hare) who came to prominence in the late 1960s and early 1970s:

May 1968 disinherited my generation in two ways. First, it destroyed any remaining affection for the official culture. The situationists showed how all of them, the dead greats, are corpses on our backs—Goethe, Beethoven—how gigantic, the fraud is. But it also, secondly, destroyed the notions of personal freedom. Freaking out and drug culture, anarchist notions of spontaneous freedom, anarchist political action: it all failed. It was defeated. A generation dreaming of a beautiful utopia was kicked—kicked awake and not dead. I've got to believe not kicked dead. May 1968 gave me a desperation I still have.[3]

Of the playwrights kicked awake into a desperate awareness of how feeble and ineffective the left was in 1968, none became as jaded about political solutions as David Hare. Instead of guardedly celebrating working-class militancy as Edgar does in *Wreckers* (1977), or offering grassroots activism as a strategy for moving forward as Brenton does at the end of *Magnificence* (1973), Hare dismisses all forms of leftist political activity as irrelevant to the real problems of society. As suggested by the interview with Simon Trussler and Catherine Itzin in 1975, disillusionment with the left gave him a powerful inoculation against seeking political answers: "It's really only as a writer that I've begun to think myself straight, work out for myself the answers to political questions. It's a rigorous discipline, playwriting, in the sense that you need to answer questions which are never answered by polemic or journalism or propaganda."[4] In view of Hare's subsequent career, the late 1960s had a formative impact on how he thought of his role as a playwright: the inoculation against political answers wore off slightly for a brief time during the mid-1970s.

Each of these early plays targets some aspect of the left and the clear unequivocal message is the same: the power of the "real" world—the capitalist system with all its institutions—totally contains and nullifies all leftist protest characterized as striving for pure "unreal" alternatives. Any attempt on the part of the left to dislodge, subvert or escape the "real" status quo is exposed as laughable, ridiculous, and impossible. Although full of clever dialogue, the humor in these plays is often aggressive and crude. Hare's disgust is so strong that instead of a bracing tonic we often get rancorous sarcasm. Hare calls these early plays satires, but satire exposes laughable departures from recognizable standards and values and there doesn't appear to be any in these plays.[5] The lack of positive value is as total as is the condemnation of the left.

In *Arguments for a Theatre* (1989) Howard Barker says "to be a satirist, one must know."[6] Barker found it increasingly difficult to write satire as he realized he knew less and less. By the mid-1970s he started writing plays (such as *All Bleeding* and *The Love of a Good Man*) that celebrate survival, the struggle to know, and at the same time the impossibility of knowing. Whereas Hare moved on to greater certainties. With *Knuckle* (1974) Hare says he started to write "with a positive sense of what I might be for rather than a purely antagonistic knocking of things I might be against."[7] However, at this early point in his career, it's not clear what Hare knew that made him less deceived then everybody else on the left.

The action of *How Brophy Made Good* takes place in London in 1968 (likely at the time of the last and most peaceful anti-Vietnam march in October) and focuses primarily on the career of Brophy, a former BBC television personality, who at some unspecified time in the past had come to the paralyzing and cynical conclusion that despite his efforts to be provocative and progressive, the media had cannibalized him and rendered him unreal and "reassuring."[8] He removed himself from public life for a year after receiving "the slobbering great big wet kiss of death" from the media in the form of an unctuous article by an admiring critic of *The Times* who said Brophy "had brought a new vitality, a breath of fresh air to the jaded business of expressing contemporary mores with a slangy bite that is the authentic sound of my generation, a generation committed to the Renaissance ethic of truth to oneself" (101). Nevertheless, being depressed about how reassuring he had become doesn't stop Brophy from trying to reenter public life to share his bleak insights about the repressive tolerance of the media with Smiles, his former female colleague at the BBC, and Peter and Leonard, two socialist intellectuals.

At the beginning of Scene Three Smiles stands alone and says in a brief speech to the audience that "media are optimistic. Media are progressive . . .

Media matters" (96). Brophy exposes the repressive tolerance of the media after Smiles says she "used not to care" until she visited South Wales with a camera crew and saw the social problems there: "They let you carry on putting out your programs of elaborate social concern. All your probing stuff. . . . Social conscience and moral outrage must be flouted on the screens at all costs. It's the perfect way to keep the public docile. Is that the comfortable chair? It reassures people to know that the media care" (97).

In further attempts to enlighten Smiles, Brophy speaks of the ability of the media to render all protest impure, unreal, and inauthentic. He tries to demonstrate the truth of this by announcing "I like fucking you" while being interviewed by Smiles on television. She says "you must be mad" whereupon he explains that his provocation will only make him more popular. The object of his little lesson is to teach her that there is nothing "pure and positive" about her "programs of elaborate social concern." All is co-opted and rendered safe: "The whole point of your awful shows is to prove how bloody liberal you all are. . . . They have to show they can face biting criticism ha ha. . . . You still think there's something pure and positive about protest. You think that screaming like a lunatic helps. You think that outrage changes things. But it doesn't. Nothing changes" (108).

The most spectacular vindication of Brophy's pessimistic analysis appears at the beginning of Scene Eight when a chorus steps forward and sings a song about how the revolution ceased to exist when "swamped with publicity": "If there is to be a revolution. Then let it happen on colour television in front of a thousand microphones with most people just sitting but an elite commentating and the whole thing mirrored into a million homes. . . . If there is to be a revolution, let it be swamped with publicity, let it cease to exist" (115).

The revolution in this case is the massive protest march through London that had fallen short of Peter and Leonard's expectations. The cause of failure eludes Leonard, yet it is clear to us that his pandering to the media is intended to be a factor as he describes to Brophy how he hired designers from the National Theatre to give his march elegance and beauty: "It was to be a sort of military ballet: very efficient and very beautiful. We got a designer from the National Theatre to draw the charts and maps and they were unbelievably elegant. Little figures, smartly dressed and very compact, making magnetic trips up and down the control board" (116).

In *Slag*, produced a year later in 1970, Hare again characterizes leftist activists as hopelessly striving for a pure, ideal alternative to the status quo. It is a measure of his rapid improvement as a dramatist that Hare finds a much more graphic and focused formal means of exposing the futility of this ambition. The utopian dream of an alternative society is played out as a series of trivial and often hilarious charades within the confines of Brackenhurst, an all-girls school with eight students and three young female teachers, Joanne, Elise, and Ann. In this scenario Brackenhurst is a microcosm of society in which Ann, the headmistress, assumes the oppressively tolerant role of the all-powerful media in *Brophy*. In order to maintain the orderly peaceful functioning of her institution, she tolerates every whim of Joanne, a radical socialist feminist intent on turning Brackenhurst into a pure alternative society without men. Every few minutes throughout the play Joanne announces the purity of her ambitions and exhorts her colleagues to rally behind her: "Brackenhurst inches the world forward. Brackenhurst is sexual purity. Brackenhurst is the community of women."[9] "Brackenhurst inches the world forward. Here at least is a pure ideal. No men" (21), "Brackenhurst is a pure ideal, pure idealism" (40), "Pure feminism, pure love Brackenhurst inches the world forward" (59).

The futility of Joanne's revolutionary ambitions is comically underscored by the unreality of the sexual behavior and speculations of these women. The play begins with the three women vowing, upon Joanne's insistence, to abstain from all forms of sex in order to establish a "truly socialist society"—an obvious take-off on the hollow vows of Ferdinand and his three lords in *Love's Labour's Lost*. Predictably enough, this utopian enterprise soon falters. Ann forgets her vows as soon as a repairman appears. Joanne's claim that the impure male Y sex chromosome would gradually disappear leaving a pure XX female gene pool appears to be borne out by Elise's mysterious self-induced pregnancy until she reveals at the end that it was just a "great wet fart"—an image that sums up Hare's estimation of the accomplishments of leftist activism in the late 1960s.

Having dismissed unorthodox, extraparliamentary forms of activism as totally irrelevant, Hare next writes about the Labour Party in *The Great Exhibition* and arrives at the same pessimistic conclusion. As suggested by the title, the central on-going conceit of the play equates politics with acting, role playing, and exhibitionism—that is, with unreality. Charles Hammett, the central character, is a 33-year old Labour MP (Member of Parliament) overwhelmed with guilt and self-loathing because his generation of politicians bungled the cause of socialism. His judgment is harsh: "I've been four years in Parliament, swept in, as they say, on the Labour landslide of sixty-five. A lot of creepy-crawlies swept in on the froth of that wave. It's like a debating society, some ghastly boy's school, with the whole grotesque inhuman game of charades magnified and ritualized to the highest possible point of futility, the most elaborate conceivable way of not actually talking to each other, of not actually saying anything."[10]

As Hammett is acutely aware, his engagement with politics was somewhat inauthentic from the start. He decided to become a politician while courting his wife Maud with eloquent speeches about socialism. "It became so clear" and "the business of speaking it all delighted me" he recalls (111). As the decade progressed and the gap between the knowledge of what ought to be and what was grew wider, Hammett's self-loathing grew until he decided to retreat from eloquence and public life altogether. The play begins with him in the sixth week of isolation from his constituency and former colleagues.

To reestablish contact with real people Hammett resolves to talk to 19 people a day. One evening he fills his quota by flashing 19 women on Clapham Common—the desperate recourse of a politician accustomed to exhibiting himself in a Parliament full of ideological flashers. We judge his gesture as grotesquely inadequate in part because we have been encouraged to read his flashing as an attempt to break out his isolation into something more real. In this exchange the detective Abel refers to "the people" in a way that suggests they might be the "real" in contrast to the unreal Labour government:

Abel: You might be my MP. (*He laughs.*) The government and the people are miles apart.

Hammett: I know this. (111)

Hammett says he knows he is cut off from "the people" and believes they are more real then himself, yet by the end of the play "the people" have been seriously undermined as a source of positive value. Maud scorns his belief in "the people" and calls it "the last great middle-class myth": "It's Charlie's belief that the stupider, dumber and more illiterate you are the nearer you are to being a real person. It's the last great middle-class myth. Somewhere there are people more real than me" (103).

How can the "real" people be an alternative to the unreal political world of Hammett if they are considered stupid and illiterate? Moments later "the people" get more scorn dumped on them in Hammett's reply to the home secretary's question about why he never visits his constituency:

Hammett: It's a long way and when you get there it's a dump. And the people resent me because I'm not working class.

Clough: They voted you in.

Hammett: They'd vote in Madame de Pompadour as long as she stood on the Labour ticket. (106)

If the Labour Party is an electoral machine supported by the unthinking robot-like loyalty of working-class voters, why is Hammett so guilty? Who did he betray? The "real" alternative of "the people" is further undermined after the home secretary informs him the party will no longer need his services—"Sunderland I think, needs something a litte more authentic" (158). Hammett's guilt doesn't prevent him from thinking himself the best man for the job and scorning authenticity as a criterion: "Why do I have to be representative? It's a hopeless idea. Where are you honestly going to find a group of people I can represent" (159).

The play repeatedly invites us to view Hammett as cut off and inauthentic, yet the possibility of authenticity explodes under a barrage of clever and cynical repartee. How can we criticize him for being isolated from a working class characterized as "aggressively real" in a drunk, stupid, illiterate sort of way? As in the two earlier plays, the satire in *The Great Exhibition* fires off in all directions, leaving nothing standing.

The play suggests another possible source of positive value. At the end of the play, just after Hammett and Maud have been rejected as candidates to represent Sunderland, she has what could be called a moment of enlightenment and seems to speak from the heart. Maud realizes that while she and Charlie have developed superb personalities, they have never actually done anything. The play closes with her proposal that they lose their personalities: "My am is superb, my does is non-existent. People's personalities . . . are little more than affectations. I suppose. If we could just bleach ourselves, lie out in the sun and lose our colour . . . Charlie. Lose our personalities" (161). Her contrast between being and doing echoes an earlier speech by Clough, the home secretary. When Hammett says he doesn't expect anyone to understand why he refuses to fulfill his parliamentary duties, Clough says that he doesn't care about personalities and motivations. What people actually do is what matters: "For myself I've no interest in motivation, why people do things, or for that matter what they want to do. I'm simply interested in what they do, what they actually do. And whether it's good. And psychology being a notoriously half-fart science can't tell us that anyway. So I don't let my motives get in the way" (108).

The Great Exhibition offers no hint as to what good action would entail for Maud or Clough because Hare was more interested in knocking things he was against than working out what he was for. Hare had just spent two frustrating years at the Royal Court and had grown to loathe their staid humanist bias for boxed-in plays in which delicate exploration of character was of paramount importance. Maud's advice to "Lose our personalities" and Clough's dismissal of psychology as a "notoriously half-fart science" expresses explicitly what is obvious in other ways (the enclosed action of Part One, Hammett's self-absorption): Hare intended *The Great Exhibition* to be "a parody of all Court-type plays."[11] This "does" versus "am" contrast resurfaces in his transitional work of the mid-1980s (most obviously in *The Bay at Nice* and *Wrecked Eggs* [1986]), in which he resolves the "debate" in favor of the "am." Twelve years later he embraced the humanist values he parodies here: personality and "being" a certain way becomes more important than political views and "doing." Speaking of his work of the 1980s in a *Plays and Players* article by Carol Homden, Hare says: "Fifteen years ago I said in response to the theatre of the left, you can't write about politics without talking about the deep problems of reaction in this country. Why are the people so reactionary? I've gone on plugging about this, I've tried to define it more and more as an emotional quality in the English."[12] In *The Secret Rapture* and in other work of the 1980s and 1990s the source of and the antidote to reaction can be found in emotional qualities of the English. However, at this early point in his career, Hare's work occupies a moral and political no-man's-land. Positive moral value resides neither in character nor in any form of action.

Anyone familiar with the countercultural movement of the 1960s may have already recognized parallels between Hare's claim that the status quo effectively contains all forms of leftist activism and Herbert Marcuse's theories about the "repressive tolerance" of advanced industrial societies. According to Marcuse in *One-Dimensional Man* (1969), liberal bourgeois states exercise a repressive control over the masses as totalitarian as that of Soviet Russia by satisfying the material needs of everyone and tolerating all dissent except violent opposition.[13] What Hare and Marcuse share is the assumption that politics as a dialectic between opposing ideologies had ceased. For both, the political universe is one dimensional in the sense that corporate capitalism neutralizes all transcendent, oppositional ideas and forces. Like Hare's total dismissal of the left, the terms of Marcuse's analysis in *One-Dimentional Man* are consistently categorical: "In the contemporary period, the technological controls appear to be the very embodiment of Reason for the benefit of *all* social groups and interests—to such an extent that *all* contradiction seems irrational and *all* counteraction impossible" (9); "Private space has been invaded and whittled down by technological reality. Mass production and mass distribution claim the *entire* individual" (10); "The status quo defies *all* transcendence" (17) (italics added).

Despite sharing key assumptions with Marcuse, Hare's prognosis is considerably bleaker. Marcuse's pessimistic analysis springs from a deep sympathy with all forms of unorthodox countercultural resistance. To show how liberal social democracies like Britain and the United States oppress people in ways they never suspected was his way of trying to open up and strengthen an oppositional consciousness, whereas Hare's pessimism appears to spring from a deep loathing of left activism. Marcuse foregrounds the awesome ability of the establishment to oppress, whereas Hare foregrounds the laughable inability of the left to oppose.

It is easy to see why Marcuse's message turned him into one of the favorite gurus of the countercultural movement: middle-class students, anarchists, and hippies found it flattering to be told they were totally oppressed and potentially revolutionary at the same time. In 1969 Marcuse published *An Essay on Liberation* in which he claims small libertarian groups of students and intellectuals possess the potential to function as catalysts of rebellion by virtue of their otherness vis à vis the establishment. He believed that the young intelligentsia had created with their language, lifestyles, and music a form of consciousness in total rupture with "the linguistic universe of the establishment."[14] For Marcuse this new sensibility derived its power and truth from its otherness and transcendence. In contrast, Hare directs his criticism at these potential catalysts of change: Smiles is a BBC commentator of liberal persuasion; as leaders of mass demonstrations, Peter and Leonard would be part of the libertarian intelligentsia; as a young pot-smoking Labour MP, Hammett could be grouped with the potentially radical forces.

According to many leftist British sociologists and political theorists, the essential problem with the analysis of Hare and Marcuse (and of others in the Frankfurt school of mass society theorists) is the fixed and total nature of its categories.[15] Both think of the relationship between dominant and subordinate forces in monolithic, static, undialectical terms. To claim that all oppositional forces are totally contained and impure is as dubious as the claim that there is, or ever was, a pure, separate autonomous space from which oppositional forces could assault the power of the status quo. People are not complete dupes of the system, neither are they capable of living in pure undefiled isolation from the system.

Is it true that the official BBC frame around Smile's documentary on poverty on Wales in *How Brophy Made Good* completely negates her protest against government policies? Is it true that publicity rendered mass demonstrations in the late 1960s unreal and reassuring? Is it true that the efforts of radical feminists to establish alternate modes of living achieved the equivalent of a "great wet fart" as suggested in *Slag*?

The answers to these questions are mixed rather than categorical. In the 1960s the BBC was considerably more liberal than it is in the 1990s, and helped prepare the ground for the countercultural movement; yet its very liberality also helped to set in motion a law-and-order backlash. The third massive march organized by the Vietnam Solidarity Committee on October 27, 1968, in London (very likely the march referred to in *Brophy*) ended with the police and demonstrators singing "Auld Lang Syne"—a reassuring sight for authorities; yet the antiwar protests throughout Britain and American certainly helped to hasten the end of the war. Feminists have not established successful alternative societies; yet they soon scored several successes (the Equal Pay Act and the Sex Discrimination Act of 1975) after they emerged as an organized movement in 1969.

Stuart Hall, in his essay "Notes on Deconstructing 'The Popular,'" invokes Gramscian theory as a means of moving beyond monolithic categories (total containment or total autonomy) to a recognition that in every cultural formation (the BBC, the Labour Party, the feminist movement) there exists a complex amalgam of dominant and oppositional forces constantly struggling with each other, each capable of producing contradictory results, and each infecting and penetrating the other. Instead of viewing dominant cultural forms as "all-powerful" and "all inclusive," Hall says:

Rather, I think there is a continuous and necessarily uneven and unequal struggle, by the dominant culture, constantly to disorganize and reorganize popular culture; to enclose and confine its definitions and forms within a more inclusive range of dominant forms. There are points of resistance; there are also moments of supersession. This is the dialectic of cultural struggle. In our times, it goes on continuously, in the complex lines of resistance and acceptance, refusal and capitulation, which make the field of culture a sort of constant battlefield. A battlefield where no once-for-all victories are obtained but where there are always strategic positions to be won and lost.[16]

In these three early plays, Hare sees the "field of culture" as a wasteland rather than a battlefield.

Significant questions remain to be explored. Why does Hare totally dismiss the left? What are the implications? And what are the continuities between these three early plays and Hare's later writing?

Hare wrote these plays in his early twenties, which partly explains why he was so harsh on the left. At that age it is not unusual for someone to have a clearer sense of what they are against than for. Hare would agree: whenever the subject comes up he dismisses these plays as forgettable juvenalia and recalls feeling at odds with just about everything and everybody during the time he wrote them. He loathed his experience at Cambridge. He found the students pretentious and narcissistic and had little respect for his tradition-bound English professors. His initial admiration for Raymond Williams turned to scorn as Williams retreated further and further from teaching to write books that Hare thought belabored the finer points of socialism in a style full of excruciating jargon and tortuous sentences. Of *The May Day Manifesto* edited by Williams, Hare says "it offered me and my despairing chums a fathomless source of satirical energy."[17] In an interview soon after Portable Theatre disbanded in 1972, Hare fondly recalls spreading massive amounts of aggravation among their audiences.[18] In his tribute to the Royal Court in Richard Findlater's book *At the Royal Court*, Hare describes his tenure there as one long, protracted battle with the leading directors about the political orientation of the theatre.[19] In the Trussler/Itzin interview in 1975 he said he was happy to "consign to oblivion" all his previous writing.[20]

However, these early plays reveal that the essential characteristic of Hare's thinking that endures with remarkable consistency in his subsequent work is the tendency to totalize moral categories. Until the early 1970s, present reality is always portrayed as a total moral and spiritual wasteland with no viable means of changing society in sight. This constant of the early work implies a constant of the later work; that is, to dismiss all leftist activism as totally inauthentic and unreal implies that if Hare were to endorse positive values they would need to be pure, authentic, and real. In this sense, these plays lay the groundwork for the later work, because starting with *Knuckle* (1974) positive moral value also operates in a total manner as a pure uncontested universal/national authority.

The question remains: Why does Hare think of morality in total rather than partial terms? I suggest the answer in this historical juncture has something to do with his being a white middle-class heterosexual male. After 1968 the struggle for progressive change splintered into many struggles as women, gays, lesbians, and blacks began speaking with a particular and local sense of identity and grievance. Having controlled the center for so long, white middle-class males were left defending it. Although the basis of this centered position is not positively identified in these early works, the reflex of defending it is already evident in the way centrifugal forces are parodied and trivialized. Why does Hare identify Leonard, who organized the march in *How Brophy Made Good*, as a homosexual? The implication could be that Leonard's homosexuality accounts for his obsession with the elegance and beauty of his protest march, which consequently became a reassuring spectacle for the TV watching masses.

Slag can be read as a comic send-up of the Feminist Movement that became prominent along with the Gay Liberation Front in the late 1960s. However, Hare counters charges that the play is misogynistic or antifeminist: "It's written as a play in praise of women. . . . The point is that it's really a play about institutions, not about women at all. . . . But it happens to be peopled with women, partly because I would enjoy going to see women on the stage, represented as I thought more roundly and comprehensively than was then usual."[21] Of this passage Ruby Cohn aptly notes that "Hare's own uncertainty of tone—a play 'not about women at all,' who are nevertheless well-rounded characters—is reflected in uncertainty of critical interpretation."[22] The play is clearly about a variety of things, (hierarchical institutions, leftist utopianism), yet it is also inescapably a comment on the women's movement.

For Hare to celebrate or ascribe any positive value to any one of the many single-issue struggles for progressive change in the late 1960s would have entailed his recognizing that positive forces had not been totally vanquished, and that the struggle for change can assume many forms on many different fronts. In other words, Hare would have moved from a Marcusian to a Gramscian sense of social change and the left would not have been dismissed as totally irrelevant. Hare's subsequent work demonstrates that the absence of solidarity with particular struggles produces positive value as absolute as his negative assessment of the left.

In the King's College Lecture of 1987 Hare says that "reading Angus Calder's *The People's War* changed all my thinking as a writer."[23] Published in 1969, *The People's War* offers a highly detailed account of how working people throughout Britain during the Second World War demanded and won vast social and political reforms only to see them compromised in the postwar period.[24] Its influence can be seen in *Brassneck* (1974) (Hare's first collaborative play with Howard Brenton), *Licking Hitler* (1978), and *Plenty* (1978). Calder may have opened Hare's eyes to the formative period of postwar Britain, yet he didn't really change the way Hare thought.

From Calder's account of how the war effort unified the nation to an unprecedented degree behind socialist ideals, Hare extracted a pure uncontested national standard of morality against which to portray postwar Britain as a spiritual wasteland. That is, Hare used the ideals generated as a result of Britain's homefront experience during the war to fill that pure authentic critical space implied by the early plays. Notice how the removal of struggle is the concomitant of totalized value in *Plenty*. The early scene with Susan in St.

Benoit, France, at the end of the war is fully charged with idealism, while all subsequent scenes portraying Susan's postwar experience are characterized as totally devoid of ideals. Apparently when Susan crosses the channel she moves from a totally authentic moral space to a totally inauthentic moral space in which her idealism burns on in isolation from an uncomprehending world. There is no sense here of Susan's ideals being contested in either sphere: they are neither won nor lost. They are simply there and then not there. Whereas the socialist ideals that came out of the war experience were contested at every stage as they rapidly became the dominant values during the war and as they were gradually displaced by other values in subsequent decades.

Jenny (*Knuckle*) and Maggie (*Teeth'n'Smiles*) also occupy a pure uncontested moral space from which they view the wasteland around them. Although their authority is not specifically rooted in the Second World War, it behaves in the same way as Susan's—as an authority that soars above partisan affiliations. As is clear from his 1975 interview with Simon Trussler and Catherine Itzin, Hare wanted to be a playwright with a national rather than a narrow leftist voice. Speaking of the transition from *The Great Exhibition* to *Knuckle*, Hare says:

I felt that in *The Great Exhibition* I'd written a play that was only intelligible to the politically minded, to anybody who cared about the future of the left in this country. If you don't care about that, the play's just a farce or satire—forgettable. So with *Knuckle* I particularly wanted to write a play which was available to everybody—it's about people for whom political rhetoric is no part of their lives. The characters aren't political—or intellectual—at all. . . . The whole play deals with moral values, and concludes that there is such a thing as moral value.[25]

What is this moral value "available to everybody" that doesn't engage one's beliefs in a political or intellectual way? It's the common moral ground of the consensus that provided a vision of national unity and purpose that informed the best sense the British had of themselves for over 30 years after the war.

To return to an earlier supposition about the role of Hare's personal identity and background: In the interview Peter Ansorge conducted with Hare and Trevor Griffiths in 1975, Hare identifies the source of his desire to write of values "available to everybody" when he speaks of feeling rootless compared to Griffiths with his working-class northern background and of his aversion to most "conventional left-wing writing":

Hare speaking to Griffiths: The fact that you can identify with a working-class culture in movement must shape your attitude to the theatre. If like me, you had been born in the thinnest soil in England—born virtually on the pavement—the theatre can come to represent a very important crucible.

Ansorge: Isn't Tagg's speech in *The Party* aimed at precisely this kind of urban middle-class intellectual without any real roots in a working-class community possessing no real commitment or ideology?

Griffiths: In part, yes.

Hare: I have no real choice about rootlessness so I don't really feel that. There's a whole lot of conventional left-wing writing which is total gibberish to me. If I'm to believe it then I'm hopelessly condemned and alienated. There are a lot of left-wing tenets which are unavailable to me because I was born into a middle-class background. I don't actually believe that left-wing middle-class intellectuals are intrinsically shallow or alienated or hopeless.[26]

While Hare is emphatic about what is not available to him as a left-wing middle-class writer, he is less certain about what is available to him. However, as his earlier comments about moral value in *Knuckle* indicate, he reconciled his perception of himself as rootless and as having "been born in the thinnest soil in England" with his assertion that middle-class intellectuals are not intrinsically shallow, alienated, or hopeless by writing plays "available to everybody."

In his book *Literature, Politics, and Culture in Postwar Britain* (1989) Alan Sinfield discusses how the urge on the part of "middle-class dissidents" in the arts, the media, and education to speak for everyone has narrowed and impoverished the range of cultural, moral, and political action and discourse. What these "middle-class dissidents" need to do, Sinfield says, is develop their own identity and recognize that they are only one of many sources of authentic leftist activism:

The 1950-60s New Left were mainly middle-class dissidents, but reluctant to identify themselves as such—hence left-culturism and the anxious revisiting. The shame-facedness of middle-class activists has persisted, and it weakens their effect. Where there is a specific, active identification with another community, on the ground, perhaps, of race, gender, nation, sexual orientation or location, middle-class dissidents may be able to work within that. But generally they should stop trying to disavow their specific constitution, and stop trying to speak for other classes and groups. . . . When middle-class dissidence is recognized as itself, it won't need to justify itself as the voice of others. . . . Middle-class dissidence has to recognize its own traditions, concerns and modes of operation, not to imagine itself as universal or as a misplaced version of someone else's politics and culture. . . . A Socialist society will draw upon economic and cultural modes developed in the dissident middle-class, as well as those from oppressed classes and groups.[27]

This is a bit too easy to say. The problem with this advice is that is seems to ignore the awesome power of the cultural and historical traditions that made middle-class dissidence a dominant universalizing force in Britain. For a gay writer, gay concerns are fairly clear. But what is the specific constituency of a writer like Hare (straight, white, middle-class) who works within a society in which very few levels of solidarity exist between the individual and a national sense of identity? Hare could think himself into a specific community or borrow someone else's, but he would be moving against the grain of his "deepest experience" to use a phrase of Raymond Williams.

In a way that is pertinent to Hare, Williams explains why it was inevitable that George Orwell remained an exile never becoming part of a believing community: "He could not believe (it is not a matter of intellectual persuasion; it is a question of one's deepest experience and response) that any settled way of living exists in which a man's individuality can be socially confirmed."[28]

3

KNUCKLE AND *TEETH'N'SMILES:* NOSTALGIA FOR CONSENSUAL VALUES

> They had feeling and imagination on their side; but they lacked a
> convincing theory to give the promptings of the heart an intellectual
> cutting edge. They could mourn the passing of the old world, and dream
> of a new one; but they could not make sense of the world which was
> actually taking shape around them.
>
> —David Marquand on the early 19th century dissenters in
> *The Unprincipled Society*, 1988

> It's a sort of presumption you have that you're different Joe. That's all.
> Nothing else. And you're not. There is nothing objectively to distinguish
> you from all the rest.
>
> —Sloman to Joe in *The Party* by Trevor Griffiths, 1974

The moral and political authority of the postwar consensus (variously known as welfare capitalism, Keynesian social democracy, Butskellism, the postwar settlement, paternal collectivism) was just about exhausted in reality by the mid 1970s, although it lived on as a compelling vision of national unity for an ever dwindling number of people until dealt a death blow by the election of Margaret Thatcher in 1979. In 1981 and 1982 the Alliance of Social Democrats and Liberals emerged to represent what was left of the middle ground. According to a wide range of British intellectuals (Raymond Williams, Stuart Hall, David Marquand, Robert Hewison, Tom Nairn, Alan Sinfield, Stephen Haseler, and others), the consensus failed largely because the socialist principles it rested on were never allowed to take root as a lived collective practice at any level of society. For reasons deeply rooted in English political traditions and its class structure, the consensus, born during the social upheavals of the Second World War, quickly evolved into a contradictory experience with paternalistic, elitist politicians and welfare-state bureaucrats administering socialist-inspired policies on behalf of people they insisted remain an aggregate of passive isolated individuals. In short, the consensus remained vaguely socialist in theory while becoming individualistic and statist in practice.

Since by definition the consensus consisted of fixed national ideals soaring above class differences and partisan politics, grassroots collective acts of solidarity were either ignored or suppressed by those administering the consensus. Less than national acts of solidarity naturally detracted from the moral authority of the national consensus from which the political parties and welfare state bureaucracies ultimately derived their legitimacy.

For those administering it, the consensus worked fairly well as long as people confined their political activity to a trip to a voting station during a national election. For those on the left unwilling to limit themselves to such narrow parameters of political activity it became progressively clearer throughout the 1960s and early 1970s that the consensus had evolved into a destructive myth responsible for political paralysis and a stifling conservatism.

Perhaps the first rumbling of discontent occurred in the mid-1950s with the Teds phenomenon. The Teddy Boys were young working-class males who appropriated the Edwardian (thus their name) style of dress favored by the upperclass. Alan Sinfield contends that, as the first rock'n'role subculture to emerge after the war, the "Teds were the first significant dent in the postwar settlement, the first sign that not everyone was feeling consensual."[1]

Frustration with orthodox parliamentary politics increased in 1961 when the Labour Party alienated those in the CND movement by refusing to endorse unilateral nuclear disarmament. Disaffection escalated sharply when progressive change failed to materialize after Labour's landslide victory in 1966 (Harold Wilson continued to support the American war in Vietnam, introduced immigration legislation, and shelved plans for nationalization of steel).

For Raymond Williams the behavior of the Labour government in 1966 precipitated a decisive change in his political thinking and practice. As he explains in an interview conducted in 1979, he gave up trying to work through formal parliamentary channels and began working exclusively with smaller activist groups that were not prepared to give up their independence for the sake of Labour Party unity:

In 1966 I decided that there was no future in the Labour Party (I worked from 1961 to 66 actively in constituency politics). The critical moment was not only what the Labour Government did in 1966, but also what happened when we got out the *MayDay Manifesto*. It was directed very much to people inside the Labour Party, and to watch the way the Party machinery shut down was a final experience really. And what I went into after that was attempting to build organizations where people can have discussions and coordinate campaigns, without giving up their group autonomy.[2]

Williams further insisted that these groups establish some sort of unity and dialogue "outside of London and the established organizations" as an antidote to a highly centralized metropolitan political culture.[3]

The massive burst of extraparliamentary activity in the late 1960s and early 1970s testified to widespread feelings and convictions that were distinctly unconsensual. David Marquand describes the mood of that period in these terms: "A growing suspicion of hierarchy, bureaucracy and complexity; a longing for the small-scale and the familiar; a growing demand for wider participation in decision making."[4] It is easy to dismiss much of the activism of that period—particularly the individualistic, anarchistic elements comprised of middle-class university students on their summer holidays—as totally irrelevant, yet few who do so press on to observe, as Robert Hewison does in *Too Much* (1986), that such irrelevance was not so much the result of political naiveté, psychological problems, or too much drugs, as it was of the ability of the managers of the consensus to marginalize and fragment radical politics. While explaining the impotence of various Trotskyist, Maoist, and Socialist groups, Hewison writes, "Excluded by the consensus from influence on 'real' politics, these groups fought among themselves, further widening the gap between revolutionary ambition and achievement."[5]

When Hare wrote *Knuckle* in 1972 and *Teeth'n'Smiles* in 1975, the countercultural movement, if it could still be called that, had moved into a much more realistic, militant, and libertarian phase. Working-class industrial militancy increased considerably. And as the pot-smoking, free-loving anarchists and hippies faded from the scene along with their utopian dreams of an alternative society, radical activists regrouped with renewed determination around single issue campaigns fighting for, among other things, the rights of women, blacks, and gays. With many of the more radical forces on the left establishing their moral and political agendas on the basis of class, gender, race, and region, it would have been a nostalgic gesture for someone to reaffirm national/universal consensual values at this time as Hare does in *Knuckle* and *Teeth'n'Smiles*. These plays affirm the paradoxical terms of the consensual political and moral framework in which solitary individuals believe in national suprapartisan values in the process of lamenting the loss of them.

The moral high ground in both plays is occupied by alienated, anguished young women possessed with burning rage at the loss of public ideals, yet their own authority is neither created nor sustained by lived experience. It appears that they partake of static, previously established moral standards by virtue of their highly receptive emotional faculties. Acts of solidarity are not only absent from the experience of these idealistic young women, they are explicitly attacked and trivialized, especially in *Teeth'n'Smiles* in which class warfare and the pop culture of the late 1960s are presented as supremely irrelevant next to the more real and enduring values of Maggie, the moral center of the play.

With Hare's leading characters of the 1970s the idea of sympathizing with a character needs to be separated from positive moral value. They come together in the 1980s when personal goodness is the basis of morality, hence the greater personal appeal of, for instance, Isobel in *The Secret Rapture* (1988). In the 1970s however, Maggie, Archie (*Licking Hitler*), and Susan (*Plenty*) are obviously cruel, selfish, and self-destructive. Such is "the cost of having a conscience"—Hare's way of describing what interested him in his history plays of the 1970s.[6] What interests me is the nature of the values that inform their conscience: the cost of having one is fairly clear.

While *Teeth'n'Smiles* endorses universal/national values by undermining partisan forms of solidarity, *Knuckle* does so by reenacting the traditional consensual relationship between the Labour Party and the Conservatives in which Labour played the role of "pacemaker in that settlement."[7] As the natural guardians of the socialist-inspired ideals of the consensus, Labour had always been able to put the Tories on the defensive morally until the mid-1970s when Margaret Thatcher and Sir Keith Joseph began openly assaulting socialist assumptions. *Knuckle*, like the Labour Party, asserts a commonly held morality with the assumption that everybody really knows that capitalism is bad and has to be modified with the more enlightened national/consensual values. The surest sign that such values retain the upper hand is the willingness of the capitalists to assume a defensive guilty posture. In *Knuckle* the entire effort of the plot is devoted to forcing Patrick Delafield, an investment banker who works in the financial district of London, to confess what he already knows: that capitalism is bad and that he has been corrupted by it.

This notion that everybody really knows what is right and wrong is important to Hare's conception of how morality operates. The claim figures prominently in Hare's discussion of *Knuckle* in an interview in 1975 and appears explicitly in a speech by Curly Delafield shortly before he forces his father to confess his guilt near the end of the play. To Simon Trussler and Catherine Itzin Hare says:

Knuckle is an almost obscenely constructive play! It says something about it being impossible to live within this system without doing yourself moral damage. That's a huge claim. It's a play about *knowing*, about the fact that *there are no excuses*, and the fact that people who are damaged by the system know themselves to have been damaged, and *are not ignorant* of what they've done to themselves. And that is a large claim, because how you feel about capitalists—whether you believe them to be knaves or fools—determines everything you believe and think politically.[8] (italics added)

While on the beach with Jenny, Curly says much the same thing:

I will tell you—the horror of the world. The horror of the world is *there are no excuses left*. There was a time when men who ruined other men could claim they were ignorant, or simple, or believed in God, or life was very hard, or we didn't know what we were doing: but *now everybody knows* the tricks, the same shabby hands have been played over and over, and men who persist in the old ways of running their countries or their lives—those men now do it in the full knowledge of what they're doing. So that at last greed and selfishness and cruelty stand exposed in a great white light. *Men are bad because they want to be.* (80) (italics added)

The claim that all the capitalists "know" (the key word in both passages) and act with "full knowledge" assumes the existence of a previously established universally recognized moral standard. The real moral battle against capitalism in *Knuckle* has already been won. Therefore the play need not present genuine moral dilemmas or real political conflict which entails a confrontation between fundamentally different moral assumptions. The phrase "no excuses left" suggests that instead of offering genuine disagreement, capitalists can only deflect the truth from themselves with "excuses" or unconvincing efforts to delude themselves and others. And people are considered bad not because they embrace different moral assumptions, but because "they want to be" despite knowing the "truth." In a world where the real battle against capitalism has been won, the political activity of those who consider themselves at the moral cutting edge can shrink to the passive task of extracting guilt from willful self-deluding capitalists.

In the Trussler/Itzin interview Hare calls *Knuckle* "an almost obscenely constructive play" and believes that to claim that capitalists such as Patrick Delafield "know" themselves to have been damaged morally is a "huge claim."[9] However, the act of extracting guilt from capitalists in the context of the early 1970s is both decidedly modest and on the verge of becoming implausible. Modest because extracting guilt from capitalists was the traditional "pacemaker" role of the Labour Party in the sense that they could always restrain the conservatives by reminding them of their commitment to social equality and full employment. From 1945 to about 1975 (when Margaret Thatcher became leader of the Conservative Party) one could say that the Conservatives "knew" that these twin pillars of the consensus represented the highest moral aspirations of their society.

However, Edward Heath's famous U-turn in 1973-1974, when he abandoned his new right economic and industrial policies, was the last time a Conservative government felt morally constrained by consensual ideals. Heath lost his nerve when unemployment rose to 1 million because, as Alan Sinfield says, "he would not risk the consequences of repudiating welfare-capitalism."[10] When Thatcher replaced Heath as leader of the Conservative Party in 1975 (the price Heath paid for his U-turn, according to Thatcher) and began her open assault on what she regarded as the corrupting collectivist morality of the consensus, it became no longer possible to claim that capitalists "knew" unrestrained capitalism was bad. Thatcher never forgave Heath for betraying free-market policies and when her turn came to confront the labor unions in the early 1980s her fighting slogan "this lady's not for turning" pointedly repudiated the entire history of the right's hedging concessions to the moral agenda of the left.

In the face of growing opposition to the consensus from both the right and left, Hare's assertion of a universal moral authority through confessions of guilt from capitalists resembles the beleaguered rearguard posture of the Labour Party establishment and welfare state bureaucrats who remained the staunchest defenders of the consensus throughout the 1970s. In the Trussler/Itzin interview Hare says "with *Knuckle* I particularly wanted to write a play which was available to everybody—it's about people for whom political rhetoric is no part of their lives. The characters aren't political—or intellectual—at all."[11] How can one write a play about the moral damage done to "capitalists" with characters who "aren't political or intellectual at all?" By proceeding on the assumption that everybody knows capitalism is bad. If there is nothing anybody can learn about morality and if it is assumed that there are ultimately no disagreements in Britain about what is right and wrong regarding capitalism, for instance, then characters do not need to be political or intellectual.

Since all is known to everybody in *Knuckle*, responses to an established truth define character rather than participation in a dialectic between beliefs or an active formation of beliefs. There are basically two types of characters in *Knuckle*: those who admit capitalism is bad and those who don't. The good characters—Jenny Wilbur and Sarah Delafield—honestly face up to what they know; whereas the capitalists—Mr. Malloy and Patrick Delafield—are those who lie to themselves and others with varying degrees of success. To equate capitalists with liars effectively depoliticizes and deintellectualizes discussion about them. The detective/thriller format of *Knuckle* is well-suited to the task of exposing guilt and assigning blame in a world of moral certainties. In the detective fiction of Ross MacDonald and Mickey Spillane (writers to whom Hare acknowledges a debt), the job of the detective is to enforce an established morality, assign blame to villains who have always known the moral implications of their crimes, and to bring about a clear resolution.

The entire life of the chief villain Patrick Delafield, the investment banker, is presented as an elaborate lie, a series of delusions and protective self-images he creates to deflect guilt and convince himself of his integrity, thus rendering the moral case against capitalism a foregone conclusion. His lies take the form of an avid cultivation of literature and the arts. He reads symphonic sheet music and has undertaken an intensive study of Anglo-American literature. He praises the novels of Henry James for their "tremendous quality of civilization" (38). His Scottish housekeeper considers him "a very Christian man" (19) and stands in awe of his culture and learning. His son Curly both loathes and envies his "state of zen" (43) which requires, as Patrick patiently explains to Curly at various times throughout the play, believing one's own propaganda and being grown-up, mature, and quiet. The stockbroker Mr. Malloy, the other capitalist in the play, doesn't disguise his guilt as effectively as Patrick. While describing Malloy to Curly, Patrick says: "Not very successful. His hands tremble. It's—bad for business" (25). The trembling in the hands is the reflex of the unsuccessful liar. After Malloy succumbed to blackmail by selling his house to developers, his burden of guilt became too much to bear so he committed suicide.

Patrick's elaborate defenses against guilt and self-loathing would no doubt have remained impenetrable had his 21-year-old daughter Sarah never discovered that he was tenuously linked to a sordid crime of blackmail in Guildford, their home town. Patrick had negotiated the bridging loan for property developers to build a large office/shopping complex in the middle of Guildford. The only obstacle was a large old house owned by Mrs. Malloy, an elderly woman assumed to be reluctant to sell. To remove this obstacle the developers offered Mrs. Malloy's son (the title was in his name for tax reasons) £200,000 pounds to sell, an offer he accepted only after the developers tried to flush him out of his house with a large vicious dog.

Since Patrick never actually commits a crime on legal terms (leaving aside the fact that he learned of the blackmail after it happened, should bankers be held responsible for the illegal actions of legitimate clients?), his only crime appears to be his complicity in the capitalist system per se, and the only evidence of this crime is his guilt betrayed by his overactive efforts to convince himself of his humanity and goodness. Nevertheless, Patrick's involvement at many removes from the crime gives his daughter Sarah an opportunity to finally break through his serene zen-like pretense of integrity and force him to confess to being corrupted morally. Apparently her youth and innocence are intended to render plausible her assumption that Patrick's banking activity inevitably leads to blackmail.

As evidenced by her faked suicide/murder designed to implicate Patrick, a superabundance of feeling charges Sarah's hostility to her father's profession, yet how were her convictions formed? The same question could be asked of Jenny Wilbur. Not surprisingly, considering Hare's three early plays, nothing is said about late 1960s activism in which they would have been old enough to participate. In the absence of any practice or of social, historical realities that might have conditioned them, it appears that they access their soaring ideals through emotional honesty. Unlike her ex-lovers Mr. Malloy and Max Dupree, Sarah can not be silenced with blackmail, her burning honesty will not allow it. "Sarah never lied" Jenny tells Curly when he doubts Sarah's version of certain events. It was the maniacal persistence of her honesty that wore Max down until he revealed that Patrick had bribed him to avoid telling her about the link between the bank and the property developers. And after Sarah's mysterious disappearance, it is Jenny's honesty that propels a wavering Curly forward with his investigation into Sarah's disappearance until he confirms his hunch that Patrick had something to do with her apparent suicide or murder.

Sarah's letter from France, which Jenny reads at the close of the play, solves the mystery of her disappearance and indicates that as far as she is concerned, extracting guilt from Patrick fulfills her moral agenda and leaves her nothing more to do. She writes:

Let us rejoice in the ugliness of the world. Strangely I am not upset. I am reassured. I think I left a finger pointing on the beach. Jenny, keep Pat on the flat of his back. On his knees, keep him confessing. Keep the wound fresh. (104)

Sarah's continued absence ensures the maximum extraction of guilt from Patrick, for it leaves him believing that he was very likely responsible for her suicide or murder. Thus, paradoxically, Sarah's moral authority is never more potent than when she travels through France alone and destitute.

According to these powerful fighting phrases—"keep Pat on the flat of his back. On his knees, keep him confessing. Keep the wound fresh"—Sarah believes she has morally overwhelmed and flattened her father with a stunning knock-out punch. This image appears a bit grandiose considering that all she has done is help force her father to confess what he already knows: the real knockout punch being the assumption that everybody already really knows what is right and wrong regarding "capitalism." Sarah's image of Patrick flat on his back presents in the starkest possible way the central paradox of the play: how can a solitary young woman be ascribed such massive moral power? How can Hare's "huge claim" about the existence of morality rest on a character who doesn't actually do anything? One answer, already proposed, is that if moral and political viewpoints are universal and fixed, then there is no need to sustain them with any kind of practice.

Hare may have anticipated this question for one of the dominant themes of the play is that action is next to impossible. It is easier to ascribe power to passionate inactivity if action is impossible. Hare's characterization of morality as all-powerful at one instant and then completely impotent in the next is contradictory in a way that upholds the consensual arrangement whereby the moral authority of passive individuals thrives under the protective umbrella of soaring national ideals. On the one hand, the power of morality has to be awesome and universal to extract guilt from the heart of even the toughest capitalists like Patrick and drive capitalists like Malloy with weaker defenses against guilt to suicide; yet, on the other hand, to justify passive individuality, morality needs to appear as a feeble and laughable force before the implacable facts of life (the forces of capitalism) whenever the issue of action is raised. When Curly wants to abandon the investigation, he explains to Jenny: "What shall we do? Rage against the beast? What good does this do? What good did it do Sarah? A crystal stream of self-righteousness and abuse. Tiny little fists banging away at the world" (80-81). Now capitalism is a "beast" and morality is equipped with "tiny little fists" (tiny fists that elsewhere deliver a knockout punch to extract guilt from Patrick). In disgust Jenny has him thrown out of the bar, Shadow of the Moon. She believes the investigation should go on.

Jenny's unwavering idealism and indignation propel the investigation forward, yet when the opportunity to do something arises at the end, her moral authority is suddenly not up to the task. In his last speech—a sort of postscript to the play—Curly says, "Jenny would go to the newspaper. They didn't believe her" (106). If she told the newspapers about Patrick's involvement, of course they wouldn't print her story for, as Patrick, Max, and Curly know, it would be impossible to convict him for providing the loan. There is simply no story here. The only story Jenny could have told the newspapers would have been about the blackmail that forced Mrs. Malloy from her home into a hospital for the insane. The question is, why didn't the newspapers believe this story for which Jenny had all the facts first hand from the key witnesses? Newspapers thrive on stories of corruption and blackmail, especially if they can be proven. The answer seems to be that the implausible rejection of her story underscores the uselessness of action thereby preserving the moral authority of passive individuals. Since the moral authority in this play is an uncontested fixed universal given, it does not depend on any political practice. Jenny's reputation as a woman of absolute integrity (while admiring her convictions, Max says at one point, "Jenny soars above us all" [36]) is allowed to remain intact as she, with good conscience, can limit her activity to managing the Shadow of the Moon.

Knuckle pulls its punches in other ways suitable for the requirements of the consensus. Since Patrick is carefully kept at eight removes from the crime of blackmail, it would seem that his real crime as a banker is his participation in the capitalist system. Yet in the following passage from the pivotal confession scene, Patrick qualifies his confession so heavily that it becomes virtually meaningless:

Curly. You may not believe it. The City of London once enjoyed a reputation for unimpeachable integrity. My word is my bond. So fabulously wealthy as to be almost beyond wealth. But in the last twenty years we've been dragged through the mud like everyone else. The wide boys and the profiteers have sullied our reputation. We work now like stallholders abainst a barrage of abuse.... We are honest men. She had always abused me. But she had never been able to fault me.
(*Pause.*)
I had to buy Dupree. Do you understand? For her sake. (93-94)

Patrick does not admit that capitalism is bad or corrupting, but only that disreputable characters have sullied the City's reputation in the last 20 years. This is a fairly bland criticism of capitalism. Room arguably exists within moderate consensual parameters to launch a sharper attack. Curly, the only one to hear Patrick's confession, aspires to be a financier like his father, so naturally he does not point out that the nature of the system, not the integrity of those currently working within it, should be the matter under discussion.

Evidence suggests that no one else would have pointed this out either. Patrick's claim in the passage above that Sarah "had never been able to fault" (94) him implies that she found capitalism more or less tolerable until she discovered that it was conducted by dishonest characters. The story seems to bear this out: why does she wait until she uncovered the facts about the blackmail to attack her father?

Sarah's towering rage that drives her to fake her suicide is arguably about more than the dishonesty of capitalists, after all, as Patrick says, she had always loathed his profession (21). Yet an investigation into the content of her loathing reveals how neatly consensual her convictions are. In one of her attempts to revive Curly's flagging interest in the investigation, Jenny bursts forth with this passionate testimony about Sarah's concern for the poor:

Jenny: She was so naive. She used to tell Patrick your wealth is built on the suffering of the poor. And she expected an answer.

Curly: All right.

Jenny (*screams*): All right.
(*She throws his clothes to the ground.*)
Always ready with an innocent question. Why don't you share what you've got? Why can't people run their own lives? Why persist with a system you know to be wrong? How can you bear to be rich when so many people are poor? (56)

One's concern for the poor can be "naive" and "innocent" like Sarah's provided a widespread public agreement exists about the best way to help the poor. It goes without saying that most people are concerned about the poor. The issue becomes political, however, as soon as people begin to disagree about how best to help the poor. In 1974 it was still possible to claim that most people in Britain endorsed the "socialist" way of redistributing wealth through social welfare programs. Sarah assumes general acceptance of this belief system with her aggressive question "Why persist with a system you know is wrong?" However, after the election of a prime minister who passionately believed that her free-market economic strategies were ultimately the best means of helping the poor, it became less credible for a passionate young person to be able to have a "naive," "innocent" concern for the poor.

In some ways *Teeth'n'Smiles* affirms the individual/universal terms of the consensual experience more emphatically than *Knuckle*. Maggie Frisby, the moral center of the play, is even more solitary, passive, and alienated than her counterpart Sarah Delafield. While everybody really knows and deep down agrees with Sarah's moral standards and therefore knows why she is outraged, nobody in *Teeth'n'Smiles* understands why Maggie is so full of rage and seems intent on drinking herself to death. Only her ex-lover Arthur gains a glimmer of understanding at the end of the play when he realizes that she is unhappy not because, as he says, "she doesn't know how to be happy," but because "she's frightened of being happy."[12] He learns, in other words, that her unhappiness stems not from some personal psychological problem, but from her feeling that it would be wrong to be happy given the moral decadence of society.

While explaining to a journalist his thinking that led to the play, Hare confirms that Arthur understands that Maggie's unhappiness is rooted in more than personal problems. In the 1950s and 1960s people were unhappy because of lightweight personal maladjustments—"they couldn't find themselves or relate"—however, Maggie's unhappiness stems from an awareness of something more significant. She is "frightened of being happy" because she feels it is "wrong." As Hare says, "suddenly I was very struck with the thought of somebody living a life in which they avoided all opportunities of being happy. It wasn't that they couldn't find themselves, or relate, or any of those boring things that people said in the fifties and sixties, it was because they were actually frightened of being happy because they felt it was wrong."[13] When Hare uses the word "wrong" how far does his moral frame of reference extend beyond the merely personal? I suggest that the values governing Maggie's sense of right and wrong are soaring national ones, because largely through her the play viciously—and sometimes humorously—lampoons and trivializes the countercultural movement of the late 1960s along with working-class solidarity. From her position of passive, totally misunderstood alienation, Maggie possesses the only true standards against which all forms of solidarity potentially hostile to the consensus are portrayed as completely devoid of moral and political legitimacy.

Most of Maggie's rage, which she tries to numb with large amounts of Johnnie Walker scotch, arises from the feeling that popular culture is not a source of progressive social change. I say "feeling," for like Sarah, Maggie arrives at her morally superior posture through a mixture of passion, intuition, honesty, and innocence. In contrast, the rational approach of Arthur and Anson (a young medical student), involving political and intellectual theories, blocks emotional access to true moral enlightenment. Arthur's unenlightenment takes the form of still believing in the counter-cultural revolution, which is why Maggie finds him a bit pathetic and no longer loves him. She says to him at one point: "You still want it to mean something, don't you? You can't get over that, can you? It's all gotta mean something . . . that's childish, Arthur. It don't mean anything" (52).

While attempting to interview Maggie for a university essay, Anson, manages to squeeze in one question about the revolutionary role of popular music that she doesn't bother responding to because to her the answer is so obvious. He asks, "Would you say the ideas expressed in popular music . . . have had the desired effect of changing . . . society in any way?" (35). The implication is that if Anson were to apprehend this sociopolitical issue with his emotions like Maggie, instead of trying to understand and articulate some theory about it, he would see that the answer is no.

Anson's question about the role of popular music is a legitimate one that has engaged many British and American sociologists (Michael Brake, Dick Hebdige, Robert Hewison, Charles Reich, Paul Willis) who contend that to some degree popular music did have a liberating and progressive impact on society in the late 1960s.[14] However, Anson's question is clearly meant to sound foolish in the context of this play, roughly 90% of which is about the mindless backstage antics of a rock band far from the cutting edge of revolutionary social change (the band plays music during the other 10%).

The four members of Maggie's band (Wilson, Nash, Smegs, and Peyote) are portrayed as if it had never occurred to them that people like Anson (and formerly Maggie) thought they were supposed to be a force for social change, thus their bewilderment about Maggie's anger. Their total ignorance of the reasons for her rage and self-destructive behavior is the measure of their total irrelevance morally and politically. Although some band members are from the workingclass (Wilson is introduced in the stage directions as "a small bearded cockney" [12]) their music is not presented as a manifestation of class consciousness. Hare undermines their oppositional potential by making the pursuit of drugs and sex—the most notorious, overestimated, and ephemeral part of the countercultural movement—the sum total of their ambition. The stage directions describe this tableau near the middle of the play: "*Laura gets up. Moves. Stops dead. The rest are sitting, staring into their mugs. Almost all comprehensively stoned now*" (46).

One may still wonder, how could Hare possibly be defending consensual ideals with an amusing parody of the zonked-out acidheads of the late 1960s? How do dropouts like Peyote, Smegs, and Wilson pose a threat to the consensus? Consider equally basic questions that expose the drift of my argument: If popular culture of the late 1960s was as unenlightened as Hare portrays it, then why bother exposing its irrelevance? And why do so in a play written in 1975, five to six years after the flakier elements had disappeared? Why kick a dead horse that everybody knows is dead? Regardless of what one may think of the impact of popular music on British society in the late 1960s, it is safe to say that the acid dreaming element of alternative culture on which Hare chose to focus had pretty well burned itself out by the early 1970s.

Teeth'n'Smiles appears amusingly pointless—little more than Hare's idiosyncratic look back on his own unhappy undergraduate experience at Cambridge University in the late 1960s—unless one considers Maggie and her band as representative of the counterculteral movement, which, at its militant core, was undeniably fed by rage at establishment values, class inequalities, and by a desire for social changes in distinctly unconsensual ways already mentioned. I suggest that Hare wrote about popular culture to bolster the consensual moral framework that in 1975 was under more stress than ever before. *Teeth'n'Smiles*, like *Knuckle* with its timorous claim that dishonest capitalists are bad, is a play that craves agreement because late 1960s popular culture, perhaps more than any other potential enemy of the consensus, provides an easy target to caricature and trivialize.

In light of the resurgence of working-class militancy in the early 1970s it is not surprising that another target of Hare's skepticism in *Teeth'n'Smiles* is the idea that the classwar is relevant to social change. Maggie's manager Saraffian is the only character who believes that what he does helps working-class solidarity. Why is he portrayed as a sleazy spiv who thinks stealing from the rich contributes significantly to an on-going class war? What is the purpose of the following episode?

After Maggie burned down the Mayball festivities tent, Saraffian enters in high spirits and says, "Bless you my dear. At a stroke the custard is creme brulee. You've totally restored my faith in the young" (81). Although it is not altogether clear why she burns the tent down (aside from fulfilling her puzzling desire to go to prison), she vehemently rejects Saraffian's interpretation of her gesture as an act of protest in the class war. The fire reminds him of a similar moment during the war 30 years before at the Cafe de Paris when he reaffirmed his lower-class origins in a political conversion that gave him a life-long faith in the class war. Yet his political epiphany, which he describes at length, involves nothing more than his watching low-life thieves loot the wealthy dead after two bombs destroyed the cafe and killed and injured many of the clientele.

My first thought is: I'm with you, pal. I cannot help it, that was my first thought. Even here, even now, even in fire, even in blood, I am with you in your scarf and cap, slipping the jewels from the hands of the corpses. I'm with you. So then a ladder came down and work began. And we climbed out. . . . I just brush myself down and feel lightheaded, for the first time in my life totally sure of what I feel. I climb the ladder to the street, push my way through the crowd. My arm is grazed and bleeding. I hail a taxi. The man is a cockney. He stares hard at the exploded wealth. He stares at me in my dinner jacket. He says, "I don't want blood all over my fucking taxi." And he drives away. There is a war going on. All the time. A war of attrition. (83-84)

Why create this nasty little story (the Cafe de Paris was actually bombed in the way described, but Saraffian's interpretation is Hare's creation) that reduces the class war to spivery and looting, except to undercut the legitimacy of working-class solidarity. What little we know of Saraffian's subsequent life indicates that he kept faith with his debased vision of the class war: he gleefully rips off his clients in the music business, and spends much of his time, while visiting his band at their Cambridge gig, stealing silver candlesticks and whatever else he can get his hands on.

Skepticism about the vanguard role of the working class became widespread after the events in Paris in the summer of 1968, yet such skepticism usually led the newly skeptical to embrace theories of social change less totalizing than set forth by Marxists and socialists of the 1940s and 1950s. In "Truth and Power" Michel Foucault describes how 1968 led leftist intellectuals to rethink their habitual role as "the spokesman of the universal": "A new mode of the connection between theory and practice has been established. Intellectuals have got used to working, not in the modality of the 'universal,' the 'exemplary,' the 'just-and-true-for-all,' but within specific sectors, at the precise points where their own conditions of life or work situate them (housing, the hospital, the asylum, the laboratory, the university, family and sexual relations)."[15] Even if Saraffian were a man of the utmost intelligence and integrity and had contributed significantly to strengthen working-class solidarity, Maggie would still have plenty of cause to feel angry. The fact is that in 1975 social and economic inequalities were as deeply entrenched as ever in Britain. Yet what values or ideas about social change inform her anger directed at Saraffian?:

What a load of shit. You're full of shit, Saraffian. What a crucial insight, what a great moment in the Cafe de Paris. And what did you do the next thirty years? (*Pause.*)
Well, I'm sure it gives you comfort, your nice little class war. It ties things up very nicely, of course, from the outside you look like any other clapped-out businessman, but inside, oh, inside you got it all worked out.
(*Pause.*)
This man has believed the same thing for thirty years. And it does not show. Is that going to happen to us? Fucking hell, somebody's got to keep on the move. (84)

Her passionate denunciation of Saraffian invites questions similar to those asked earlier of Jenny and Sarah in *Knuckle*. What convictions inform Maggie's anger? What is it (aside from her aforementioned emotional aptitude) that prevents her from being blinded by Saraffian's comforting theories about the classwar? Is there an objective moral difference between her burning someone else's tent down and his stealing jewelery from the dead and wounded? What has Maggie done or thought of doing that gives her the convictions and authority to demand of Saraffian, "and what did you do the next thirty years?" She says "fucking hell, somebody's got to keep on the move," yet she says this just before she willingly goes to prison. What does she have in mind with this advice? Maggie offers no analysis of her frustrations and there is no evidence of how a practice in a "specific sector" (Foucault's phrase) enlightened her, yet the nature of her protest is not therefore mysterious.

Her moral authority is a function of her solitude, passivity, and powerful feelings about the need to restore larger authentic and enduring ideals that exist apart from popular culture and the classwar. This individual/universal mode of protest fits the consensual framework, yet the story Maggie tells Saraffian of a glorious childhood memory suggests that the taproots of her ideals also draw upon a vague totemic emotional sense of Englishness evoked by the English countryside. As a polite way to ask about her self-destructive behavior, Saraffian asks Maggie where the "need" has gone when they find themselves alone together on stage. He thinks her suffering has something to do with being a failed or unsatisfied artist. She asks him "where did we get this idea that one human being's more interesting than another," and then tells him a touching childhood story about a doll village she made in her aunt's garden by the Thames River (71). The story indicates that her pain is not merely personal, but about something lost that she feels was the birthright of all English children: "I took the local priest down there, I wanted him to consecrate the little doll church. The sun was shining and he took my head in his hands. He said, inside this skull the most beautiful piece of machinery that god ever made. He said, a fair-haired English child, you will think and feel the finest things in the world. The sun blazed and his hands enclosed my whole skull" (72). Maggie says she does not believe one human being is more interesting than another, yet her romanticized pastoral vision of a small fair-haired English child in a garden by the Thames being blessed by an Anglican priest suggests otherwise. Is this the kind of memory that Saraffian or her working-class musicians can draw upon. Who are the "we" in her question "What have we ever known?" How does her garden experience allow her to speak for what others have or have not known and to criticize them?

This tableau of a child in an English garden evokes a vision of lost national unity and purpose more suspect than the consensus that was rooted, at least for a brief time during the war, in genuinely popular and collective action. Maggie's nostalgia for her aunt's garden, where she learned to expect to "think and feel the finest things in the world," fits into the tradition of "abstract upper-class kitsch" described by Tom Nairn in his discussion of English nationalism and Enoch Powell. This tradition, perfected in the poetry of A. E. Houseman and echoed in less pleasing terms in the poetry of Enoch Powell, celebrates a synthetic "Old English" identity that, according to Nairn, floats off into a "rustic English limbo" redolent of a "Disney-like English world where the Saxon ploughs his fields and the sun sets to strains of Vaughan Williams."[16] The "finest things in the world" are effectively depoliticized, dehistoricized, and universalized with the assumption that the nature of the "finest things" would be self-evident to a naive, innocent child.

The tragedy of postwar Britain in *Knuckle* and *Teeth'n'Smiles* is intended to be that Jenny, Sarah, and Maggie never experienced the "finest things" because various regressive elements of society failed to keep faith with the nationally unifying ideals formed during the Second World War, yet their profoundly individualistic manner of lamenting the loss of collective national ideals indicates that Hare doesn't know why such ideals never materialized. The real tragedy of postwar Britain from the perspective of intellectuals such as Raymond Williams, Stuart Hall, and David Marquand is that collective ideals never took root largely because of the individualistic way they were upheld and defended.

4
FANSHEN: A POSITIVE MODEL FOR CHANGE

If a factory worker or even a suburban executive wanted to fanshen, how would he go about it? As I say, it makes you think.
—Catherine Itzin, Review of *Fanshen*, 1975

Like *A Map of the World*, written eight years later, *Fanshen* (1975) sprang from Hare's urgent need for a change from writing about England. As he says in the Trussler/Itzin interview in 1975, he needed something positive to write about: "I was sick to death with writing about England—with writing about this decadent corner of the globe. The excitement of *Fanshen* was to write about a society and to cover a period of time in which one felt that people's lives were being materially and spiritually improved, in a culture that was completely different to anything we knew about. We wanted to write a positive work using positive material."[1] Hare says much the same thing in stronger and more self-revealing terms in the preface to the 1976 edition of *Fanshen*: "Writers have been trapped in negatives, forced back into sniping and objection, or into the lurid colors of their private imaginations. At some stage they will have to offer positive models for change, or their function will decay as irrevocably as the society they seek to describe."[2]

It appears a likely possibility, in light of the raging despair of his three early plays, that Hare is generalizing here from his own experience as a "sniping" writer "trapped in negatives." As a glowing portrayal of the Chinese revolution in the forties, *Fanshen* is a clear departure for Hare, yet distinctive characteristics persist. His portrayal of the Chinese revolution is as positive as his earlier portrayal of leftist activism is negative. The uncontested soaring values of Sarah and Jenny in *Knuckle* (1974) reappear with the difference that everybody in *Fanshen* rallies around them.

Perhaps with his earlier works in mind, William Gaskill and Max Stafford-Clark were both surprised when Hare agreed to adapt William Hinton's documentary novel, *Fanshen*, for a Joint Stock production that premiered at the ICA Theatre in April 1975. As Gaskill says, "neither of us thought he would do it. Well, he read the book, liked it very much, agreed to work with us and from then on his commitment was total."[3] From William Hinton's moving and celebratory account of how nearly 600 million Chinese abolished, within roughly a decade, a repressive feudal landlord/tenant system that had been rigidly intact for over 2,000 years Hare extracted an even more positive version in which oppositional forces are largely edited out, leaving little sense of how revolutionary ideals achieved ascendancy.

After discussing the potent religious, economic, and psychological barriers to land reform in the first 107 pages, Hinton proceeds with the assumption that everybody in the village of Long Bow believed in the ideals of the revolution. His account is tremendously exciting and optimistic because it focuses primarily on the implementation rather than the formation of new positive values. From Hare's comments in the Preface to *Fanshen*, it appears that Hinton's assumption of a common unquestioned moral ground appealed to him and governed his conception of how to proceed with the adaptation:

On stage people are defined by what they cannot do and say, as much as by what they can. Look through the text. See what is missing in their experience. Then see what is assumed. Hinton himself points to one simple example: nobody in the book ever questions the value of the revolution, they only question its direction. After the barbaric experiences of the past, it simply never occurs to them to question the actual fact of the fanshen.[4]

"Fanshen" is a Chinese word meaning "to turn over." Hare, even more than Hinton, is interested in what happens after the essential turning over, when, as he says, "it simply never occurs to them to question the actual fact of the fanshen."

By beginning his adaptation after page 107, Hare skips over the most remarkable fact conveyed in these early pages of Hinton's account: the fact that change took place at all in China. The title of Hinton's second chapter—"Can the Sun Rise in the West"—was the stock reply of the gentry before the revolution when anyone mentioned change.[5] The question expresses the supreme confidence of the gentry that nothing could threaten the established order. Such confidence rested on what Hinton calls the "three pillars of Heaven": Confucian thought combined with a widespread belief in geomancy, gentry control over local government, and the threat of physical violence.[6] According to Confucian thought, earthly success demonstrates the moral law that virtue and "right thinking" bring rewards. Consequently, it was immoral for the poor peasants to question the power and wealth of the gentry. Confucianism was thus a system of thought perfectly suited to preserving the status quo. Geomancy also helped the peasants resign themselves to their fate by claiming that the configuration of the heavenly bodies at one's birth determines one's destiny. Local governments also preserved the status quo, for they were extensions of the power of a handful of wealthy landlords. In the absence of any central government authority, the gentry enjoyed nearly absolute control with literally the power of life and death over the peasants, who comprised roughly 90% of the village and national population.

The stage directions at the beginning of Act One say that *"Fanshen* is an accurate historical record of what once happened in one village four hundred miles south-west of Peking."[7] *Fanshen* is indeed accurate according to Hinton's version of events, yet with the negative material edited out, the spirit of the play becomes even more biased toward the positive. For instance, the crowd does not cheer, as Hare indicates, at the beginning of Act One when several young cadres arrest Kuo Te-yu, the puppet mayor backed by the gentry.[8] According to Hinton it was several days before the boldest peasants had worked up the courage to overcome deeply engrained psychological and religious inhibitions and speak against their oppressors.[9] Hinton's revolution begins with a crawl; Hare's at a run. With a similar selective handling of history, Hare could have extracted equally positive models of change from revolutionary periods in English history during the past 150 years: the Chartist movement in the 1840s, the rapid growth of labor movements between 1911-1920, or the achievements of the 1945-1951 Labour government.

Fanshen has been called Hare's most Brechtian play.[10] The spare set and use of slogans at the beginning of most scenes clearly suggest a resemblance to Brecht's work, but beyond this it is easier to see the dissimilarities. With its microscopic focus on one village during a narrow time frame (1945-1949), *Fanshen* is one of Hare's least epic plays. Larger historical realities are only glancingly referred to so that it is not clear how "social being determines thought," to cite one of the qualities of epic theatre according to Brecht.[11] And while there is process in *Fanshen*, it is a process of bureaucratic implementation of established values rather than a dialectical process in which value is contested and affirmed.

In later plays—*Licking Hitler* and *Plenty*—Hare embraces the ideals that elected the 1945-1951 Labour government, yet what is more problematic?: to claim that such ideals completely died in postwar England, or to suggest that the revolution in *Fanshen* was totally positive and successful—the result of isolating the glorious revolutionary events that occurred in the village of Long Bow in the late 1940s from the many inglorious ways China failed to live up to them in subsequent decades. I suggest that it was the remoteness of the revolutionary period in China from European consciousness that allowed Hare to believe it could be bracketed off from subsequent historical developments and presented as a plausible model of change.

It appears from Hare's statements about *Fanshen* that he thought the Chinese revolution offered a model of change highly relevant to Europe. In the Trussler/Itzin interview he says: "I had deliberately written a text that was as resonant of Europe as was possible, so that people might make their own analogies, about political leadership and so on."[12] A year later, in the Preface to the 1976 edition, his claim about its relevance to Europe is more emphatic:

It is a play for Europe, for the West. Besides trying to explain as deftly as possible the aim and operation of land reform in China, to show how it changed men's souls as well as their bodies, the play is much concerned with political leadership, with the relationship in any society between leadership and led. In the political climate of Europe where the distrust between the people and their bureaucracy is now so profound, this seemed a subject of extreme urgency. For *Fanshen* seeks to explain to an audience who have no real experience of change what exactly that change might involve and how it can in practice be effected.[13]

On a general level the relationship between the leaders and the led in *Fanshen* is relevant to Europe or any part of the world. From the example of Secretary Ch'en and the Work Team, Hare seems to be saying that the bureaucrats in Europe need to subordinate personal needs to collective needs and to be open to self-criticism in order to secure the trust of those they lead. For a country as centralized and politically and culturally top-heavy as Britain, this model of participatory democracy is particularly apposite. However, a model of change based on redistribution of land is of marginal relevance to Britain or Europe, where power does not rest primarily with owners of land.

In-so-far as land reform is an issue in Britain, John McGrath had already addressed it in a play directly relevant to Scotland. *The Cheviot, the Stag and the Black Black Oil* (1973) calls for land reform in the Scottish Highlands, where wealthy landlords continue to be a source of oppression for the local inhabitants. Several dozen vast estates of over 100,000 acres still exist in England, Ireland, and Scotland. With a wealth of historical material presented from the perspective of the working people, *The Cheviot* encourages Highlanders to resist the latest form of exploitation at the hands of large corporations developing the North Sea oil deposits. It follows the history of exploitation that began in the middle of the eighteenth century, when landowners literally drove tenant farmers off the land to make way for the newly imported and far more profitable Cheviot sheep capable of surviving the cold Scottish winters. In later years, the land was cleared of people for the stag-hunting gentry.

In the 1960s and 1970s, Highlanders again found themselves legally and economically defenseless against the commercial interests of oil companies that disfigured coastal towns and created property speculation, making it very difficult for local people to buy homes or land. Between April 1973 and June 1974, McGrath presented *The Cheviot* at 60 different locations throughout Scotland. The play was a resounding success because issues of utmost importance to Highlanders were presented by Scottish actors in the traditional Highlander form of entertainment, the ceilidh.

Hare may have derived his sense of *Fanshen's* relevance to the West from Hinton's claim that the Chinese model of revolution, based on land reform, would be imitated by all third world nations that would in turn bring about world revolution. World relevance is a persistent theme in Hinton's Preface. Within the same sentence he moves from the credible proposition that the events in Long Bow form a microcosm of the Chinese revolution to the much grander claim that the transformation in China has "unleashed political and social forces so tremendous that they continue to shake not only China but the world."[14] Hinton's sweeping prognostications reach their height of grandiosity in the following passage:

The relevance of Long Bow's history to the present day can hardly be overemphasized. The story revolves around the land question. Without understanding the land question one cannot understand the Revolution in China, and without understanding the Revolution in China one cannot understand today's world. . . . But the impact of the land question on world affairs is not a function of China's specific gravity alone. Who shall own the land? Who shall rule the countryside? These are primary questions in the revolution that is sweeping the whole of Asia, Africa, and Latin America. That revolution, far from dying away, is intensifying. Sooner or later, all those countries where agricultural production is a main source of wealth—and the relation between owners and producers a main source of social conflict—will undergo great transformations. An understanding of the issues involved and the solution already applied by one great nation is therefore important. . . . Land reform is on the agenda of mankind.[15]

In the Preface and in other writings Hinton reveals himself as a zealous partisan of an orthodox Chinese political theory that claims the spread of revolution throughout the world will pattern itself on the Chinese revolution; that is, just as the revolution in China started with the peasants and spread to the urban centers, so will world revolution be achieved with the spread of revolution from third world agrarian nations in Asia, Latin America, and Africa to Western industrialized nations.

With vastly inferior material and financial resources Mao Tse-tung defeated the Kuomintang under Chiang Kai-shek because he knew that success depended on winning the hearts of the peasants and that land reform was the only way to do this. Undoubtedly this was an astute strategy on the home front, but it is evidence of Mao's ignorance of the rest of the world that he believed land reform to be the key to world revolution.

Mao's recipe for world revolution, known as the "national liberation" theory, is one of the chief identifying theories of a political faction, formerly led by Mao, that has not always been in the ascendancy in China. According to most Western historians, China's "Great Leap Forward" (begun in the late 1950s) and the "Cultural Revolution" (begun in 1966) were, among other things, attempts by the Maoists to reassert the control they enjoyed in the early 1950s. The struggle was essentially between "redness" and "expertness": the one being Maoist, agrarian, highly theoretical, and prone to cultworship of Mao, the other being industrial, urban, intellectual, and pragmatic.

Hinton clearly places himself in the orthodox Maoist faction. His claims of world relevance, even his phrasing, echo this statement, published by the Chinese Communist Party in 1963, that sets forth the "national liberation" theory: "The various types of contradictions in the contemporary world are concentrated in the vast areas of Asia, Africa and Latin America; these are the most vulnerable areas under imperialist rule and the storm centers of world revolution dealing direct blows to imperialism."[16]

The fact that China has been largely unsuccessful at exporting its model of revolution and that in the 1960s and 1970s it remained one of the most politically and culturally isolated countries in the world apparently did not give Hinton or Hare a more realistic sense of the relevance of Chinese land reform to the world. According to Richard Walker, China's foreign relations throughout the 1960s had been frustrated by Mao's national liberation theories: "It is difficult to build lasting relationships with the new states of Asia and Africa if Maoist doctrine claims that they are 'ripe for revolution,' and implies a threat to overthrow the present leaders. Again it is doubtful whether Peking can gain respect for its position as a superpower in world affairs when its representatives insist that the Thought of Mao Tse-tung is the pinnacle of modern scientific achievement."[17]

Within ten years of writing *Fanshen*, Hare developed reservations about its relevance to the West, which cannot be said of Hinton, judging from his claim (made in the early 1970s) that as a result of the "Great Proletarian Cultural Revolution" (1966-1969), "China's revolutionaries now stand at the cutting edge of history."[18] Only a true believer in the infallibility of Maoist thought could make such a statement about a period that by all conventional cultural and economic standards was an immense failure. Hare, on the other hand, concedes ten years later, in his Introduction to *The Asian Plays*, that his former claim of relevance was ill-conceived: "Once in a phrase I now think both pretentious and unfortunate, I called *Fanshen* a play for Europe. . . . But I hope readers will know what I meant."[19]

5

LICKING HITLER:
THE BOOMERANG EFFECT
OF BLACK PROPAGANDA

> With *Licking Hitler* and *Plenty*, Hare has reached a dazzling creative
> peak.
> —Peter Ansorge, *Plays and Players*, 1978

For the historical content of his first successful TV play *Licking Hitler*
(1978), Hare turned to the relatively unknown activities of the black
propaganda radio stations that broadcast to Germany from southern England
during the Second World War. Those responsible for British propaganda (the
Political Warfare Executive under the control of the Foreign Office) soon
learned that overt white propaganda (for example, BBC broadcasts or leaflets
with the imprint of the British government dropped by the RAF on Germany)
was not as subversive as covert black propaganda that was "black" to the degree
it appeared or sounded unlike propaganda. As Hare explains in the introduction
to *The History Plays* (1984), he was led to this subject as a result of a chance
meeting with Sefton Delmer, the director of several propaganda stations during
the war, who was largely responsible for creating broadcasts that convinced
quite a number of Germans that they were eavesdropping on a private wireless
transmission from an ordinary patriotic German disenchanted with a corrupt
and self-serving Nazi leadership. They met while working at the same table in
the Weiner Library. Delmer introduced himself with what Hare thought a "fine
opening line" from a heavy-set "thundering asthmatic": "I am Sefton Delmer. I
bet you have never heard of me. Yet I have sat as close to Adolf Hitler and to
Winston Churchill as you are to me now."[1]

Soon thereafter, Hare read Delmer's account of his propaganda work in
Black Boomerang (1962).[2] It was a highly fortunate encounter because *Black
Boomerang* provided Hare with a narrative ideally suited to represent the forces
of wealth and privilege that effectively inhibited a radical transformation of
society after the war.

Angus Calder's argument in *The People's War* (1969) that the forces for change were exploited in the interests of the national war for survival against Hitler is also the argument of *Licking Hitler*. In his recreation of Delmer's propaganda activities, Hare concentrated the forces for change in Archie Maclean, a tough-minded Scot from the Red Clyde and the star writer of the unit, who suppresses his desires for change in the interests of defeating Hitler. Calder claims that the pattern of capitulation we see in Archie's experience was a general phenomenon of the war:

The war was fought with the willing brains and hearts of the most vigorous elements in the community, the educated, the skilled, the bold, the active, the young, who worked more and more consciously towards a transformed post-war world. Thanks to their energy, the forces of wealth, bureaucracy and privilege survived with little inconvenience, recovered from their shock, and began to proceed with their old business of maneuver, concession and studied betrayal. Indeed, this war, which had set off a ferment of participatory democracy, was strengthening meanwhile the forces of tyranny, pressing Britain forwards towards 1984.[3]

While *Licking Hitler* is clearly indebted to both Angus Calder and Sefton Delmer, it is distinctly Hare's own creation and one of his finest. The tendency to both individuate and universalize moral value persists, but this time there is a near perfect fit between this tendency and the historical moment evoked. Archie's solitary act of repression plausibly carries the weight of national significance, because during the war national ideals were born at the very time they were being compromised. In the somewhat clumsily conceived postscript to the film, a woman who loved Archie Maclean finally understands 30 years later that his repression of his ideals represents the postwar national habit of lying.

This notion of a nation lying to itself bears a close resemblance to the assumption in *Knuckle* that all capitalists are liars for they really know capitalism is wrong. The crucial difference between the plays is that a national consensus did in fact exert considerable moral force for about 30 years after the war, thus making the national lie credible in *Licking Hitler;* whereas *Knuckle*—set in the early 1970s—tries to shore up a national consensual morality at about the time it was beginning to dissolve in an increasingly fragmented and polarized social and political environment. To assume capitalists really know what is right and wrong in this fractured context is problematic.

While history fully supports Anna Seaton's (Archie's assistant) claim that Archie's lie resonates with national relevance, the monolithic undialectical handling of moral value in *Licking Hitler* arguably undermines this claim. As in *Plenty*, we see burning ideals set against a total spiritual wasteland: Archie's aspirations—like Susan's—exist amid the totally uncomprehending status quo represented by his oxbridge-educated colleagues. One might well ask how can Archie's repression of ideals represent lying on a national scale if all his colleagues clearly have no grasp of his ideals and thus have nothing to repress or lie about?

Sefton Delmer wrote *Black Boomerang* to dispel the "legend of the good generals and the good Wehrmacht who were always against Hitler" by arguing that the legend arose as a result of his propaganda activity.[4] The legend grew from vicious rumors that Delmer spread about the corruption of Nazi Party functionaries. As evidence of the effectiveness of his work, these rumors took on a postwar life and provided the German people scapegoats to blame for the war. In this way Delmer's propaganda returned like a boomerang with increased force in postwar Germany.

Hare saw an equally insidious boomerang effect in postwar England from the failed social revolution on the home front. The deliberate lying of the propaganda broadcasts becomes a metaphor for the loss of faith and ideals in postwar England—for what Anna, the conscience of the play, calls "the thirty-year-old deep corrosive national habit of lying" (54). Delmer jokingly applies the metaphor to himself as he gazed with shock at his own disfigurement upon shaving his beard off at the end of the war. Apparently he was not allowed his war-time civilian dress code for his postwar reconnaissance job in Germany. "As my razor shaved the soap-sodden whiskers from my face I gazed into the mirror with all the horror of Dorian Gray confronting his tell-tale portrait. There staring at me was the pallid, flabby mouthed face of a crook. Was this, I asked myself, what four years of "black" had done to Denis Sefton Delmer?"[5] In *Licking Hitler* the characters, notably Archie, lose the Dorian Gray pact with the devil. Their wartime game of spreading filth and obloquy across Europe deeply affects the way they behave after the war; the game is the seed for later lies at personal, political, and artistic levels.

While propaganda serves as a general metaphor in *Licking Hitler*, Hare's most significant borrowing of Delmer's account is found in his descriptions of the privileged and aristocratic British Secret Service network that he so much enjoyed being a part of. For long stretches in his book, Delmer seems to forget his intention of dismantling the myth of the good Wehrmacht in the interests of describing the romance and excitement of intelligence work and the daring battle of wits with Goebbels.

His work brought him into frequent contact with admirals, BBC directors, important naval intelligence officers, and ministers of the Special Operations Executives. To underscore the fact that he was associating with the best and the brightest people in the British political and military establishments, he never misses the opportunity to point out Oxbridge connections or that certain young men later became powerful or famous. For example, Hugh Gaitskell, the self-effacing young secretary, later became the leader of the Labour Party and died in 1963. Dick Crossman, the future Labour MP and cabinet minister, was a director of one of the propaganda units. The three clerks to Admiral John Godfrey (responsible for Naval Intelligence) later became the editors *of The Sunday Telegraph, The Observer,* and *House and Garden.* Ian Fleming of

James Bond fame was the chief clerk, and so on. These and others appear as composite characters in *Licking Hitler*.

Secret Service work not only put Delmer in distinguished company, it also removed him from the harsher realities of the war. He frequently met colleagues at the posh London restaurant Frascati's. He says that, "my most successful 'black' ventures were born there under the inspiration of a Moët Chandon 1919 and a superb Ausone 1923."[6] His privileged removal from typical hardships of the war is most clearly typified by the comfortable country estate he was given to house his propaganda unit. (Later in the war his unit was moved to a larger unused BBC studio with a more powerful broadcasting capability.) Here he describes his delighted surprise upon seeing the estate for the first time:

Twenty minutes later we stepped out again in what looked like a London stockbroker's more than comfortable retreat. Rhododendron bushes, spreading chestnuts, and a few venerable monkey-puzzle trees hid a lawn from which came the click of croquet mallets. "You're sure this is the right place?" I asked the driver. And I was even more puzzled when I went inside. For there, confronting my astonished eyes, were a shiny mahogany table with books and a vase of cut flowers, a large settee and easy chairs, an elegant staircase leading to what would be the bedroom stories, and a grand piano, with a fresh and pretty blonde tinkling something that sounded like Mozart's "Eine Kleine Nachtmusik." Nothing suggested that this was a recording studio of the Secret Service.[7]

Hare seized upon this country house setting and the upper-class old boy network to evoke in *Licking Hitler* the aristocratic, conservative values that were the real enemy of so many who, like Archie Maclean, wanted to see real social changes during the Second World War. In English drama and fiction the country house has long been the most resonant metaphor for aristocratic values. Its place in British literary iconography is as important as the Wild West is in the American imagination and literary iconography.

According to Robert Hewison in *In Anger: Culture in the Cold War 1954-60*, the country house appeared in English literature with increased frequency in the 1950s as a result of a resurgence of "Mandarin values." The similarity between Hewison's claim and Calder's argument that conservative forces survived the war stronger than ever is striking:

Thanks to the war and its consequences, Mandarin values dominated the early 1950's. Having abandoned the mild socialism that had given Bloomsbury a radical edge up to 1945, the intellectual aristocracy fell back on a system of values that was more appropriate to the function they performed, and the caste from which they came. These values were truly aristocratic in origin, in that they were conservative of tradition, pastoral as opposed to industrial, and most detectable when it came to nuances of class.[8]

Hewison mentions a variety of works from the 1940s and 1950s in which the country house figures prominently: Evelyn Waugh's *Brideshead Revisited*, Agatha Christie's *The Mousetrap*, Nigel Dennis's *Cards of Identity*, William Douglas-Home's *The Chiltern Hundreds*. The setting continues to be seen in works such as Trevor Griffiths' *Country: A Tory Story*, Tom Stoppard's *The Real Inspector Hound*, and *Arcadia*, and Hare's film *Paris by Night* (1988).

If the country house setting had not been so vital to Hare, *Licking Hitler* might have become a stage play or a video instead of a film shot on location. With the exception of several outdoor scenes and the brief documentary-style portion that moves the action into the 1970s at the end of the film, all the action takes place within a country house. The BBC wanted to shoot *Licking Hitler* in a studio to save time and money. However, the impact of the play would be greatly diminished onstage or on video because there has to be the sense that this propaganda unit operates from a real country house set in the lush English countryside. A studio cannot match the visual sophistication of film on which Hare depends so much to evoke with setting alone the enduring mandarin values in which Archie found himself immersed.

In the film the house is set near Aylesbury, about 15 miles east and slightly north of Oxford, yet the actual setting is Compton Verney—"a fine country house," Hare says in the Introduction to *The History Plays*.[9] In his essay "Ah Mischief" he says, "I waited a year and would have waited five years to avoid putting *Licking Hitler* through the studio."[10] The wait was well worth it. *Licking Hitler* won the British Academy of Film and Television Arts Award (BAFTA) of 1978.

Lingering tracking shots of the interior and exterior frequently remind the viewer that the propaganda emanates from a magnificent country house. The movie opens with a shot of this calm tableau described in the stage directions: "*An English country house. Perfect and undisturbed. Large and set among woods. The sun behind it in the sky*" (11). Twenty-one scenes later the camera rests on the same tableau on a moonlit night as the "ranting" voice of Karl's German broadcast can be heard. A third outdoor tableau of the house and grounds shows the staff members enjoying a moment of relaxation "*sipping long cool drinks*" while watching a game of croquet. No studio could replicate these scenes.

The game of croquet is one of many references to sport that Hare uses to embellish his portrait of the English upperclasses at war in this country house. The first indoor scene begins to establish a close association between sport, propaganda, and the upperclasses. After a convoy of military vehicles and a voiceover break the calm of the opening tableau, the camera moves indoors to search out the source of the voiceover. It turns out to be Archie reading his latest broadcast on Rudolf Hess's surprise flight to Scotland in May of 1941:

Nobody really believes that Hess flew to Britain on the Fuhrer's instructions. Hess flew to Britain for one simple reason; because he's a criminal lunatic.
(*The camera pans slowly round to a bare passage leading down to the servants' quarters. A few hunting and military pictures hang at random on the cream walls. At the bottom of the passage the sun shines brilliantly through the glass panes of the closed door of the gun room, from which Archie's voice is coming.*) (11-12)

As Archie continues to read a draft of his broadcast the camera moves into the gun room which is described as *"full of fishing rods, tennis racquets, golf clubs, mosquito nets, sola topees, croquet mallets, polosticks, riding boots, skis, deerstalkers, wellingtons and husky jackets"* (12). These opening shots provide the first glimpse inside the estate of old Lord Minton, who in his younger days had clearly been an avid sportsman in the best tradition of the English gentry.

In *Black Boomerang* Delmer speaks of his propaganda activity in sporting terms—as an exciting contest of the wits with his brilliant rival Goebbels. With shots of hunting pictures on the walls and sporting equipment such as croquet mallets, polo sticks and deerstalkers in the gun room, Hare develops the propaganda-as-sport metaphor with a distinctly upper-class coloration. It is no accident that Archie writes his scripts in the gun room with a "large and magnificent portrait of Goebbels" before him (15). The actual broadcasting takes place in the billiard room. Fennel, the highest ranking officer with the unit and the sole link to the Political Warfare Executive, is described as *"almost forty, fat, boyish, an enthusiast, an intellectual enjoying his war"* (17-18). There are parts of Delmer in this description. Langley, the next in command, is a sportsman in the obvious sense. While talking with Fennel over a predinner beer, he says the war ruined his chances to compete in the 1940 Olympics. However, he had a "half-blue" in fencing (an award from Oxford) and still hoped for national honor after the war.

These references to sport point to the truth in the old saying that English military battles are really fought on the playing fields of Eton. From a very young age, English public school (private schools in the United States and Canada) boys are taught to associate sport with the exercise of power which they also learn is the prerogative of their class to exercise in society. These well-placed references to sport suggest that this propaganda unit is the epitome of the ruling class in wartime action.

In a later English play, *Another Country* (1982) by Julian Mitchell, we see even clearer parallels drawn between public school games and the behavior of the ruling class—particularly the behavior of a thinly disguised Guy Burgess who defected to the KGB. Mitchell's implicit argument is that Burgess' attraction to the secretive and powerful KGB found its roots in the ruthless power games he played as a boy in public school in the 1930s.

Under Marek Kanievsha's direction, the film version sharpens Mitchell's mild critique on public school institutions. Marek says of the response he hoped to evoke: "Hopefully people get the feeling that the games people play when they are at school are insane. When you think that for hundreds of years, the people who have governed this country have come from a public school background, where they are obsessed with the fact that they are going to be part of the hierarchy, and with ruthlessly manipulating themselves into positions of power, it seems absurd."[11] While Marek captures very well the absurdity of the serious fight for power among young boys and of the rituals they are forced to observe, he does not engage the issue of how the public schools perpetuate upper-class power in society as a whole.

Licking Hitler addresses these wider implications. By casting propaganda as an elaborate game or sport for these upper-class Secret Service officers, Hare suggests that they are oblivious to the revolutionary desires that inspired a majority of the population during the war. In a game one defeats an opponent according to unquestioned and therefore unchanged rules. In this sense Langley and Fennel exercise their wit against Goebbels but never question the power or right of the institutions from which they play their war games. Sport becomes a profoundly conservative metaphor in *Licking Hitler*.

In several departures from Delmer's account, Hare heightens the snobbish and racist attitudes of the officers to complete his portrait of a class oblivious to the need for a more egalitarian society. Delmer found Jewish refugees, along with German prisoners of war and defectors, very useful for the information they could provide about Germany. According to Delmer, although he makes no special point of it, the Jews were treated the same as the others who assisted the research teams. They lived in the same quarters and were no more or less free than anyone else associated with the secret stations.

In *Licking Hitler* the two radio broadcasters are Jewish refugees from Germany. They are not treated with the impartiality described in *Black Boomerang*. After a particularly successful broadcast the entire team is seen relaxing in the drawing room. Langley is reading *The Times*. The engineers are playing chess. Archie is serving drinks. Eileen (Archie's secretary) is reading *Wellington Wendy*. And Anna simply sits listening to Jungke, the Jewish broadcaster, playing Chopin on the Steinway. Lotterby appears at the door and announces that a car has arrived for Herr Jungke, whereuon Langley, the senior officer, offers Jungke a Sambuca, then turns to Lotterby and says, "Ian, would you take Herr Jungke back to the internment camp?" (33). This brief episode casts an unsavory light on the English upper class. There is no reason, other than that of race or class, to account for Jungke being placed in an internment camp. With this small departure from Delmer's account, Hare suggests that Langley and his fellow officers were not fighting on behalf of progressive changes in society.

Hare points to an affinity between the conservative forces in England and Nazi Germany with several other small but significant details. At the end of a tracking shot up the corridor into the gun room, the camera comes to rest for a moment on a *"Nazi notice board"* nailed onto the door which the stage directions describe as a "trophy." The sign says, "JUDEN BETRETTEN DIESEN ORT AUF EIGENE GEFAHR" or in English, "Jews enter at their own risk" (28). Old Lord Minton could only be sympathetic to the Nazis to collect such a sign as a "trophy."

Upper-class affinities with Nazi Germany are further hinted at when Archie conducts his own vetting of his young assistant Anna Seaton upon her arrival. It was to be her job to translate his scripts into German, a language she learned while vacationing with relatives along the Rhine. "My cousin was married to a German. I spent my summers in Oberwesel. They had a schloss on the Rhine," she tells him (16).

Anna's intimate family connections to Germany, Lord Minton's "trophy," and Jungke's confinement point to an affinity between Nazi Germany and England which has a basis in historical events alluded to in Archie's speech about Rudolf Hess. Archie's broadcast makes Hess look a fool to the German people in order to undermine their confidence in the party leaders. By stressing affinities between the Nazis and English upper-class attitudes, Hare plays on the disturbing implications of Hess's true intentions. When Hess flew alone to Scotland in a Messerschmitt fighter in May 1941, he was confident he could convince the English to accept Hitler's terms for peace, which he thought were being refused because they were somehow not getting through to the right leaders. Hitler did not want to fight the English. He admired them and thought they might help him fight Bolshevism.

Hess made the mistake of overestimating English sympathy because he had taken a reading of the English mood primarily from the conservative proto-Fascist element of the upper classes—notably from personal contact with men such as Lord Beaverbrook whose newspaper, the *Express*, was the mouthpiece of the Tories during the war. Thus it was no accident that Hess landed within 12 miles of the home of the Duke of Hamilton, the Lord Steward, whom he thought would help his cause. Hare suggests that Lord Minton, Fennel, and Langley belonged to that reactionary strata of English society Hess expected to be sympathetic to his peace-feeler. If their class was not inspired by any ideals or moral principles in the war against Hitler, then they may as well have remained neutral or even helped Hitler against Russia.

The only person in the propaganda unit who knows what he should have been fighting for is Archie Maclean. As a Scotsman from the Red Clyde it is nearly axiomatic that he would be antagonistic toward the English upper class. The industrial Clydesbank area just west of Glasgow has been for a long time the backbone of radical left union power in Britain. Because of his writing talent (he had fought his way up to become a successful journalist in London) Archie found himself enlisted to fight the war in a setting with people who represented everything he despised.

Archie's suppression also operates in his attempt to turn propaganda writing into a game. He could forget his anger if what he did was a mere game in which he did not have to think about the real world. When he first explains Anna's duties to her he says, "The game is. We are a radio station" (20). Later in the campaign Langley learns that one of Archie's broadcasts had precipitated a run on winter clothing in Berlin. The broadcast had spread rumors of special clothing privileges for Nazi party officials. As he was about to tell Archie of his success Anna stops him and says, "He wouldn't want to know. It would spoil the game" (40). Archie could function at his job precisely because of the self-induced illusion that what he did was a game and therefore had no real consequences. To learn of the real havoc he created in Germany would destroy the illusion that the suppression of his socialist ideals had no real consequence in England.

The work also becomes a game for his secretary Eileen and remains so until she learns that her brother was killed in the war. Part of their research involved reading letters written by Germans to friends and relatives in America. The news of a death in one letter provokes this frivolous response: "Whoops, Somebody's dead" (35). After the news that her brother had been killed, she is overwhelmed by the implications of what she has been doing. She rocks in Anna's arms "hysterical with grief, wild, out of control, like a drowning woman." When she stops screaming she says "I can't stand what we've done" (45).

That night Eileen leaves the propaganda unit for other work. Archie ignores her departure and says nothing of the episode. Anna reproaches him for this callous behavior: "You should have said goodbye to her. . . . That was the decent thing to do" (46). He ignores this and simply asks her to take on Eileen's secretarial duties in the morning. Her curt response—"no I won't"—provokes Archie's only direct statement about his suppressed feelings:

I set maself [sic] the task. Get through the war. Just get through it, that's all. Put it no higher than that. Accept it. Endure it. But don't think, because if you begin to think, it'll all come apart in your hands. . . . This house is the war. And I'd rather be anywhere, I'd rather be in France, I'd rather be in the desert, I'd rather be in a Wellington over Berlin, anywhere but here with you and your people in this bloody awful English house. (46)

Archie refuses to acknowledge Eileen's departure because he saw in her hysterical response to the death of her brother the trauma he would suffer if he thought too much about where he was and what he was doing. His strategy of enduring and accepting—of turning his writing into a game—would collapse if he were to show any compassion for Eileen. He is able to continue working in this house that stands for everything he really wants to fight by suppressing all revolutionary thoughts and desires. To show the slightest compassion for Eileen would touch him at this level of suppression. For Archie, opening up his emotions would be like taking the top off a volcanic mountain.

His callousness toward Eileen is consistent with the repressed way he conducts his affair with Anna. The subtext in her reproach about his callousness toward Eileen is really her protest about his callousness toward her. Their affair starts with him crashing into her room late at night. It was the first night she left her door unbarracaded against him. Despite this small degree of complicity on her part, what followed was very much a rape. He begins with this drunken announcement: "The Scot makes love wi' a broken bottle. An' a great deal a'screamin'" (34). He leaves without having said anything more to her. Drunken, silent visits at night remain the extent of their relationship. Soon she has a row of empty whisky bottles lined up in her closet. During the day he never acknowledges their affair; talk between them is restricted to their propaganda work.

The affair that began with a rape assault develops into an intolerable contradiction in Archie's life. He finds himself in love with a naive innocent 19-year-old girl with an upper-class background who did not know how to make tea when she first arrived. As the play progresses she makes it very difficult for him to maintain his state of repression as she begins to love and respect him. When Fennel apologizes to her for making her work for a savage, meaning Archie, she replies, "He seems . . . he just seems a very extraordinary man to me" (39).

As a testament to the power of his anger, she tries to move closer to him in understanding. During one nightly visit she talks freely of her sheltered background and admits she knows nothing about the world. She tells him that it had never occurred to her that people had to pay for things like gas, electricity, and water until one day when Eileen mentioned that electricity prices had risen. As he walks out the door without saying anything, she calls out, "Archie. I am trying to learn" (35).

To resolve the contradiction between his growing affection for her and his effort to suppress all emotion, he asks Langley to request Anna's resignation. Archie tells Langley that Anna had been trying to seduce him. Rather than lose his best writer, Langley asks Anna to resign. She denies the accusation, but resigns without telling the truth, which would not have been believed anyway. Archie's lie to Anna reveals that his strategy of enduring and accepting without thinking or feeling had damaged his integrity. The lie was a refusal to recognize the growth and change in Anna which was precisely what he claimed he wanted to fight for on a larger scale. With this lie, his endurance act—his game—becomes an excuse for his own failure to act. If he had openly loved her, then it would have been difficult for him to rationalize further suppression of revolutionary feelings.

The last scenes of the screenplay that move forward in time claim that Archie's lie to Anna represents the tragic loss of nerve of all those who wanted a transformed postwar society. The play suggests that the nation as a whole lost its convictions in the process of suppressing them. The only criticism of the screenplay has been directed at the postwar scenes. "Wise friends," says Hare, point out "that the last part of the film in which I bring the lives of the central characters up to date is the weakest."[12] The last scenes are weak and rather obviously so; they merely announce, as in a biographical epilogue, the essential facts of each character's postwar life. And they intrusively claim a national postwar significance for the propaganda/lying metaphor instead of allowing dramatic situations to develop such significance. Hare agrees that the end is clumsy in execution yet adds, "But I cannot concede that the intention was wrong."[13]

As soon as Anna resigns, the film begins the transition to the present with conventions used to update narratives. The screen goes blank and what follows is an expanded version of those telegraphic biographical notes preceding the credits at the end of historical films and documentaries. An anonymous narrator then introduces the closing scene as the final broadcast of the propaganda unit. The updated biographical sketches begin to appear as short, narrated film sequences after the narrator says many of those who worked in the Intelligence and Propaganda services later became prominent in various professions.

Fennel is seen campaigning in a council estate from an election van while the narrator gives a synopsis of his political career with obvious parallels to the career of Labour MP Dick Crossman; Fennel achieved cabinet rank in 1968 which he lost with the Labour defeat in 1970. Langley is seen in a wheelchair on the lawn of an expensive nursing home. Like Ian Fleming, he became a famous thriller writer in the 1950s. Eileen became a successful business woman and the president of the Guild of British Businesswomen. She never married.

The remaining nine sequences are devoted to Archie and Anna. Archie became a highly successful film director in the same way John Boorman, John Schlesinger, and Ken Russell did. He started out making documentaries at the Crown Film Unit before moving on to commercial, feature length movies in the 1950s and 1960s. One sequence is taken from his most famous documentary *A Kind of Life*, which the narrator describes as "a loving and lyrical evocation of his own childhood in Glasgow" (52). The sequence shows a small boy watching his father being washed in a tin bath by his mother. Anger over the poverty of his childhood had given way to sentimental nostalgia. The next sequence is from a later commercial movie. We see a runaway car speed off the end of a pier into the water as the narrator explains that his recent work, featuring Hollywood stars, received little critical attention and respect. Archie's game of suppressing his anger and convictions during the war had permanently damaged his integrity. The mandarin atmosphere Archie thought he had to endure only for the war in Lord Minton's estate became even more entrenched after the war.

In the brief sequences evoking Anna's postwar experience we get the sense of ideals being contested in an ongoing struggle as she tries to live according to Archie's convictions that touched her so deeply. Yet these cryptic scenes tacked onto the play in a sort of epilogue are not enough to offset all the previous scenes set during the war in which ideals are totally contained. In the first of five black-and-white stills she is seen at work in the layout department of an advertising company. In 1956, after ten years, she resigned out of distress "at the compromises forced on her by her profession" (53). Then we see her semi-detached suburban home in Fulham while the narrator informs us that her husband left her after she told him she was having an affair with another man. She then entered "a period of lavish promiscuity," which put her in the hospital with an infected womb. In 1968, after several years of doing research for the Labour Party, she went to live in Wales with a young unmarried woman.

The last of the five still sequences brings the movie into the mid-1970s. A much older Anna is shown playing on a Welsh hillside with a small child. The narrator says she was propelled to write to Archie for the first time since 1942 after she saw his latest movie at a seaside Odeon. She complained "of the falseness of his films, the way they sentimentalized what she knew to be his appalling childhood, and lamenting, in sum, the film's lack of political direction" (53-54).

Anna begins to read the last paragraph of her letter as the camera moves us back into Lord Minton's deserted country house. The country house achieves its clearest significance as a metaphor for the ascendant values in postwar Britain as it forms the visual counterpart to Anna's indictment of that society:

Since that first day at Wendlesham I have been trying to learn, trying to keep faith with the shame and anger I saw in you. . . . Over the years I have been watching the steady impoverishment of the people's ideals, their loss of faith, the lying, the daily inveterate lying, the thirty-year-old deep corrosive national habit of lying and I have remembered you. I have remembered the one lie you told to make me go away. And I now at last have come to understand why you told it. I loved you then and I love you now. For thirty years you have been the beat of my heart. Please, please tell me it is the same for you. (54)

Archie never responded to the letter the narrator tells us. It would not be credible if he did after 30 years of failing to act upon his former convictions.

For the audience much of this letter is redundant. By the end of the propaganda scenes it is clear why Archie lied to Anna. And we already know from the hints of racism and the references to sport that Langley and Fennel are not fighting for any progressive social change. Yet the letter is significant for several reasons. It explicitly claims Archie's private lying as a national reflex. And it marks the culmination of Anna's remarkable growth, which testifies to the transformative power of Archie's convictions.

6

PLENTY: HARE'S DEFINITIVE STATE-OF-THE-NATION PLAY

> Conrad described the world as it exists better than anyone else. He also pulled into it a tremendous longing for what men could be.
> —David Hare, quoted by Mel Gussow in
> *New York Times Magazine*, 1985

When *Plenty* premiered at the Lyttelton Theatre (one of three theatres that comprise the National Theatre) in April 1978, Peter Ansorge noted the "critical vacuum" surrounding Hare's work and offered a large claim that I believe still stands today: "The plays are eminently worth taking seriously and with *Licking Hitler* and *Plenty*, Hare has reached a dazzling creative peak."[1] Of all Hare's many subsequent "tribal pieces" about the moral and political state of British society, none captures the interplay between personal despair and national decline as convincingly as *Plenty*.

Instead of the constricted static scenes of earlier work, *Plenty* presents an epic sweep of action with 12 scenes covering 19 years from 1943 to 1962 in which all is dramatized rather than claimed or assumed. As usual the loss of national ideals is filtered through a single character; this time the source of ideals and the causes of their loss are grounded in the experiences of Susan Traherne, who remains fully engaged in events of central importance to Britain during and after the war. Hare's own estimation of *Plenty* is high for this reason:

Certainly compared to *Teeth'n'Smiles* I would say that *Plenty* is a much better achieved play, in the sense that the actions of the central characters are presented on the stage, in dramatic scenes. You don't just have claims made from a character's own mouth. You actually see the protagonist do things that are the crucial incidents in her life. It's not a play in which a woman sits in a chair and recollects flying into France. I actually show her flying into France.[2]

As in *Knuckle, Teeth'n'Smiles*, and *Licking Hitler*, the basis of moral value in *Plenty* is both individual and national and as such constitutes a form of radicalism within mainstream liberal/consensual parameters. However, *Plenty* is Hare's most powerful and convincing indictment of postwar Britain because at every stage of Susan's postwar experience she remains actively engaged with public realities that resonate with truly national significance.

In Scene Seven, to portray Susan's near suicidal despair as a response to the Suez Crisis is a brilliant stroke: no other event in postwar British history is representative of a national, as opposed to a partisan, collapse of ideals. Although not quite as national a phenomenon, the "spivery" of Mick the cheese grater salesman also testifies to a widespread cynicism in the 1950s. With an unerring grasp of the defining events and essential characteristics of postwar Britain Hare demonstrates in *Plenty* the truth of Stephen's claim in *A Map of the World* that Britain "died in its heart" after the war.[3] In contrast to the passive idealism of Jenny and Maggie (neither do anything to demonstrate how their ideals were created or how they might be acted upon), Susan's ideals are not only clearly born during the war, she also remains active after the war in ways that are idealistic, yet nonpartisan. For 18 months she tries unsuccessfully to conceive a child with an acquaintance with the expectation that society would soon become a more hospitable place for bastards—to use her word. She helps organize the Festival of Britain in 1951, which was a national celebration of hope and renewal. She then takes a job in advertising, an industry that in the early 1950s appeared to be an agent of progressive social change.

It is fitting for a playwright who gravitates to the common moral ground that the "cost of having a conscience" became more significant as fewer and fewer people were willing to believe in public values as the 1970s wore on.[4] The increased difficulty of appealing to a national sense of unity and purpose in 1978 is registered in the much darker mood of *Plenty*. Susan pays such a high psychological and emotional cost for trying to live according to ideals forged during the war that *Plenty* can be read as a farewell to consensual values as much as an endorsement of them: *Plenty* is the last play in which public consensual values define the common moral ground.

In *Plenty* it appears that Hare projected the mood of the late 1970s onto the 1950s because Susan's protest is much more desperate and costly than that of any character in Osborne's or Rattigan's work set in the 1950s. This play takes us well beyond the anger of the "angry young men" of the 1950s. Susan gradually descends into madness as each rebuff by society throws her back further into her own world. She ends up wandering in the Midlands in a state of dementia, alone, and penniless.

In Hare's next two works set in England this pattern of futility, impotence, and escape into madness is reworked in an even darker moods. The title of his TV play *Dreams of Leaving* (1980) announces its central theme: escape. Caroline, the heroine, collapses into madness at the end of the film. Her madness comes as an escape or reprieve from living in the impoverished moral climate of London in the 1970s. William, her ex-lover and the narrator of the film, struggles on in sad accommodation to a society stuck in a deep rut of social and political paralysis. He concludes the play with these words that also capture the mood of *Plenty* and *Wetherby*: "Our lives dismay us. We know no comfort. (*Pause*) We have dreams of leaving. Everyone I know."[5] The last scene of *Plenty*, set in the French countryside in August 1944, is literally Susan's "dream of leaving." As she escapes England for the last time through her madness, the action flashes back to a scene from her brief years of happiness when she worked as an undercover agent in the French resistance.

Escape and dreams of escape become even more central to the structure and themes of Hare's first feature film *Wetherby* (1985) set in Yorkshire of Thatcher's England. As a shocking and violent metaphor for all desperate urges to escape in the film, John Morgan, a young man in his mid-twenties, shoots his brains out in the home of Jean Travers, a stranger in whom he recognizes his own loneliness and despair. The structural preoccupation of the film is to exhume with frequent flashbacks the painful memories Jean Travers spent 30 years suppressing. The film ends with Jean and her friend Stanley sharing a quiet lunch hour in a pub. Jean tells him about one of her sixth formers who ran away that morning. They wish her good luck and then drink to Stanley's toast: "To all our escapes."[6] Their toast is a sad gesture emblematic of the despair governing the mood of *Plenty*, *Dreams of Leaving*, and *Wetherby*.

"Escape" remained the central impulse in Hare's work about England until the mid-1980s when he severed the connection between the state of the nation and the emotional state of individuals and began to define, as he says, "the deep problems of reaction in this country . . . as an emotional quality in the English."[7] With the weight of English society removed from their shoulders, the mood of morally enlightened characters changed from despair to inner peace and happiness. Not surprisingly, the sense of impotence and the patterns of escape in *Plenty*, *Dreams of Leaving* and *Wetherby* express Hare's personal anguish about living in England in the late 1970s and early 1980s. In an interview with Benedict Nightingale of the *New York Times* (introducing Hare to New York theatergoers a week before *Plenty* opened at the Public Theater in October 1982), Hare says he found political developments under Thatcher's Conservative government heartbreaking: "England breaks my heart. My irritation is so great that I spend a lot of time abroad. How could people have become so unprotesting, so apathetic, so resigned to whatever Mrs. Thatcher and her government fling at them?"[8] After *Dreams of Leaving* Hare took a five-year break from writing about England: the film *Saigon: Year of the Cat* (1983) is set in Saigon at the time the Americans left in 1974, and the play *A Map of the World* (1983) is set primarily in Bombay, India.

The brief postscript scenes of *Licking Hitler* can be considered one of the fruitful failures in Hare's development as a playwright because they anticipate the structure and thematic concerns of *Plenty* and *Wetherby*—his most accomplished work along with *Licking Hitler*. We begin to see in Anna's experience the articulation of personal despair, a pattern of escape, and political impotence set against the politically inert 1950s and 1960s covered in *Plenty*. The symbiotic relationship between *Licking Hitler* and *Plenty* is underscored by the fact that Hare wrote *Plenty* just after finishing *Licking Hitler*. While filming *Licking Hitler*, he would spend mornings writing *Plenty*.[9] *Plenty* premiered at the National Theatre in April 1978, just four months after *Licking Hitler* was first shown on BBC TV.

The essentials of Susan's experience—her recoil from society and her subsequent descent into madness—appear in embryonic form in the five truncated scenes devoted to Anna's postwar life in *Licking Hitler*. After Anna leaves the propaganda unit she works in advertising, just as Susan does in the early 1950s. And for both women physical sterility represents the sterility of their efforts to "move on" or live up to their ideals. Anna's retreat from London during the Vietnam demonstrations to live in Wales with a young unmarried mother anticipates Susan's final disengagement from society.

On March 5, 1978, Hare gave a lecture at King's College, Cambridge which was his first extensive assessment of his accomplishments and objectives as a playwright. The fact that Hare bases his comments primarily on *Plenty*—a play he had just finished writing and which was to receive its premiere performance a month later at the National Theatre—suggests that Hare felt he had hit his stride with *Plenty*, that the tentative working-out of a new thematic emphasis in *Licking Hitler* had come to fruition in a play with a structure fully adequate to the new emphasis on historical movement. Hare clearly refers to the structure of *Plenty*, not of *Licking Hitler*, when he describes how a playwright can use dramatic structure as an antidote to political stasis:

When I first wrote, I wrote in the present day, I believed in a purely contemporary drama; so as I headed backwards, I worried I was copping out, avoiding the real difficulties of the day. It took me time to realize that the reason was, if you write about now, just today and nothing else, then you seem to be confronting only stasis; but if you begin to describe the movement of history, if you write plays that cover passages of time, then you begin to find a sense of movement, of social change, if you like; and the facile hopelessness that comes from confronting the day and only the day, the room and only the room, begins to disappear and in its place the writer can offer a record of movement and change.[10]

As Hare spoke these words on March 5, 1978, the only play of his (aside from *Brassneck* which he coauthored with Howard Brenton five years before) that offers a "record of movement and change" over a span of many years is *Licking Hitler* in the postscript scenes devoted to Anna. *Fanshen* presents change and movement, but primarily in theme rather than in structure and scope of action.

The intense focus on individual despair and madness in *Plenty* has puzzled several American theatre critics. They view Susan as eccentric and her madness as primarily a personal psychological problem with mysterious causes. Mel Gussow in a *New York Times* review says: "Susan is not a representative figure, and she is certainly not heroic, at least not after her moment of teen-age valor. During peacetime her actions could be regarded as offhanded and even self-indulgent."[11] It's fair to say that for someone without a close familiarity with postwar British history, the national and representative dimension of Susan's experience would not be immediately apparent. Susan is indeed neurotic, selfish, cruel, self-indulgent, and eventually goes mad, yet the structure and movement of the play counterpoint each stage of her long descent into madness with specific historical realities so that the cause of her madness is found in society as much as herself.

The counterpointing, in more specific terms, sets Susan's efforts to "move on" against a morally impoverished society. Every frustrated attempt to move forward and somehow realize her ideals results in her being pushed further into the past. Twelve scenes rework and amplify this pattern of thwarted forward movement and subsequent recoil from the present into the past.

The play begins with a scene that, except for Scene Eleven near the end of the play, marks the furthest forward point in time. The time is Easter weekend 1962. Susan, with the help of her friend Alice, has spent the night packing all the contents of her Knightsbridge apartment into shipping crates as a prelude to walking out on her husband, who lies drunk and naked on a bare mattress in the middle of a room stripped of all its furnishings, even its wallpaper. Susan hands the house over to Alice to use as a refuge for unmarried mothers and then walks out. Three months later, as we see in Scene Eleven, she ends up in a hotel in Blackpool with Lazar, a former Special Operations agent she hadn't seen since their brief romantic encounter in St. Benoit, France, in November 1943.

It becomes progressively clearer throughout the play that Susan's strange leavetaking in the opening scene is one of many of her desperate attempts to "move on," and to live up to her ideals formed during the Second World War. Her life with her diplomat husband and all their fine possessions had come to epitomize their materially comfortable yet spiritually impoverished society. In Scene Eleven, the chronological sequel to Scene One, Susan explains to Lazar that she "stripped away everything" because "there's only one kind of dignity, that's in living alone."[12] The image of a naked man lying on a mattress in the middle of a bare room of a posh Knightsbridge apartment provides a striking visual equivalent to Susan's effort to strip away her disappointing postwar life. Scene One ends with her embarking on her quest for solitary dignity as she walks out with nothing except the clothes on her back.

Scene Two immediately cuts to St. Benoit in November 1943, the happiest period of Susan's life, when she worked with a Special Operations unit assisting the French resistance. The emotional logic in the juxtaposition of these first two scenes becomes apparent from subsequent repetitions of this pattern: first the attempt to move on and then the escape to the past. The tragedy for Susan is that moving on and escape to the past become the same thing as soon as the war is over. Stepping out of her Knightsbridge apartment

in 1962 is in emotional terms Susan's culminating recoil from the present back
into wartime France.

What Scene Two in St. Benoit does not reveal about Susan's past is as
important as what it does reveal. Hare does something rather unusual in
modern and contemporary British literature: he avoids defining her according
to social pedigree or political tendency. Like Maggie and Jenny before her,
Susan Traherne cannot be clearly positioned on that highly formalized and
delicately nuanced class map that English audiences use to mediate their
responses to fictive characters. When she marries Raymond Brock, a career
diplomat, she takes on an upper-middle professional class coloration, but we
learn nothing about her family, educational background, or political party
affiliation.

Against this conspicuous lack of biographical exposition, St. Benoit stands
out as her formative experience from which all her ideals were formed. For
Susan "moving on" in postwar England means somehow recapturing the sense
of fulfillment she experienced as a secret agent in France. Although Susan's
role as a special agent meant she was alone much of the time in France, she
shared in the exhilarating new hope for the future that the war created in
England and throughout Europe. Aside from Angus Calder's account of the
war in *The People's War* (1969), I know of no better description of the spirit
that Susan draws upon than Frank Thompson's letter to his brother E. P.
Thompson sent from Cairo at Christmas of 1943:

There is a spirit abroad in Europe which is finer and braver than anything that tired
continent has known for centuries, and which cannot be withstood. You can, if you like,
think of it in terms of politics, but it is broader and more generous than any dogma. It is
the confident will of whole people's, who have known the utmost humiliation and
suffering and have triumphed over it, to build their own life once and for all. I like best
to think of it as millions—literally millions—of people . . . completely masters of
themselves, looking only forward, and liking what they see. . . . There is a marvelous
opportunity before us—and all that is required from Britain, America and the U.S.S.R.
is imagination, help and sympathy.[13]

To use Hare's praise of Conrad, frequent echoes of Susan's experience in
France pull a tremendous longing into the play for what England could have
been. Whenever disturbed about the cynicism of postwar Britain, she invariably
invokes some aspect of her experience in France.

The scene in St. Benoit opens with her nervously waiting at night in the
French countryside for a parachute drop of explosives and guns. What should
have been her drop turns out to be an English agent on his first assignment. His
pilot had to drop him 80 miles before the intended drop spot because of a fuel
shortage. He took advantage of Susan's light signal. While waiting for her drop
she tells him how various aspects of his training have become anachronistic
and he tells her about the situation at home. Within minutes the expected drop
arrives, whereupon a Frenchman hiding nearby attempts to steal it. This

provokes Lazar, the English agent, to threaten him with Susan's pistol. After the tensions of these few minutes—Lazar's unexpected arrival, the fear of discovery by the Gestapo, and the close call with the Frenchman—Susan breaks down, crying on the shoulder of Lazar. She breaks the code of silence on such matters by telling him that a friend in her unit had recently been captured and sent to Buchenwald. He decides to stay and help out for a few days. The scene ends with his asking her the French phrase for "a mackerel sky." "Un ciel pommele," she replies (19).

Echoes of this scene from the smallest action and phrase to the general situation appear throughout the play. Susan periodically cleans her pistol and keeps it nearby; she also finds a place to slip in the phrase "a mackerel sky"; she seeks out strangers to recreate the excitement and passion of her brief sexual encounter with Lazar; her "stripping away" everything at the end is a desperate attempt to recapture the fulfillment she felt in France.

Scene Three presents the first variations on the ongoing tension between the moral stasis of postwar British society and Susan's attempt to move on, a tension first established by the juxtaposition of Scenes One and Two. From St. Benoit the action jumps forward five years to the British Embassy in Brussels in June 1947. Susan finds herself in an uncomfortable situation: she was about to begin a two-week touring holiday of Europe when her companion suddenly died of a heart attack while loading their luggage at the hotel. Her companion was Dr. Tony Radley from her Secret Service unit during the war. The fact that they were not married and that he had a wife and three children living in Crediton, Devon makes the disposing of his body a particularly delicate predicament for her. She poses as Radley's wife at the British Embassy, yet the problem of how to spare his wife the painful knowledge of her husband's affair remains. At the embassy she is assisted by Third Secretary Raymond Brock, an ingenuous young man of thirty with "a natural energy he finds hard to contain in the proper manner," and the Ambassador Sir Leonard Darwin, a "silver-haired, immaculate" man in his "late forties" (20). When Darwin leaves the office to reserve her flight, Susan seizes the opportunity to tell Brock the truth and ask him to lie to Mrs. Radley for her. Sparing Mrs. Radley would be reason enough for lying in this context, yet Susan invokes her war experiences as further justification. She assures Brock that being Tony's mistress was incidental and secondary—"I was barely even his mistress"—to their shared desire to escape England for several weeks. Because of the war experience they share, she says "we're rather intolerant, we don't suffer fools. And so we get rather restless back in England" (24). Their holiday is not only an escape from England but a move into a shared past of St. Benoit that represents meaningful action, excitement, and freedom from conventional social constraints. This is the first of Susan's many escapes from England cast in terms of recreating the past.

The end of the scene with Brock and Susan about to have sex on the floor of the ambassador's office would be somewhat perplexing if it were not seen as part of Susan's effort to "move on." When Darwin returns from arranging Susan's return flight, Brock abruptly leaves (to cancel the flight, we soon learn) and Susan is left alone with Darwin, whose glowing description of the "New Europe" under reconstruction—"Jobs. Ideals. Marvelous time to be in Europe"—lends Brock an aura of dynamism that attracts her and motivates their sexual encounter a few minutes later (27). To suppose that Susan would make love to Brock on the spot as payment for his lie would diminish her and trivialize the scene. I suggest that Brock's "natural energy," his willingness to circumvent diplomatic protocol, the progressive aura of the diplomatic service in light of Darwin's description of "New Europe," and the daring of the situation itself that echoes her sexual encounter with Lazar, together provide Susan with the feeling of hope, and of moving on.

The contrast between stasis and Susan's desperate desire to move on deepens in Scene Four. The setting is Susan's small "well maintained but cheerless" (28) flat in Pimlico. Although only three months have passed since Brussels, the tone is much darker in this scene—the first, in chronological terms, to be set in England. The freedom of Brussels and the hint of something new and exciting in a relationship with Brock gives way to greater emphasis on stasis, impotence, and frustration.

The setting here is far from gratuitous. It would be difficult to imagine an area of London more apt than Pimlico to mirror Susan's frustrations at this point. It's the area just south of Victoria Station that features wide straight avenues lined with identical plain, stucco houses. According to David Piper, the author of the Prentice-Hall guide to London, Pimlico is noted for its melancholic atmosphere: "Pimlico has its own peculiar flavour and atmosphere: insecure and uneasily vibrant and lonely as telephone wires where migrant birds collect on autumn dusks. . . . Pimlico has an odd air of barely, even dangerously, prevented permanent decay in a nostalgic middle-age; certainly without 'sights' for the seer in the accepted sense, it is richly melancholic for the expert sniffer of metropolitan atmosphere."[14]

It must be remembered that the year is 1947. Rationing reached a new level of severity in the wake of the harshest winter of the decade. In this scene Hare holds obvious partisan political realities in abeyance—nothing is said of Clement Atlee's leadership, of Labour's small victories to secure real change, of the reactionary retrenchment of the right—and foregrounds the national reality of austerity. They are still eating omelets made from powdered eggs. Brock's beautifully wrapped gift for Susan stands out in sharp contrast to its drab surroundings. Images of austerity within a naturally melancholic Pimlico prepare us to understand why, in Scene Five, Susan seizes upon the Festival of Britain and advertising as harbingers of change and progress.

However, the chief interest of this Scene Four set in Pimlico is in how it sustains the contrast between stasis and Susan's need to move on. The scene begins with several seemingly insignificant details that anticipate the action of the scene and of the play as a whole. Its opening tableau strangely evokes Scene

One with Brock stretched out naked on the bare mattress. Alice sits on the floor. Susan sits on the bed. And Brock lays stretched out asleep across two chairs. Repetition of this tableau signals a repetition of action: Susan leaves Brock in this scene as she does in the opening scene.

The embrace of Brock and Susan at the end of the Brussels scene, repeating the embrace of Lazar at the end of Scene Two (later echoed by her embrace of Mick on the Embankment and her final rendezvous with Lazar at the end of the play) infuses seemingly random events with an emotional rhythm and logic. For instance, her embrace of Brock in the Brussels embassy is obviously a moment of hope with the image of her embrace with Lazar in St. Benoit in the background. Repetition of emblematic moments, words, or images such as the embrace, the tableau of three characters, the phrase "a mackerel sky," and fondling of the gun keep the spirit of France alive as a critical perspective on the present.

Several emblematic and prophetic details, giving Scene Four its own unity, appear in the radio announcement prefacing the scene. The announcer for the BBC Third Program obliquely refers to stasis—the key motif of the scene—and Susan's eventual madness in his comments about the next musical piece *Les Ossifies* composed at the time of the Paris Commune by Vorichef, who died from senile dementia in 1878. Hare fabricated this account of Vorichef (no reference to him or his music can be found in existing English music dictionaries or encyclopedias) to sound the obvious note of the scene: *Les Ossifies* means stasis or death. The central tension of the play between stasis and progress is quickly established as soon as the the announcement ends. Susan's first words, opening the scene, express acute frustration with her life in a society that had fallen away from the hope and ideals of the war: "I want to move on. I do desperately want to feel I'm moving on" (29). These words become the refrain of the scene as she repeats them four times. Vorichef's "senile dementia" looks back to Susan's dementia in Scene One as she strips the flat, including the wallpaper off the walls, and forward to her complete dissociation from present reality at the end of the play.

Some of the details that contribute to the contrast between stasis and progress in this scene are fairly obvious. For instance, Susan's search for something progressive in her life explains her attraction to Alice, who is in every respect the opposite of Brock. She proclaims herself "the only bohemian in London," dresses in men's suits, smokes a foul-smelling hookah, fancies herself a writer, refuses to work at a regular job, and is busy overcompensating for getting a late start sexually. Also, Susan's job is obviously dull and unrewarding: she handles export and import invoices for a shipping company.

Yet Hare provides clear indications that "moving on" for Susan is not simply a matter of getting rid of Brock for more exciting companionship or finding a new job. Alice tells Susan to "just go," leave her job. Susan's response indicates that frustration with her job is symptomatic of frustration with much larger public realities: "I'd like to change everything but I don't know how"

(31). And while Brock sleeps, Alice suggests she leave him for someone younger, as if lack of sexual compatibility was the source of her dissatisfaction. "That's not what I mean," Susan replies (31). Susan never explicitly defines what she means by changing "everything" or "moving on." Hare's reluctance to make Susan articulate sets him apart from other leftist play-wrights—particularly David Edgar and Trevor Griffiths and to a lesser degree Howard Brenton and Howard Barker—who often define the hopes and aspiration of their characters in terms of specific class and/or ideological affiliations.

Susan's war experience gains greater and greater significance as a national standard of excellence in her life as she confronts impasse after impasse in the present. After she says "I'd like to change everything but I don't know how" for the second time, the stage directions reveal this unconscious reflex to turn to the past as if searching for a solution there: "She leans under her bed, pulls out a shoebox, starts to oil and clean her gun" (31). Her decision to leave Brock appears to arrive out of an unconscious process of rationalization mixed with memories of France. Her dissatisfaction with Brock and her intention to leave him are implicit in the language she uses to describe her experience as an agent in France during the war: "People I met only for an hour or two. Astonishing kindness. Bravery. The fact you could meet someone for an hour or two and see the very best of them and then move on. Can you understand?" (36). After she tells him about her moving encounter with Lazar and that she wonders every day where he is, it comes as no surprise when she announces "I think we should try a winter apart" (37).

One of the cumulative effects of this scene, deepened in subsequent scenes, is the sense of isolation, marginality, and even eccentricity of Susan's desires. Her closest companions fail to comprehend the significance of her oft-repeated refrain, "I do desperately want to feel I'm moving on" (29). For Alice "moving on" means a different job or a new relationship. Brock displays even less understanding in a richly ironic observation about Susan's aggressive style and her ability to get what she wants when he says, "The very day I met her, she showed me you must always do what you want. If you want something you must get it. I think that's a wonderful way to live don't you?" (33). He is obviously remembering that day they met at the embassy in Brussels when her boldness in asking him to lie for her provoked a corresponding sexual boldness in him. His glowing praise for her ability to get what she wants follows her lament that she gets nothing she wants. Not only does he fail to understand that she gets nothing she really wants, but he is the victim a few minutes later of her single act of boldness in the scene when she ends their relationship for the next several years. The inability of Alice and Brock to fathom that there are wider implications to Susan's desire to "move on" adds to a portrait of a society oblivious to World War Two idealism.

Scenes Five and Six depend—more than any other portion of the play—on specific historical events for their significance, yet the relative obscurity of these events makes them perhaps the least accessible in the play. Those who grew up in the 1950s and after would likely fail to grasp the significance of Susan's participation in the Festival of Britain and the fact that Scene Five takes place on May 4, 1951, the opening day of the Festival. Would Susan's decision to quit the Festival and take a job in advertising in Scene Five and her rage at the profession 18 months later in Scene Six be understood without the knowledge that advertising, as we know it today, was a relatively new phenomenon in the early 1950s, responsible for creating a powerful myth of progress based on material wealth—a myth more potent in Britain after its decade of austerity than in America? And what possible significance could Mick's attempt—in the opening line of Scene Five—to sell Susan 500 cheese graters for the Festival have if the deal is not identified as part of an extensive black market buying and selling known as "spivery"?

Scenes Five and Six heavily underline the national significance of Susan's postwar experience by playing out the ongoing tension between cynicism and hope against historical realities (the 1951 Festival, advertising, and spivery) that defined the spirit of the late 1950s in a way that went well beyond partisan politics. The central ostensible action of both scenes is highly personal: Susan attempts and fails to conceive a child. In Scene Five, Susan meets Mick, a working-class youth she had met through Alice, on the Embankment opposite the Festival, to ask him if he would be willing to father her child without marriage or any responsibilities beyond conception. He is wary, but flattered. He agrees to the arrangement. In Scene Six, set 18 months later, we learn that the experiment has failed and brought heartbreak to both of them. He appears at her Pimlico flat, after having promised not to see her again, to reproach her for using him. She becomes extremely annoyed and tells him that she chose him in part to avoid having "to drag through this kind of idiot argument . . ." (47). When he doesn't leave after repeated requests, she pulls out her pistol and fires four shots in his direction. In a later scene we learn that she wounded him and she ended up in the Maudsley Hospital with, apparently, a nervous breakdown. Her desire to have a child in such an unconventional manner represents her enormous hope and expectation of social change.

Their sterility signals yet another failure to move on, a failure linked in Susan's mind with national sterility. In her response to Mick's question "What about the kid?" she explicitly links her expectation of social change with having an illegitimate child:

Susan: The child will manage.

Mick: How do you know?

Susan: Being a bastard won't always be so bad . . .

Mick: I wouldn't bet on it.

Susan: England can't be like this for ever. (41)

The contrast between Mick's cynicism about the possibility of social change and Susan's optimism in the last three lines resonates with national significance when put in the light of his class, his illegal trading activities as a "spiv," and her connection to advertising and the Festival.

The idea for the Festival of Britain grew from plans to celebrate the midpoint of the 20th century and the centenary of the Great Exhibition in 1851. However, the social and political realities of 1951 dictated that this backward-looking purpose became secondary to celebrating the future. By 1951 Britain had begun to recover psychologically and economically from the war. Thus the Festival stood as a promise of better things to come for the entire nation. In the words of Michael Frayn, "the Festival was a rainbow—a brilliant sign riding the tail of the storm and promising fairer weather. It marked the ending of the hungry forties and the beginning of an altogether easier decade."[15]

It is far from incidental that Susan and Mick stand talking about having a child while looking across the Thames at the Festival on opening night. Although the heart of the Festival was a vast sprawl of exhibits covering 27 acres on the South Bank, including the newly opened Festival Hall and the area where the National Theatre now stands, it was celebrated in some way in every village and city in the country. The BBC alone devoted 2,700 programs to the Festival.[16] Susan's decision to have a child becomes her personal covenant with a better future in the context of this national celebration of its creative achievements and spiritual healing. We can assume from her frustration in Scene Four that she left her job in the shipping office by late 1947 or early 1948. She then could have spent at least two years working for the Festival, which took three years to launch.

When Susan leaves the Festival the day it opens to work in advertising, the progression is natural. Both appeared as harbingers of social change. Except for the optimism in mood and setting in Scene Five, there is little indication that Susan expected advertising to be a way of "moving on." Of her plans to work for Bovril, she casually says to Mick, "I doubt it it'll stretch me but it would be a way of having some fun" (39). ("Bovril" is the trademark of a company she assisted with their advertising at the Festival.) Yet her rage at her new profession 18 months later in Scene Six clearly reveals former high expectations.

In sharp contrast to the buoyant mood of Scene Five, Scene Six begins with Susan at this high pitch of anger and disgust: "This is hell. . . . I am living in hell. . . . Why do I lie" (43-44). This outburst anticipates her stripping away of all material possessions in the last scenes. Jaded as we are to the blandishments of advertising today, it could be puzzling why Susan had high expectations attached to it without knowing that in the early 1950s advertising possessed a powerful aura of progress. The British social historian Richard Hoggart argues in *The Uses of Literacy* (1957) that in the 1950s advertising—what he calls the "shining barbarism"—helped weaken the springs of collectivist action and particularly working-class protest by perpetrating a dubious analogy between social progress and the growth of material wealth: "'Progressivism' holds out an infinite perspective of increasingly 'good times'—technicolor T.V., all-smelling, all-touching, all-tasting T.V. 'Progressivism' usually starts as a 'progressivism' of things, but cannot stay there; it ineluctably spreads beyond things, by dubious analogies. . . . Like the concept of unlimited freedom, the notion of unlimited progress survives with the popular publicist."[17] We see Susan seduced by this "dubious analogy" between social progress and material progress when she moves from the Festival into advertising.

Throughout the 1950s the Conservatives successfully exploited this dubious analogy: as long as social progress could be defined in terms of material progress, real progress would be deflected and placated, and the status quo preserved. In *Paper Voices* (a study, published in 1975, about the popular press and social change in Britain from 1935 to 1965), Anthony Smith attributes the successful conflation of social and material progress to the conservative press, particularly to Lord Beaverbrook's *Express*. During the 1955 election the *Express* not only colored prosperity blue but also encouraged its audience to believe that in a era of peace and plenty all battles had been won, that the demands of the socialists within the Labour Party were a quaint thing of the past:

The *Express* sang a psalm of prosperity, "an outward and visible sign of an inward financial grace." News from abroad, where great power conflict was abating, and from at home, where rationing had been ended in 1954, alike blended into an image of booming Britain. "The British people never had it so good," said the *Express* in a phrase that [Harold] Macmillan would make famous in the following election. . . . "Who would change governments in the midst of this prosperous stream?" William Barkey demanded.[18]

The assumption that progress equals material comfort also appears in an article written for May Day 1954 by the *Express* gossip columnist William Hickey:

I remember pre-war May Days in Hyde Park. There would be 100,000 or more workers marching along with their banners. It was a brave sight. There were bands and bowler hats. Slogans about the workers of the world uniting. . . . Ah! They were brave days! But now times have changed. You cannot have giant demonstrations when the battle has been won. You cannot sing the Red Flag when one union is fighting another about wage differentials. . . . And the rain dissipated what little ardour may still be left to destroy the capitalist system. . . . This is, essentially, a satisfied country. The basic problems of sharing wealth in an industrial community have been solved. The working class—to use an antiquated phrase—doesn't march in Hyde Park in the rain. In the comfort of their home they watch politicians arguing on TV for their favour. Watch with the amused contempt of men looking at performing fleas in a circus side-show.[19]

The chorus of voices from the Conservative Party, the conservative press, and advertising that sang "psalms of prosperity" and "progressivism" in the early 1950s began to falter only in the late 1950s. Susan's vision of advertising as an opportunity to "move on" becomes credible in light of this buoyant happy chorus. The only thing that might strain credibility is the fact that she steps off what Hoggart calls the "band-wagon of progess" so soon. By 1952, after only 18 months in advertising, she discovers what Hoggart announces in 1957: that "the wagon loaded with its barbarians in wonderland, moves irresistibly forward: not forward to anywhere, but simply forward."[20]

Through Mick, Hare opens up another social phenomenon of the late 1940s and 1950s as regressive as the myth of progress orchestrated by the conservative press and the world of advertising. The stage directions identify Mick as a clean-cut working-class youth of 20 from the East End. And the opening line of Scene Five, his greeting to Susan—"Five hundred cheesegraters"—announces his profession or lack of profession (39). He is a spiv. "Spivery" was a term given to the vast network of black market crime that sprang up during the war to circumvent government rationing regulations. Practically anything from chocolate and nylons to a new suit or a luxury automobile could be bought on this market that depended primarily on stolen goods. It is estimated that £13 million—of recorded thefts—worth of property was stolen in 1947 alone; while in 1938 the figure was £2.5 million pounds.[21] Most of the "traders," known as spivs, were working-class Londoners.

As spivery continued to grow unabated after the war, it revealed more disturbing implications than a gleeful and widespread disrespect for the often absurd rationing policies of the Labour government. Spivery became symptomatic of a widespread and profound disbelief in public morality, collective values, and the possibility of genuine social change. Having been repeatedly disappointed by promises of social change—the failed revolution during the Second World War being the last of many such failures—the working people stopped believing in its possibility. Such resignation to a fixed place in the social and economic tapestry of the nation removed wartime idealism from the national agenda as effectively as the "psalm of prosperity" sung by the Conservative press.

With a few deft strokes—Mick's spivery and his cynical response to Susan's hope that "England can't be like this for ever"—Hare creates a character who displays the deepening postwar cynicism among the working classes described by Hoggart in *Uses of Literacy*. Hoggart suggests that a relatively benign prewar skepticism among the working classes had turned after the war into a much more trenchant cynicism before which all values beyond the private sphere stood suspect:

The new attitude is frequently a refusal to consider any values, because all values are suspect. "I dissent" becomes "It's all boloney," a mockery of all principles and a willingness to destroy them. Cheerful debunking becomes an acid refusal to believe in anything. . . . The use of such attitudes appears to have been extended latterly, as a saving armour against a world in which much is suspected, in spite of its obvious improvements; an armour behind which most of its wearers are puzzled before they are self-indulgent. Where domestic or personal roots are weak or have been forcibly broken, these attitudes can quickly lead to an extensive moral "spivery." . . . Eventually, nothing in this big world can move the "common man" as a "common man." He is infinitely cagey; he puts up so powerful a silent resistance that it can threaten to become a spiritual death, a creeping paralysis of the moral will. . . . This disillusionment presents as great a danger now, and one which (this cannot be said too often) they share with other classes. Outside the personal life they will believe almost nothing consciously; the springs of assent have nearly dried up. . . . There is then a loss of moral tension, a sort of release in accepting a world with little larger meaning.[22]

When Stephen, the idealistic young journalist in *A Map of the World*, says England is "a country that has died in its heart—over twenty, thirty, forty years ago" (22-23) he is talking about the "moral spivery," the "spiritual death," the "creeping paralysis of the moral will," and "the loss of moral tension" that Hoggart argues set the tone of the nation in the 1950s. Susan, with her inarticulate anger and hope, is the foil that exposes this death at many levels of society in *Plenty*.

While Scene Four reveals the isolation of Susan's commitment to change against the incomprehension of friends in a domestic setting, Scenes Five and Six begin to define a larger circle of moral collapse with her ideals further isolated against working-class cynicism and a fraudulent myth of progress created by advertising. The second half of the play—Scenes Seven through Twelve—about the Suez Crisis and the diplomatic world define an ever-widening collapse of "moral tension" to use Hoggart's phrase. When the senior civil servant Sir Andrew Charleson says to Susan that in the Foreign Service there is little to believe in after the loss of empire and that "behavior is all," we see the cynical counterpart to Mick's working-class moral spivery among the ruling class. A total lack of commitment to social change is exposed at both ends of the social and political spectrum.

Greater isolation precipitates a corresponding increase in Susan's sense of desperation and self-delusion, which can be gauged by looking at how echoes of France signal a progressively greater estrangement from her present reality. In Scene Four she merely fondles and cleans her gun, while at the end of Scene Six she actually uses it to shoot Mick. In Scenes Three and Four she uses France as a relatively innocuous justification for lying—first about her relationship to Tony Radley and later for moving on from her relationship with Brock; while in Scenes Five and Six, echoes of France reveal a more radical dissociation from present reality.

The first echo of France in Scene Five merely suggests a movement of escape in Susan's progressive notion of having an illegitimate child with Mick. As she and Mick stand looking over the Thames at the end of the scene, he says, "Great sky. . . . The light, those dots" (43). Susan tells him they call it "a mackerel sky," which is the phrase Lazar taught her. The resurfacing of this phrase comes as an eerie sign of an undercurrent pulling her into the past at the very moment she is in a highly optimistic mood. Her attempt to have an illegitimate child with the expectation of vast social renewal is delusional; yet the phrase indicates that her delusion should be seen as part of her nostalgia for France rather than a quirky personal whim.

The second echo of France in Scene Five confirms the suggestion of the first. Much is revealed about Susan's state of mind when Mick complains of feeling dirty and used by the 18-month experiment and she responds with this question: "Scrabbling about on bombsites, you think I enjoy that?" The audience has good reason to agree with Mick's reply: "Yeah. Very much. I think you do" (47). The unusual length of the experiment—18 months—and the unusual location for their sexual encounters—bombsites—suggest that Susan wanted more than just a child out of the experiment. She wanted to recapture the significance of France by recreating its romantic/sexual encounters. The enormous gap between the excitement and romance of France and the pathetic "scrabbling about on bombsites" with Mick provides a measure of her dissatisfaction with her present life and her dissociation from it.

From the alarming tableau at the end of Scene Six with Mick lying wounded on the floor and Susan waving her pistol at him, Scene Seven moves forward four years to late October 1956, several days after the Suez crisis began. The setting is Susan and Brock's Knightsbridge flat on the night of a dinner party for select friends and colleagues from the diplomatic service. Although the Suez crisis began as a relatively minor military skirmish between the Egyptians and Israelis (cooked up by the French and British to justify their "peacekeeping" military presence and joint recapture of the Suez Canal from Gamal Abdel Nasser who had nationalized it four months before), no other event since the Second World War symbolizes with such clarity the diminished world status of Britain, and, more important for Hare, the profound cynicism at the heart of its ruling establishment.

It soon became obvious to the world that the so-called collusion between France and England, designed to justify their peacekeeping presence with a phony war, was an inept attempt to deflect attention from their imperialist efforts to maintain economic and military control over increasingly nationalistic third world countries: France feared that Nasser's nationalism would continue to influence their colony Algeria; Britain wanted to regain control of the canal and reassert her traditional influence in the Middle East.

The Suez adventure turned into a "crisis" or major international embarrassment for Britain for two reasons. Before landing troops in Egypt on November 5, Britain and France issued an ultimatum to Israel and Egypt that had little bearing on the realities of the war and thus exposed the contrived nature of the conflict. The ultimatum instructed both sides to retire to positions ten miles either side of the canal at a time when Israel would have had to retreat 40 miles and Egypt advance about 80 to follow the order. Through sheer incompetence of their intelligence services, the French and British had underestimated Israeli strength, overestimated the Egyptians, and had failed to reword the ultimatum drawn up in Paris several weeks before. However, primary cause for embarrassment came from the fact that Britain, under pressure from the United States, called a cease-fire after only four days into the conflict, with its troops within 25 miles of Port Said.

By bowing to U.S. pressure, England essentially announced to the world that, in addition to having no moral ground to stand on in this adventure, it no longer possessed the economic and military power to call the shots in the Western world. The expedition was carried out with borrowed money in the sense that England was at that very time negotiating a massive loan from the International Monetary Fund to help stabilize the value of the pound. Also, the crisis came just two weeks before the U.S. elections, with Dwight D. Eisenhower running on a platform of peace. It didn't look good if close allies were conducting thinly veiled imperialistic military adventures at the same time. Both sides, of course, indulged in pious rhetoric to advance similar imperialist interests.

Arguably, the main bone of contention between the British and the Americans was over control of Middle East oil. David Widgery, a British historian, characterizes the Suez adventure as "sordid and incompetent," yet concedes no moral superiority to the Americans. Secretary of State John Foster Dulles, he says, "was using an anti-colonial rhetoric to enable U.S. firms to replace British in the Middle East."[23] (The French were outraged at the British decision to abort the mission because their economy was healthier and their foreign policy more independent of U.S. influence.)

English historians offer conflicting accounts of how the crisis actually unfolded and often disagree about the relative importance of political causes and consequences, but they generally agree that the crisis turned 1956 into an *annus mirabilis* because it stunned the nation into a painful awareness of its reduction in world opinion from a first- to a second- or third-class power. Accordingly, the lessons of Suez for most British historians have mostly to do with the manner of conducting diplomacy and with finding a more realistic and modest role in world affairs. For P. J. Madgwick in *Britain since 1945*, the lesson of Suez is largely a matter of tidying up diplomatic procedures: "Suez affords a splendid example of how not to conduct foreign policy."[24] For Sir Pierson Dixon, Britain's UN representative at the time, the Suez Crisis was to be lamented primarily because it diminished world respect for Britain's integrity. He wrote in his diary in 1957:

At the time I remember feeling very strongly that we had by our action reduced ourselves from a first-class to a third-class power. We revealed our weakness by stopping; and we threw away the moral position on which our world status largely depended. We were greater than our actual strength so long as people knew that we went to war in defense of principle—which is what we did in 1914 and 1939.[25]

Even for David Widgery, who writes from a leftist perspective, the international implications are of greater significance than domestic ones. He considers the colonial military ambitions of the Suez Group ludicrous: "An important wing of the Tory Party, the Suez Group, were reluctant to relinquish the zones the British Army occupied at the end of the desert war and wanted an armed colonial presence in the Near East. Their reasons were military. They still ludicrously wanted Britain to rule the waves."[26] However, Widgery does not ask why such a powerful formation of 30-45 Tory MPs, eager to sustain the British Empire, was doing in Parliament in the first place and why the Tory government remained intact and in power after the crisis.

In Scenes Seven through Nine, Hare ignores the international implications and comes to grips with the more disturbing fact—rarely discussed by historians—that nothing changed within Britain after the Suez Crisis. While Suez provoked sweeping changes in the way most British viewed their role internationally, it initiated very little change in the way they were governed or in the values of its ruling establishment. By 1956 the empire had conclusively disappeared, yet the elitist Foreign Service—with its rhetoric of service and sacrifice for country and empire—remained intact. But, most revealing, the Tory government remained in place and unrepentant: it conceded failure in execution, yet believed the intentions justified. Only four elected officials resigned. Prime Minister Anthony Eden resigned on grounds of ill health, although he lived into his eighties. Anthony Nutting and Sir Edward Boyle—both noncabinet Tory ministers—also resigned. Of the Labour MPs only Stanley Evans resigned from both Parliament and the Labour Party on account of his support of the government. So in spite of much discussion, and albeit weak and belated Labour opposition, there was scarcely a ripple of change within the government.

According to several well-known public figures at the time, if such a massive blunder in the direction and execution of foreign policy had occurred before the Second World War, it would have caused the resignation of the government and a rigorous investigation. In his essay "Parliament and the Establishment," published in 1959, Tory MP Christopher Hollis finds it extraordinary that no investigation followed the crisis and even more extraordinary that the Labour opposition didn't press for one. He argues that to publish a White Paper setting forth the facts should have been in the interests of a Tory Government so confident that its actions would be ultimately justified if all were known:

If the full story is a story which would show that the Government was abundantly justified, one would have thought that here, if ever, the usual precedent would have been followed. A White Paper, setting out all the facts—facts which on this hypothesis would have justified the Government in all that they did—would have been issued and the Socialists would have been dared to challenge this uncontrovertible case on the floor of the House. Nothing of the sort has been done. Why not?[27]

Hollis answers his own question by observing it is at least intelligible, "though not perhaps very glorious," that the Government prefers very little said about its blunders. By implication he finds the Labour response both inglorious and unintelligible:

But what is wholly extraordinary is not so much that the government should be reluctant to publish its defense of its conduct as that the Opposition should be almost as reluctant to demand that they should do so—that, though in general terms the Socialists at the time denounced the action at Suez as wholly disreputable, it should yet, when that action is proved a failure, allow its whole case to go by default and leave it to Mr. Randolph Churchill in a newspaper to expose the failure with no serious support except from a few highly irregular Socialist back benchers.[28]

Hollis offers this peculiar parliamentary inertia after Suez as an example of how Parliament in the 1950s "has almost ceased to function as a real element of our political life."[29] Both parties, he argues, had too many skeletons in their closets to encourage frank discussion about anything except trivial matters. The joint understanding was along the lines of "we won't press you on Suez if you won't press us on our confused policies on nuclear weapons and therefore expose massive splits in the party."

With the empire gone and the country enjoying unprecedented prosperity, the Tory and Labour Parties found very little to believe in except power. For those in Britain still committed to a socialist transformation of society, the Suez Crisis offered a stunning example of the cynicism of the establishment. In 1958 J. B. Priestley published an essay disguised as "a dialogue" entitled *Topside or the Future of England*, which was no doubt inspired in part by the unprecedented display of government inertia after the Suez crisis. The dialogue takes place over dinner between an elderly man, Jordan, and his young nephew, Nigel, who has just received a posting, much to his delight, in the Foreign Service. In a Socratic question/answer form of instruction, Jordan gradually undermines young Nigel's happy confidence that a civil service that selects only "men with the right background and necessary experience" is a good thing for the country. Jordan calls the thing "Topside" and likens it to "a sort of gigantic human polyp. . . . It feeds on all the P's—power, place, privilege, patronage."[30] Jordan sees "Topside" as primarily a postwar phenomenon that would ruin the country because it relegates to the fringes of society all creative protesting forces—"any rebellious, radical, nonconforming type" who believes in something, is willing to act on conviction, and possesses an acute sense of social injustice.

Jordan draws young Nigel's attention to the Suez crisis as the most revealing example of how "Topside" England holds on to power regardless of the integrity of its actions and remains impervious to criticism. I quote Jordan's comments at length because he is shocked and dismayed by Suez for the same reason as Susan is: nothing changed within the country after the fiasco. For Priestley and Susan, Suez established 1956 as a spiritual and moral *annus horibilis* when the establishment "fully revealed itself" as being no longer capable of believing in anything but power.

Jordan: An episode possibly unique in modern British history because, no matter from what point of view it's regarded, it appears equally idiotic and disastrous. No enemy of Britain is clever enough to have designed for her such a supreme piece of imbecility.

Even Topside, hurrying to its defense, hardly knew what to say or how to say it. But what happened afterwards? It was then that the new England of these Fifties, Takers controlled by Topside, fully revealed itself. It was then I realized I was living in a different country. For after Suez nothing happened.

Nigel: Except that Eden, a sick man, resigned, and Macmillan took over.

Jordan: Yes, but the whole sick government ought to have resigned. And in your father's time—and most certainly in my father's time—there'd have been such an outcry that the government would have fallen like coal down a chute. But all we were expected to do was to keep quiet and foot the bill. This was the new Topside England with everything nicely under control. As you say, Harold Macmillan took over. Himself a Suez man, unrepentant and bland, he quite coolly took over.[31]

It is interesting to consider why no other contemporary British playwrights—notably John Osborne, Trevor Griffiths, David Edgar, Caryl Churchill, Howard Barker, and Howard Brenton, all of whom consider English history a concern of theirs—have written about the Suez Crisis, an event so central to postwar British history. Their silence on the matter illustrates the difference between Hare's desire to speak from an unaffiliated national perspective and the explicitly partisan perspective of more radical socialist playwrights.

Suez resists a partisan approach because it arguably exposes a collapse of politics. The Suez fiasco resulted from a complicity of both Tory and Labour Parties and was thus not a partisan political disaster, but a national disaster that revealed, as Priestley and Hollis argue, a cynicism pervading both parties and the ruling establishment as a whole. A playwright such as Edgar, who is much more firmly grounded in a nonconsensual socialist perspective, would, not surprisingly, find other historical events more suitable to write about because the Suez Crisis illustrates neither the failures nor successes of party politics or partisan political theory. A partisan of the left could not use Suez as an auspicious or inauspicious event in the history of the left. To criticize the Labour Party, as Widgery does, for a "parliamentary performance" that "was a sickly mixture of rectitude and utopianism,"[32] does not begin to touch national implications—the larger collapse of moral tension addressed by *Plenty*.

With his partisan perspective, David Edgar bypasses the crucial national event in postwar British history in *Maydays* (1983), touted by the press as "Edgar's epic play of political life since 1945." The setting for Act One, Scene One is simply *"Mayday 1945 England."* Act One, Scene Two takes place at *"A military barracks in Budapest 5 Nov. 1956."*[33] The Suez Crisis, taking place at the exact same time, goes unmentioned. He instead turns to the Soviet suppression of the Hungarian uprising, an event much more pertinent to the shifting theoretical Marxist positions of the protagonists Martin Glass and Jeremy Crowther. Scene Three moves ahead to Easter weekend 1962 with the CND campaign as the central issue of the scene. In *Plenty* Susan walks out on Brock and begins her two month wander in the Midlands the same weekend.

Hare pointedly underlines the irrelevance of the CND to Susan at this stage by having Alice glancingly refer to the Aldermaston March as the latest enthusiasm of her former friends (74).

It is only within Scenes Eight and Nine of *Plenty* that the significance of Suez, as an indicator of the impoverished moral climate of the establishment, is fully driven home. Both scenes show how Susan's hopes for change within Britain after the Suez Crisis, deliriously expressed at the end of Scene Seven, once again go unfulfilled. Structurally, these two scenes illustrate (like the paired Scenes Three/Four and Five/Six) what Hare means by epic writing when he says in an interview with Julian Petley in 1985, "A number of young writers seem to think that if you write a great many monologues and short scenes, that's epic writing. But epic writing on stage is actually about juxtaposition, about what you put next to what."[34]

Scene Eight is set in Susan and Brock's flat in Knightsbridge in July 1961, four years after Suez. The occasion is Darwin's funeral, which Susan insisted on attending even though it meant traveling from Iran where they had been living for the past three years. Brock was posted at the embassy there. The scene begins with the voiceover of a priest concluding Darwin's funeral service as Brock, Susan, Alice, and her pupil Dorcas—all in black—enter the unused Knightsbridge flat. Moments later the point of the scene is hinted at when Brock assures Alice that it was all right to bring Dorcas to the funeral. "She swelled the numbers," he says (59).

The question for the audience is, why do so few—just the four of them—attend the funeral of a former ambassador and senior civil servant in the Foreign Office? Rather than answering the question by having Brock, Susan, and Alice tell each other what they already know—a form of exposition Hare mocks in *The Great Exhibition* with an allusion to Ibsen—Hare introduces a new character, Dorcas, who raises the necessary question. No one attended the funeral because as Susan explains to Dorcas, "he spoke his mind over Suez. In public. He didn't hide his disgust. A lot of people never forgave him for that" (61-62).

In Scene Eight Susan begins to see for herself what Sir Andrew Charleson tells her in Scene Nine: "behavior is all" where there is little to believe in (72). A government willing to ostracize Darwin for resigning in protest clearly stands opposed to change.

Susan's behavior throughout Scene Eight is strangely subdued. Her conversation is terse and unemotional. Her request of Brock to make tea to wash down her pill is the first sign—aside from her suppressed behavior—that she is on medication. Later scenes reveal that Brock gained the authority to have her confined to a mental institution sometime after her spectacular rudeness to both Darwin and himself at their dinner party. No doubt to avoid having to do so, he put her on the tranquilizer Nembutal. By the end of the scene it's clear that the old anger lurks beneath her placid exterior. It's significant that when Brock brings the tea she doesn't take her pill. Just minutes before they expect to begin the return trip to Iran, she reveals her startling decision—made before they left Iran she secretly tells Alice—not to return. She thus forces Brock to desert his post in Iran, which, like Darwin's protest, is unacceptable behavior in the Foreign Service. He is punished with a reassignment to a relatively insignificant job backing up the team negotiating entry into the European Economic Community (EEC).

Susan's abrupt decision sets up the highly revealing encounter in the next scene when she confronts Sir Andrew Charleson at Whitehall about Brock's faltering career. She doesn't want him punished on her account. However, the key reason for juxtaposing Scenes Eight and Nine is to deepen the post-Suez despair of Susan with her encounter with Charleson. Scene Nine begins with Susan being interviewed on BBC radio about her resistance activities in France. Only after she sees the establishment for what it is by its conspicuous absence at Darwin's funeral, does she fully understand the significance of her activity in France. The radio interviewer asks her to respond to allegations that "Special Operations was amateurish, its recruitment methods were haphazard, some of its behaviour was rather cavalier. Did you feel that at the time?" (67). After some reluctance to respond, Susan says she had no opinion at the time, but now believes "that it was one part of the war from which the British emerge with the greatest possible valour and distinction" (67). Susan does not mention Suez, yet the contrast between the loss of integrity at Suez, of which we are reminded in the previous scene, and the "valour and distinction" of France is implicit.

The interview segues into Susan's appointment with Charleson, the head of personnel, at Whitehall. In Charleson Susan meets her complete antithesis. He possesses the qualities—aside from the right background—ideally suited for achieving success in a profession where "behavior is all": impeccable manners and poise, and the ability to dispense with personal conviction in the interest of official policy. Plus he is absolutely free of any illusions about himself or about the nature of his profession. He personifies the collapse of moral tension she has fought since the war. He proves to be her nemesis. After confronting such an articulate and unapologetic spokesman for cynicism at the heart of the government, she can no longer entertain hopes for change.

As soon as he finishes telling her that "behavior is all . . . this is a lesson which you both must learn" (72), she announces her intention of behaving exceedingly bad, the perversely logical thing to do if moral reasons for behavior no longer matter: "I must however warn you of my plan. If Brock is not promoted in the next six days, I am intending to shoot myself" (72). Charleson and his aide try to take her down to the doctor's office which only increases her hysteria. Charleson's lesson completes the lesson of Suez. From this point forward Susan rapidly withdraws from society, first mentally, then physically.

After the shattering interview with Charleson in January 1962, four months lapse until Scene Ten, which takes place the evening before Susan walks out at six in the morning in Scene One. Meanwhile, Brock has lost his job on the EEC team. We gather that Susan has been put back on Nembutal, for the scene begins as a quiet evening in the Knightsbridge flat with Brock and Alice on duty guarding Susan. Brock and Alice exchange small talk while he fiddles with his financial accounts and she stuffs envelopes for her charity appeal. Except for a strange noise from the next room, all is calm and relaxed. Eventually Susan enters the room, a bit dusty and with bloody hands, and calmly announces that she needs the room. Would they please leave momentarily, she asks. Brock assumes from the blood that she has slashed her wrists. A glance in the next room tells him the truth. She has stripped the room completely, even the wallpaper off the walls, thus the bloody hands. Fine vases, artifacts from Persia, books, cutlery, crockery, and lampshades lie broken and jumbled together in crates.

The situation provokes the only burst of outrage from long-suffering Brock: "Your life is selfish, self-interested gain. That's the most charitable interpretation to hand. You claim to be protecting some personal ideal, always at a cost of almost infinite pain to everyone around you. You are selfish, brutish, unkind." "You might really move one," he continues, if you admit that you have "utterly failed" in the "very heart of your life" (79). Brock is right; yet what he says is only half the truth. The claim of the play, insisted upon by implicating society at every stage of Susan's descent into madness, is that the failure at the very heart of Susan's life is largely caused by the failure at the very heart of her society.

In her numbed and withdrawn state, Brock's outburst makes no impression on her. While he goes to call the doctor with the resolve to have her committed, she calmly pours him a "spectacularly large scotch." She knows the Doctor won't be in Easter weekend. She wins again. He ends up lying drunk and naked in the middle of the floor the next morning.

What is not clear at the end of Scene One is clear now: walking out on Brock is her last desperate attempt to move on. This time "moving on," in her advanced state of dementia, becomes a complete escape into the past. The first step is her attempt to replicate her experience in France. Wandering alone in the Midlands for several months with no money and no destination, she pathetically reenacts her solitary existence as an undercover agent.

Scene Eleven in its entirety is her attempt to relive the happiness of her encounter with Lazar, this time with Lazar himself, who tracked her down with a lead from the BBC. He heard the interview and felt compelled to find her. They meet in a seedy hotel in Blackpool, a coastal town just north of Liverpool. The scene opens with Susan lying on the bed with her *"dress crumpled round her thighs."* She murmurs, "Jesus. Jesus. To be happy again" (81). For both of them the encounter is an obsessive recreation of the brief time they spent together in France. Repetition of the very manner of intercourse helps create the fantasy for Lazar. "Don't take your clothes off whatever you do. . . . That would spoil it hopelessly for me," he tells her (81). Susan sustains the illusion by blocking out present reality. She doesn't want to know about his personal life. Yet Lazar continues to share feelings of despair about his life as Susan slips away from him into a vision of France with the aid of cannabis rolled into her cigarette.

She collapses on the bed, he shuts off the lights and walks out. As he opens the door *"the room scatters,"* the stage directions say, and *"where you would expect a corridor you see the fields of France shining brilliantly in a fierce green square"* (84). The action of the final scene flashes back to St. Benoit on a bright August day in 1944, Armistice Day. This situation with one character hating his life, yet stuck, and another escaping is repeated in *Dreams of Leaving* and *Wetherby*. In *Dreams*, William, like Lazar, remains sane yet stuck in a comfortless compromise with society while Caroline escapes to a mental institution. *Wetherby* ends with Jean and Stanley offering a toast to all escapes—Morgan's suicide being the most obvious of several in the film. Susan's escape in *Plenty* takes her to the most radiantly happy time of her life just as she is poised at the beginning of a miserably unhappy life. The short scene shows her on a hill overlooking the countryside. She greets a middle-aged French farmer who finds her exuberance a bit puzzling after he learns she is English: "The English . . . have no feelings, yes? Are stiff" (86). She assures him that "we have grown up. We will improve our world." As they walk down the hill together she says, "my friend. There will be days and days like this" (86). Of these last words from Susan, Howard Brenton says, "that line is irony with an almost tragic weight. You're thinking, 'Indeed Susan, there will be days and days like that—and you're not going to have any of them.'"[35]

This is true in another sense Brenton may not have intended. The idea of tragedy can be used to identify the fine achievement of *Plenty*. In *Modern Tragedy* Raymond Williams says most modern literature is either social or liberal tragedy, rarely both. He explains: "If the reality is ultimately personal, then the crises of civilization are analogues of a psychic or spiritual maladjustment or disaster. If the reality is ultimately social, then the thwarted relationships, the destructive loneliness, the loss of reasons for living, are symptoms or reflections of a disintegrating or decadent society."[36] In *Plenty* the personal and social define each other in an active process without either sphere being relegated to a passive reflective role. Susan's ideals are born and lost as she participates in and responds to the social and political events of her time. As a tragedy about a society in decline because of seemingly intractable social and political causes, *Plenty* doesn't offer the consolation that comes with the resolution of disorder or the restoration of what is lost. However, the tragic rhythm of its action with causal counterpointing of the personal and public expresses the optimism that Britain's postwar malaise can at least be understood.

7

DREAMS OF LEAVING: PRIVATIZATION OF MORALITY BEGINS

> Why do journalists all become cynics? Is it really the things that they
> see? Isn't it more likely . . . the cause of their unhappiness . . . is
> something to do with a loss in themselves?
>
> —William in *Dreams of Leaving*, 1980

Hare wrote *Dreams of Leaving* within two years of completing *Plenty*. It was commissioned by the BBC and broadcast on January 17, 1980, as the "Play for Today" evening feature on BBC-1. It has never been rebroadcast in either Britain or America, which partly explains why it remains one of Hare's more obscure works. Also, as a love story on a very quiet and intimate scale it is rarely referred to in critical discussions that tend to focus primarily on his more obviously political works.

The two TV critics who reviewed the BBC broadcast recognized *Dreams of Leaving* as a clear departure for Hare, which it is, yet I will point out how this is so in ways more radical than they appear to realize. Peter Fiddick of *The Guardian* begins his review as follows: "It was certainly as advertised, a change of pace, mood, pre-occupation, from *Licking Hitler* and others that have come before, generally tagged as having public themes. You could scarcely get more private than *Dreams of Leaving*."[1] Michael Ratcliffe of *The Times* likewise comments on the unusually private focus of the film. He says that, except for Caroline's madness at the end, "Hare was playing dangerously with the Hollywood convention of wretched lover and femme fatale."[2]

Fiddick and Ratcliffe are right ostensibly. *Dreams* contains no references to specific historical events such as the Suez Crisis or Rudolf Hess's flight to Scotland in 1941. The concerns of its characters are more personal than Archie's or Susan's. With an intensity of focus not found in any of the earlier plays, all the action in *Dreams* revolves around a single love affair in London during the summer of 1971 between William Cofax, a naive 24-year-old newspaper reporter recently from Nottingham, and Caroline Alexander, a beautiful and sophisticated woman, also about 24, who moves with ease through a variety of professions.

William narrates the entire film which consists of 105 brief episodes, thus personalizing the love story even further. The first 97 episodes are William's memories of the love affair in 1971, while the last seven episodes jump forward to 1980 and show William's comfortable, married, suburban life—the point in time from which he remembers the summer of 1971. Most of the first 97 episodes portray Caroline's increasingly desperate attempts to suppress her love for William because the existence of needs and desires poses an intolerable contradiction in her life. Within six months she moves from being perfectly at ease and happy to the point of being permanently brain damaged as a result of starving herself in the attempt to control and suppress her love for William.

William's response to love is much less drastic and, befitting the role of narrator, more typical. He moves from emotional innocence to uneasy acceptance of his comfortable conventional life in 1980. Loving Caroline taught him the necessity of curbing his needs and desires. After visiting her in a mental institution, months after he had broken off the relationship, he says, "thank God she was mad."[3] Relief at her madness betrays an attempt to repress his unrequited love. Viewing her as mad allows him to pity her, and pity is much less threatening than love. Nine years later in the updated scenes (all in voiceover) he admits that memories of Caroline still haunt him and create dissatisfactions with his present life. The mode of narration itself, with the past safely contained in a memory that never interferes with his profession or his marriage and never intrudes into his daily conversation, testifies to his powerful defenses against the ongoing subversive impact of his former desire.

Yet *Dreams* is not simply a story of unsuccessful love. The film claims a public significance by showing that the existence of love between Caroline and William raises their political awareness, which throws them into a painful dislocation with a society in which all critical consciousness has been leveled down, to use William's words (32). This linkage of private emotion and public realities rests on an assumption found in Hare's earlier work: the capacity of people to respond to romantic love is profoundly connected to their convictions about society. However, *Dreams* is a significant departure. Love is now the primary transformative experience that leads to the possession of a public moral perspective, while in previous works the way characters express love merely illustrates the way they possess such a perspective. For example, Archie's repression of love for Anna is a function of his repression of political beliefs. And in *Plenty* Susan's physical sterility and inability to love Raymond is emblematic of a widespread failure to live up to national ideals created during the war.

Dreams of Leaving is the first work in which Hare uses romantic love alone as the origin of common moral values because by the late 1970s he no longer believed that collective radicalizing experiences were capable of creating them. As a more optimistic playwright to the left of Hare on the political spectrum, Howard Brenton continued to celebrate collective public experiences as the basis of morality throughout the 1970s and 1980s (industrial strike action in *Weapons of Happiness,* 1976, and grass-roots community activism in *Sleeping Policeman,* 1984). By making love the catalyst for moral enlightenment, Hare takes the first decisive step toward the privatization of morality, a process pressed much further in later works of the 1980s. Although the private sphere is now paramount, essential continuities persist. As in his earlier work from *Knuckle* forward, only two levels of reality come into focus: the very private and the national with no mediating intermediate levels.

How is love isolated as the agent of public moral enlightenment in the lives of William and Caroline? By showing them in contented easy adjustment to a morally impoverished London society before they fall in love. William's initial easy adjustment to the way things are flows from his innocence and naiveté which is somewhat unconvincingly established by his having a provincial background. Apparently, in Nottingham his emotional needs and professional expectations were either so minimal or so readily fulfilled that he never needed to develop defenses against their possible denial. Caroline, on the other hand, is a hardened London veteran. Before meeting William, her uncritical adjustment to London society is a function of her complete repression of emotional needs.

The film begins with several shots of a train hurtling through the English countryside with William looking for a seat in an open carriage. In the accompanying voice-over, William stresses his innocence upon entering London nine years before in 1971. He defines himself in terms that make him an ideal foil to illustrate the subversive impact of love that erupts into his life after he first sees Caroline ten episodes later. "At the time I had no idea what I was doing. I didn't know if it was breakfast or lunch" (11). This is an unusual claim for a leading character in a Hare play to make. Recall the passionate certainty of Jenny and Curly in *Knuckle*, Maggie in *Teeth*, Archie in *Licking Hitler*, and Susan at the end of *Plenty*.

William's befuddled innocence is also unusual in light of his historical context, his age, and his experience as a reporter. Most young men of 24 entering London in 1971 would not be quite so raw, innocent, and apolitical. They would likely have some opinions about the countercultural movement that had peaked in strength only a year or two before. Hare himself was 24 in 1971 and ample evidence indicates that the late 1960s deeply affected him and most of his generation. However William's blank innocence implies that Hare no longer believed history could provide the generation growing up in the 1950s and 1960s with any experiences capable of morally rejuvenating society. The quiet 1950s drive Susan Traherne to madness, while the activist 1960s produce complete indifference in William. Until he falls in love with Caroline, William is an unthinking acquiescent product of the postwar society that Susan ruins her life passionately criticizing. William was born two years after the Second

World War ended so he couldn't have experienced it directly as Susan did, yet surely there were other social or political events or movements that could have given him a critical moral perspective. Hare's thinking had clearly undergone a sea change between *Plenty* and *Dreams of Leaving*.

My reading focuses on two ways the source of public moral value has been relocated from national consensual ideals to the emotional capacities of individuals. First, William and Caroline's new moral consciousness arises not from their participation in events with national significance, but from a private moment when love is spontaneously and mysteriously born. Second, the public dimension of this new consciousness is revealed through their responses to events and realities on a domestic and interpersonal rather than national level. Larger historical realities need not come into focus when the authority for assessing the spiritual health of society springs from subjective states of mind.

In the eight episodes that cover William's brief period in London before meeting Caroline, he describes a life of casual promiscuity with minimal needs and expectations. "At the beginning," he says, "girls were easy to meet" (11). A brief episode in his bare apartment off Cambridge Circus shows him lying in bed with an American girl he picked up in the cinema. In response to her question "All right?" he says, "What? (*Pause.*) Yes. Yes I'm fine" (12). His surprise and incomprehension at her question suggests he couldn't conceive of their encounter being other than fine because of such minimal expectations. He got exactly what he expected: sex. Later Caroline responds to his pleas for greater emotional contact with the same uncomprehending "What," followed by a pause.

While seen dashing after a bus in front of a large newspaper office, he casually describes the termination of a relationship with Angela, a woman he had been living with: "It was six days before I realized she'd left me and another six before I could get over it" (12). This emotionally flat response to the breakup with Angela enhances by contrast the intensity of his love for Caroline and helps isolate it as the crucial transforming experience of his life. William recovers from Angela in six days, yet nine years later admits that memories of Caroline still break his heart.

In the next episode, William falls in love with Caroline with the suddenness often seen in Elizabethan drama (Bel-Emperia and Horatio, Rosalind and Orlando, Romeo and Juliet). For William it is love at first sight. It happens at night in the newspaper offices. He has just handed some of his writing to the editor, Stievel, to check over when he notices Caroline and Aaron 30 feet away negotiating a sale of hash to Colin, the gossip columnist. As the stage directions repeatedly indicate, William stands watching Caroline throughout the sale while Stievel sits reading the copy. After a few minutes, as Colin prepares to pay in the next room, Caroline notices William and returns his stare with an "absolutely level" gaze:

Colin: Are you coming . . .

Caroline: Caroline. (*Pause.*) Yes. I'm coming. (*But she still doesn't move. She just stands, staring at William, and then suddenly turns lightly to Colin, and they go.*) (14)

It's a provocative moment when she completes Colin's question by saying her name while looking straight at William. A trace of her later urgent need to deflect emotional intensity is already seen in her light cheery manner when she "suddenly turns lightly" to Colin before leaving.

The episode ends with a moment that captures the predicament William finds himself in for the rest of his life. He suddenly has greater needs and expectations that extend beyond the personal realm. After Caroline and Aaron leave, William turns to Stievel for his opinion on his writing: "Well? What d'you think? D'you think I should cut it?" Stievel replies, "It's fine. It's absolute rubbish (*He smiles.*) Congratulations. You have the house style" (14). William has just been gripped with what proves to be the passion of his life when Stievel praises him for writing "absolute rubbish"—that is, writing without passion or integrity. William soon understands the significance of this moving encounter with Caroline. As he walks home in the rain in the next episode, he says in voice-over: "From that day on things were never easy. Something had changed for the rest of my life" (14). By "things" he means relationships with women and his newspaper reporting. Love for Caroline escalates his expectations about the quality of his writing and about the ethical conduct of his life in general.

A love story exists in nearly every Hare play, yet this is the first time he uses the cliched convention of love-at-first-sight. The staring may be portentous and faintly ludicrous, but it establishes romantic passion as the single unmistakable cause of William's subsequent discontent and Caroline's strategies of control and repression. By compressing the formation of love into a three to four minute scene, Hare gains maximum dramatic time to deal with William and Caroline's responses to this sudden intrusion of love into their lives. As usual, Hare places greater emphasis on the deformation and repression of desire and ideals than on their formation. The analogous scene in *Plenty* is Scene Two set in St. Benoit, France. In that three to four minute scene we see the formative time in Susan's life and the source of all her subsequent discontent with postwar British society.

The power of love to open up a critical moral perspective on society is revealed in how it alters William and Caroline's behavior in small seemingly insignificant ways in their daily lives. After the fateful exchange of stares in the newsroom, William contrives, with the pretext of writing an article, to meet Caroline at the art gallery where she works as a salesperson. The first sign of her powerful defenses against emotional needs and desires appears in her matter-of-fact explanation of how paintings are sold in a logical way without any regard for particular painterly qualities. She explains that price depends entirely on size, square footage. When he asks if they would have to charge more "if Bacon painted a masterpiece," she replies with a smile, "Good Lord no, what, hell are you mad? . . . It's just logical. It's a business" (16-17). Her emphatic and happy endorsement of a logical marketing system that sells the art of Henry Moore, Barbara Hepworth, David Hockney, and Francis Bacon as if it were lumber indicates that she is denying vital ethical and affective faculties. The contrast between William's higher expectations, implicit in his amazement that there is no ethical criteria, and her easy acceptance, recurs in a personal key when at last he gets to the point of the interview and asks her out to dinner. She stops, looks at him and asks, "Why do you find it so hard to ask?" (17). This episode begins to demonstrate what William means when he says "things were never easy" after falling in love in Caroline.

Following their dinner date they go to William's flat where the gap between their expectations become painfully obvious. William's awkward politeness and eagerness betray his high emotional investment, which confuses and then alienates Caroline, who wants a casual sexual encounter:

William: I'm really pleased you decided to come back with me.

Caroline: What?

William: Just feel . . . (*Pause.*) . . . a good time. (*She looks straight across at him.*)

Caroline: William, I want to make love to you. (18)

A few moments later she impatiently interrupts his rambling description of his next-door neighbor with "William let's get into bed" (18). As she undresses she says, "I love more than anything to make love to strangers. It's the only time I forget who I am" (19). Before she finishes undressing, her brother calls and asks her to help him get out of prison on a charge of drunk driving. No doubt thankful she left him William's number, she seizes the opportunity to escape William's imploring neediness. Contrary to her assurances, she never returns that night, nor does she call to explain. He calls a week later but she resists making plans.

He sees her by chance several weeks later at a news conference for a rock star just released from prison. In the episodes devoted to this encounter, Caroline reveals the destabilizing and subversive nature of desire in her life with the desperation of her strategies of control, her mounting hysteria, and her increasingly blunt deflations of William's idealism and his desire for her. Her effort to maintain her easy acceptance of everything as it is, without indignation, requires increasing amounts of psychic energy.

In the intervening weeks she had taken a job as a photographer for a rock group after being fired by the art gallery for running off three unauthorized lithographs. While showing William a series of her photographs taken in various brothels in London, she says with apparent disregard for his feelings: "You should go. They're wonderful places. I know the addresses. I could soon fix you up" (24). He manages to reply, "Well I would rather . . ." before she cuts him off with commentary on another slide. It becomes progressively clearer that fear of her own emotions causes her to deflate his ideals and his effort to invest their relationship with meaning. In her explanation of why the gallery sacked her, she vehemently rejects William's effort to elevate her petty crime—an "error of taste"—into a protest against the gallery marketing system. "Well in a way you were making a protest." She stops him and says, "No William. No. I was ripping them off" (24). In contrast to the vast arena of national events in which Susan rages, William's tentative protest against cynicism in the art market provides a cameo portrait of Britain's social and political malaise.

Later that evening at William's place Caroline comes as close as she ever does to freely loving William, yet her abrupt shift from a flat to a hysterical emotional state upon confessing her love to him indicates that opening herself up to desires poses a considerable risk to her mental stability. She begins the evening with her defenses intact. As she agrees to go home with him she says, "I like it to be easy. . . . If it just mattered less to you, then you'd be fine" (25). Later, on the bed she withdraws from his embrace and says: "You have that look. I really can't kiss you. . . . The look that says 'help me.' I'm sorry. I can't" (25). At this point, William becomes very angry about her complete disregard for his feelings. She then reveals that she rejects his needs out of fear of her own. Speaking very quietly, she says, "I'm very frightened. I'm in love with you" (26). This admission of love precedes her first manic release of emotion. As she rocks "with grief and joy" in his arms, with tears streaming down her face, she says, "Oh God Jesus William I love you. You're the only man who's ever been kind. You're the first friend . . . the first friend I've trusted. God how I love you" (26). After this eruption of enormous emotional energy, Caroline's strategies of repression become more desperate and obvious. She sleeps with her clothes on that night and all subsequent nights with William. To combine sex with love would be too threatening. The refusal to consummate their love helps rob it of reality.

Her confession of love occurs sometime in May, perhaps as much as four or five weeks after their initial encounter in the newsroom. The remainder of William's narration follows her increasingly desperate attempts over the next six months to reestablish control of her needs and desires. She resumes her promiscuity and complains to William about the neediness of other men in a way that clearly reveals her own fear of love. She calmly explains to William while having dinner at a restaurant that she had to say to one lover who wanted to "drag" her down with "talk about love" that "we had a good night together, why can't we leave it" (28). One might well ask why William tolerates this cruel treatment for three months. At moments such as this, with William behaving with implausible wretchedness, it is easy to agree with Michael Ratcliffe's opinion that "Hare plays dangerously with the Hollywood convention of wretched lover and femme fatale."[4] William explains his dogged perseverance several episodes later as he and Caroline lay on his bed (both fully clothed the stage directions specify) reading Yeats: "always implicit there was always the promise, if I held on, the moment would come" (29). However, other than this scene of happiness reading Yeats together, the play presents little evidence of such promise.

Toward the end of the summer, William protests to his fellow journalists and editors about the pressure to "level everything down" (32). After meeting Caroline he found it difficult to write "rubbish." When he tells her about his protest, she rejects his expectations of praise with a "hysterical" violence that signals her complete withdrawal soon thereafter: "Whenever you do something virtuous, you seem to think you're entitled to come to me and collect some reward. (*A pause, She is hysterical, on the verge of tears. She suddenly spits out her words with great violence.*) Well that sort of weakness disgusts me. Do what you have to. Be your own man" (33). She realizes that his protest at the editorial meeting was also about his dissatisfaction with her pressure to level down needs and expectations in their relationship. For her to recognize any truth in his protest would entail facing her own threatening emotions. The vehemence of her reply betrays the desperation of her need for control. When she says, "that sort of weakness disgusts me," she is really feeling disgust for her own weaknesses. And her advice "be your own man," anticipates her next defense of actually disappearing to be alone, to stand on her own. Several episodes later, William says in voice-over that late in the summer she disappeared for two weeks before she called to say she had been "on her own" (34).

Caroline's experiment in independent living is the first stage of her external physical means of controlling her emotional needs. After she calls, they meet for lunch at her dance studio. As she unconsciously admits, she was attracted to the discipline of dance for the sense of order and control it could give her: "I'm really pleased. I'd forgotten the discipline" (34). In her rejection of his offer of help, it is clear that the "discipline" of dancing gives her the emotional lightness and control she enjoyed before meeting him: "Why would you help me? I'm absolutely fine" (34). Being "absolutely fine" means being absolutely free of any troublesome emotions that could frustrate one's adjustment to the way art is sold or to the lack of integrity in journalism. William's decision to end their relationship fails to penetrate her newly strengthened defenses: Her calm acceptance—"well that's it"—disappoints him. "I'd come for hysterics and loss of control," he says (35).

After William leaves her she maintains control but at the cost of her sanity and nearly her life. Four months after the breakup, around Christmas time, she was found alone in her room weighing 98 pounds. She had starved herself until her mind was permanently damaged and would have died had someone not found her. Her defenses against threatening emotions had become focused and externalized into a preoccupation with controlling her eating, clearly a serious case of anorexia nervosa.

William's response to love exacts a substantial price, although much less than madness. The romance leaves him with a permanent dissatisfaction with his job and later with his marriage and suburban life. Within a few weeks of falling in love, he matures from not knowing whether "it was breakfast or lunch" to being acutely aware of a connection between private emotional poverty and public amorality and cynicism. The clearest instance of his new awareness appears in his angry protest to his colleagues about the pressure to "level everything down" (32) in the newspaper. His protest sets forth the clearest link in the play between private and public morality.

William vents his frustrations during a morning editorial conference with 12 journalists sitting around a table. Stievel opens the meeting with the question, "What do we have to set the world on its ear?" (31). A Miss Collins answers by reading with complete seriousness the first item on the list: "The Queen's in Moose Jaw" (Moose Jaw is a small city in southern Saskatchewan, Canada) (31). Perhaps it's the triviality of such topics that triggers William's long outburst about the cynicism and "smell of bad conscience" on Fleet Street: "Why do journalists all become cynics? Is it really the things that they see? Isn't it more likely . . . the cause of their unhappiness . . . is something to do with a loss in themselves? (*He looks round. Silence.*) I dread a lifetime randomly producing something which we all distrust and despise. I dread the effects on my person of a lifetime given over to royalty and dogs" (32).

William makes this speech at the height of his frustrations with Caroline—after she resumed her promiscuity and just before she disappeared to be on her own. The parallels between what he sees in his colleagues and in Caroline are obvious: the pressure to level down expectations, the cynicism, the "bad conscience," and the "loss in themselves." This protest, however, cannot be seen as merely a projection of temporary personal frustrations with love, because William recalls his immediate sense of shame when the parallels hit him. A colleague, Xan, catches William as he leaves in order to congratulate him, but he goes out without responding. In voice-over he says, "I wasn't speaking to anyone present. I was ashamed. I was speaking to her" (32). He is ashamed because he knows the speech should not be merely a projection of frustrations with Caroline.

He recognizes that his criticisms of the newspaper should be valid independent of his love life. The essence of William's experience is that love has created in him a permanent critical perspective on society that will continually frustrate his adjustment to it. In this regard, William's experience is remarkably similar to Lillian Hempel's in Hare's film *Strapless* (1989). Her love for Raymond Forbes first enlightens her emotionally then transforms her into a political activist fighting against budget cuts in the National Health Service. Both *Dreams of Leaving* and *Strapless* depend on two assumptions: Love is capable of transforming people politically, and a direct correlation exists between the capacity for love and the possession of moral authority.

Dreams ends with an episode that testifies to the permanence of William's discontent. It's the last of the seven episodes that portray his life nine years later. He is married, has two children, and commutes daily by train from his pleasant suburban home. It is clearly a good life and no doubt typical for a successful London journalist. "I haven't done badly," he says. "Laura and I have had some very good times together . . . holidays, parties, evenings at home" (40). Yet memories of Caroline—the substance of the entire play—intrude into the idyll. As he sits reading in the evening with his wife, he says in voice-over: "Obviously Caroline is much with me. I mean it's something I shan't ever forget. What I always took to be her self-confidence, now seems a way she had of hiding her fears. . . . It breaks my heart that she couldn't reach out to me" (40-41).

The play then ends with William and his wife getting into bed while he sums up the impact the summer with Caroline continues to have on his life: "Our lives dismay us. We know no comfort. (*Pause.*) We have dreams of leaving. Everyone I know" (41). The pronouns in the last four sentences—"our," "we," "we," "everyone"—are significantly either plural or indefinite. The film closes—like *Licking Hitler*—with a claim of national relevance. Anna Seaton's realization that Archie's lie became a national habit of lying parallels William's realization that everyone he knows shares his despair and dreams of leaving.

Although a quiet, delicate chamber piece in comparison to the full orchestral blast of *Plenty*, *Dreams of Leaving* is considerably darker. Susan's raging anger and desire appear rousingly optimistic next to this film in which the "springs of action"—to use Richard Hoggart's phrase[5]—have unwound so completely that the passion for a morally and spiritually fulfilling life remains locked up in the purely subjective reality of memory and dream. William's covert act of narration is thus the perfect symbiosis of form and content.

8

WETHERBY: FIRST EVOCATION
OF THATCHER'S BRITAIN

I just wanted to write something very much from my subconscious; a lot
of work I'd been doing had been willed.
                                        —David Hare on *Wetherby*, 1986

During the 1979 general election, the Tories equated a drab Orwellian
totalitarian state with a Labour Party win in a poster posing the question:
"Where will you be in 1984 if Labour wins?"[1] In the film *Wetherby*, set in the
town of Wetherby in Yorkshire in 1984, Hare offers a more despairing portrait
of England under Margaret Thatcher than Orwell's vision of England as Air
Strip One under the watchful eyes of Big Brother.

In Orwell's *1984*, human capacities for love and hope together with a sense
of history and time remain surprisingly robust amid the oppressive bureaucratic
and urban nightmare. Winston Smith displays an acute memory of the
prerevolutionary period. The act of remembering for him is not only free of any
psychic barriers but is a compulsion that prompts him to keep a diary. Despite
nearly insurmountable obstacles, love flourishes between Winston and Julie
after she slips him a note that says simply, "I love you."[2] Winston even
entertains hope for a counterrevolution in this diary entry: "If there is hope it
lies in the proles" (60). This entry precedes a thinly disguised Marxist analysis
of the revolutionary role of the "proles"—clearly the working classes.

The totalitarian state in *1984* forces love, mutual trust, hope, and memory
out of the public sphere, yet they exist relatively undamaged within a strictly
private one. Survival for Winston demands a disguise of self, not an emptying
or transformation of self. His acquiescence to Big Brother is thus partly an act.
When Julia furtively passes him the "I love you" note, Winston betrays no
emotion: "Not to let one's feelings appear in one's face was a habit that had
acquired the status of an instinct" (89).

While individual survival in *1984* requires escape into private memory and spaces, in *Wetherby* it requires a willed impoverishment of consciousness—an escape from self. Memories, a sense of history, hope for the future, needs, desires, and emotional contact with others—all constitute a liability for the characters in *Wetherby*. With images of madness, emotional numbness, and repression in *Licking Hitler, Plenty, Dreams of Leaving,* and *Wetherby,* Hare charts an increasingly bleak assessment of the resources of hope and idealism until they no longer exist in *Wetherby,* even on a subconscious level. The nearest thing to a primary resonating image in *Wetherby* is John Morgan's face with its "central disfiguring blankness" (28). His suicide is the most desperate of the many escapes from consciousness carried out by the chief characters in this film.

What is the particular relevance of *Wetherby* to Thatcher's England? How is the moral climate of England in the early 1980s evoked in images of retreat from consciousness and collapse into solipsism?

According to Arthur L. Morton in *The English Utopia,* a writer, such as Hare, who desperately wants to see social change, yet fully abandons "the belief that a just and decent society is possible and can grow out of existing society," is left with essentially two modes of creative response to his society: He can project his hopes in utopian models of individual and/or social transformation, or he can create "the highest form satire can take" which "is to assume the apotheosis of the policy satirized and make our shuddering humanity recoil from the spectacle of the complete realization of its own ideals."[3] *Wetherby* arguably offers this highest form of satire. Its spectacle of "disfiguring blankness," loneliness, and solipsism can be seen as the apotheosis of Thatcher's "policy"—her social and political ideology. *Wetherby* evokes in images of individual alienation the atrophication of a public consciousness and the sense of belonging to a community as a result of an aggressive reassertion of 19th-century liberalism and a free-market ideology.

In an interview with Jim Hiley of *The Observer* in 1985, Hare says his obsession with trying to evoke in *Wetherby* the climate of Thatcher's Britain "in a tone that is of the 1980's" began as an effort to disprove the charge "made by my former neighbors in Clapham" that he could not write "ordinary people." Of the attitude of "ordinary people"—university students, housewives, solicitors, schoolteachers—under Thatcher, Hare says: "She has bought them relief in a confusing world. She's absolved them from worrying about other people's lives."[4] Absolution "from worrying about other peoples lives" was at the heart of Thatcher's revolution that encouraged a withering of social consciousness. She largely dissolved the social-democratic consensus, in place since 1945, that had been sustained by the widely accepted belief in public and collective means of achieving an equitable distribution of power and wealth. According to Stuart Hall, she was able to cut public spending, privatize major industries and utilities, encourage private medicine, and substantially alter the tax structure, largely because of a successful strategy "to disconnect, in the popular mind, the word 'public' from its association with anything that is good or positive, and to harness it instead to a chain of negative associations which automatically connect it with everything that is nasty, brutish, squalid and bureaucratic—and to exalt, in its place, the private market as the sole criterion of The Good Life."[5] To equate Orwell's vision of a bureaucratic dictatorship with a Labour Party electoral win on campaign posters was part of her strategy to discredit the word "public."

Hare's special talent as a playwright is the ability to limn the national pathologies of Britain in the affective capacities of individuals such as Archie Maclean and Susan Traherne. In *Wetherby* the disturbing legacy of Thatcher's attack on public and collective values can be seen in the alienation of individuals from each other, from their past, from memory, and from the future. Before 1979 Hare felt he was living in a society in which desire for change was out of fashion. In the years after Thatcher's election in 1979 he was confronted for the first time with a society finally moving, but going, in his words, "in reverse."[6]

Writing a play in response to a society going "in reverse" plunged Hare into even greater despair. Benedict Nightingale, who interviewed Hare for the *New York Times* in 1982, says that "Mr. Hare finds it impossible to write about England at all at the moment." It was at that time Hare told Nightingale "England breaks my heart. I find it almost impossible to live here."[7] His writing in the early 1980's reflects this aversion. After *Dreams of Leaving* in 1979, he wrote *A Map of the World* (1982), set in Bombay India, and the TV play *Saigon: Year of the Cat* (1983) about the last days of the American withdrawal from Saigon, before taking up the challenge of his Clapham neighbors to write about England from the perspective of common people.

As a measure of Hare's deepening despair, the critical perspective on contemporary Britain is now buried deep under many layers of repression or is so remote in the past that it becomes a matter of pure nostalgia. In *Dreams of Leaving*, sexual love is the catalyst for William's dissatisfaction with his life in London in the 1970's. However, in *Wetherby*, the capacity William displays for falling in love and for voluntarily remembering the experience nine years later no longer exists. Now, genuine emotional contact at any level is difficult to achieve.

Hare relies heavily on form itself to preserve and express states of repression, inarticulacy, and resistance to consciousness. The story in *Wetherby* could not be told without the freedom of film to excavate in flashbacks deeply repressed memories. Involuntary filmic flashbacks are the most obvious means of propelling the story forward despite the silence and repression of the key characters: At many junctures, the narrative would grind to a halt without the catalyst of a coincidental encounter, a whimsical decision, a fortuitous event, or the amateur curiosity of a detective trying to understand the causes for a mysterious suicide after it had been officially "solved." Thus both forward and backward movements proceed independent of the will of individuals eager to suppress painful memories.

The central event of the play, John Morgan's suicide in front of a stranger, is fraught with a fortuity that suggests it could have happened in front of nearly anyone anywhere in Britain. He intrudes into Jean Travers' life like a randomly shot explosive projectile capable of unearthing pain and suffering wherever it lands. Thus it seems the town of Wetherby is only one of many possible locations for a story of repression.

Morgan (Tim McInnerny), a 25 year old graduate student from the University of Essex, travels north by train to the town of Wetherby in the relatively affluent West Riding of Yorkshire. With extraordinary luck, and a good dose of English reticence on the part of the guests, he manages to crash a small dinner party without being exposed as an intruder. Jean Travers (Vanessa Redgrave), an unmarried middle-aged schoolteacher, hosts the dinner in her cottage—"a perfect Yorkshire farmhouse, rather dilapidated, set in the crook of a hill" (10). Her guests include two middle-aged couples: her lifelong friend Marcia Pilborough (Judi Dench) and her husband Stanley (Ian Holm), the local solicitor, and Roger Braithwaite, a fellow schoolteacher, and his wife Verity. The next day, in the early evening, John returns to Jean's house with a gift of a pair of pheasants. She invites him in for tea and is shocked and amazed upon learning that he was not a friend of Marcia's as she had assumed. As she protests the absurdity of the situation, he calmly puts a gun to his mouth and blows his brains out.

Several hours later the police arrive and begin their investigation. The detective, Mike Langdon (Stuart Wilson), asks the two essential questions of the film, subsequently answered on many levels of investigation: "Why did he do it?" and "Why did he do it here?" (25). On a forensic level, the case is closed in several days. It was obviously a suicide. John's fingerprints are the only ones on the gun and it is established that he was a perfect stranger to those at the party. Logical methods of police investigation are totally incapable of providing the real answers to Langdon's two questions: why did he do it?, and why in front of Jean?

After the suicide, four lines of inquiry gradually reveal that the true crimes in *Wetherby* are emotional crimes people inflict on themselves and on others. Flashbacks move three directions into the past: to Jean Travers' first love for a young airman thirty years before; to John Morgan's life at the University of Essex, and to his activities in Wetherby before the dinner party, and to the dinner party. The flashbacks are woven into postsuicide events spread over three weeks that are primarily concerned with a fourth forward moving line of investigation haphazardly kept alive by Mike Langdon's persistent curiosity about the mysterious suicide.

The ten episodes before the suicide contain clues that anticipate the emotional crimes uncovered by the flashbacks. The idea of emotional lying (a familiar motif in Hare's work starting with *Knuckle*) first appears in the opening scene in which Jean and Stanley sit in a pub idly reminiscing about Nixon. "He was a distinquished member of my own profession" says Stanley (9). Jean responds with a lame pun "liar or lawyer?" that is echoed much later in the film when she watches a TV discussion program about lying in which a panelist says lying by not saying something—"lying by omission"—is morally equal to speaking untruths (70). An unsavory parallel between Jean and Nixon emerges as her own emotional lies of omission to John Morgan and Jim Mortimer (her first love) become exposed later in the film. "Lying by omission" plagues other relationships as well: Roger Braithwaite has an affair with a colleague from Home Economics, and Chrissie, Langdon's girlfriend, leaves him for her former husband, whom she had continued to see all along.

In the first scene of the dinner party, Jean and Marcia steer the conversation onto a theme elaborated in nearly every episode in the film. Jean's observation that nobody loves people with opinions reminds Marcia of a new girl at the library where she works who is "vacant," "distant," and "doesn't really have a personality, she just has a way of suggesting to men that she'll be whatever they want her to be" (12). Marcia finds the vacant new girl typical of a younger generation she cannot understand: "I look at the young—truly—and I am mystified. Want nothing. Need nothing. Have no ambitions. Get married, have children, get a mortgage. . . . That isn't right, is it? Can anyone tell me?" (12). A drip from the ceiling interrupts the conversation so her question—"That isn't right is it?"—goes unanswered. However, Morgan's suicide and the flashbacks into his life at the University of Essex provide a powerful and clear answer—one of many in the play. He becomes obsessed with a vacant young woman, like the one at the library, whose inability to connect emotionally drives him mad.

In a schoolroom scene on the day after the dinner party and just hours before the suicide, Jean bases a lesson, for her fifth formers, on the question, "can you read a person's character in their face?" Ostensibly, the discussion arises from a study of Duncan's comment on the Thane of Cawdor in *Macbeth*: "There's no art . . . to find the mind's construction in the face" (16). Later flashbacks to the dinner party reveal the highly personal relevance of the question to Jean. It emerges that while Jean and John were alone upstairs replacing a broken tile—the cause of the leaking ceiling—he told her that he saw loneliness beneath her "cheerful resolution" and "wonderful enlightenment" (87). After spotting her face in a crowd days before, he followed her with the hope of contact with a person at his level of despair. We see in retrospect that Jean's choice of lesson topic anticipates her ability to disguise feelings to which she thought she had long been hardened. In a sense, the entire film is an exploration into the loneliness and despair beneath the faces of Jean and John.

Langdon's first question, "why did he do it?" is partially answered in a series of flashbacks about Morgan's lonely existence at the University of Essex. A still shot through an uncurtained window shows him sitting at a desk in a room on the twelfth floor of a tower block. His block sits in a row of "sinister, desolated" tower blocks that could be part of the bleak urban landscape of Orwell's *1984* (63). These scenes of desolation and alienation mirror the poverty of Morgan's emotional life. In his desperation for human contact, late one night he breaks into the room of a young woman named Karen Creasy (Suzanna Hamilton) whom he had dated several times. She awakens in a panic, struggles to get away from him, and screams repeatedly, "get out of here," "fuck you, get out," while he pleads, "I only want to talk to you . . . I want some feeling! . . . I want you fucking near me!" (65). This confrontation recurs in an equally desperate key when Jean rejects Morgan's demand for contact on a level of shared despair.

Hare indicates with a small detail that an acute knowledge of medieval English history contributes to Morgan's sense of alienation. As he unpacks his suitcase in a rented room in Wetherby we see the title of his doctoral thesis: "The Norman Village in the Thirteenth Century" (33). Life in England six centuries ago was undoubtedly brutish, yet the title evokes a time when emotions were supposedly expressed more freely and directly and when many communal ties bound people together into a genuine connectedness—the values conspicuously absent from Morgan's life at the University of Essex.

In a flashback to the dinner party at its most lively, Stanley draws Morgan into the conversation as it turns nostalgic. The era of the Norman village is implicitly Morgan's historical perspective that judges the present when he speaks of the remote past with an enormous sense of loss. With his thoughts and inhibitions loosened with much wine and gin, Stanley becomes nostalgic about the "good" he rarely sees in people:

Stanley: When I find good . . . my first feeling is one of nostalgia. For something we've lost. Ask John Morgan.
(*He turns to Morgan. There's a pause.*)

Morgan: Well, I don't know. I only know goodness and anger and revenge and evil and desire . . . these seem to be far better words than neurosis and psychology and paranoia. These old words . . . these good old words have a sort of conviction which all this modern apparatus of language now lacks. . . . We bury these words, these simple feelings, we bury them deep. And all the building over that constitutes this century will not wish these feelings away. (79, 81)

Morgan kills himself within 24 hours because he can no longer feel these "simple feelings"—"goodness," "anger," "revenge," "evil," and "desire." His contrasts between the "modern apparatus of language" versus the premodern, "this century" versus previous centuries, plus the reference to 13th-century English life and Stanley's claim that the "good" has been lost—all move the capacities for goodness and genuine feeling into the remote past . . . and nearly out of consciousness. For it is with great reluctance that Stanley and Morgan speak of what they feel has been lost. Drunkenness induces Stanley to speak. And Morgan speaks because he is pressed to. The film (as opposed to the screenplay) enhances Morgan's reluctance to talk with Stanley's interjection of "come on" after Morgan's hesitation "well, I don't know." Morgan's ensuing speech is the only time in the film he says more than a few words at once.

It's a measure of Hare's despair and understandable concern about where viable public moral values will come from that the remote English past is offered as a vantage point from which to evaluate what is lost in the present. The creative interaction between individuals and the public realm operating in *Plenty* is absent from *Wetherby* because that which is "good" was formed and lost in the past and persists at a very deep level whether people acknowledge it or not. As the repository of the good, the 13th century is a less confident variation on Hare's tendency to abstract moral value from a historical process and treat it as a fixed uncontested totality with national/universal relevance that is accessible through intuition and feeling. John Morgan could be talking about Jenny's soaring vaguely consensual values in *Knuckle* (1974) or Isobel's soul in *The Secret Rapture* (1988) when he says that old words such as "anger," "goodness," "revenge," "evil," and "desire," "don't need defining. If you can't feel them you might as well be dead" (81).

The causal linkage between Morgan's acute knowledge of the past and his suicide stands as the most extreme illustration of an equation borne out by the behavior of the leading characters in *Wetherby*: the greater one's knowledge of the past and inability to suppress memory of it, the greater their despair. Morgan's awareness of what has been lost literally kills him. His suicide in turn pushes Jean unwillingly into her past, to confront her own sense of loss, and thus into a severe depression. Marcia is better equipped to resist troubling memories by temperament and design, for she numbs herself to the present with a flurry of activity. When Jean asks Stanley, while sharing a bottle of wine in a pub, how Marcia is, he answers with a distinct trace of irony: "Oh, she's tremendous. Yes. The Charity Bridge Tournament takes all her time" (91). He intimates that being married to Marcia enhances his loneliness. "If you're frightened of loneliness, never get married," he says to console Jean after she admits that her loneliness attracted John (36).

The past disturbs Marcia when she is forced to confront it in the form of old clothing gathered for a jumble (rummage) sale. On the way to the sale she says to Roger, "It was funny. Cleaning out all my stuff began to upset me" (58). With her resistance to memory, Marcia is similar to the vacant younger generation she criticizes at the dinner party. Marcia's retreat from consciousness is more complete than Jean's or Morgan's; however, Karen Creasy is portrayed as the character best equipped to survive in the 1980's. She has willed herself into a state of emotional blankness. With absolutely no needs or expectations, she is incapable of being disappointed.

The suggestion that Margaret Thatcher is the epitome of the survivor appears at the beginning of the dinner scene in which Stanley and Morgan speak of lost values. Stanley suggests that the true source of Thatcher's policies that wreak a "terrible revenge" on the country is found in her emotional scars and deformities: "Some deep damage. Something inside" (78). The phrases "terrible revenge" and "deep damage" suggest parallels between Thatcher and the central action of the film—Morgan's suicide. Stanley seems to believe that a certain emotional disfigurement accounts for Thatcher's dogmatic, harsh personal style—she is the "iron lady"—and for her political ideology that rests on the assumption that people are motivated only by greed and selfishness and not by any sense of public responsibility. Although it is not convincing to reduce the ideological agenda of the Tory government to a function of the emotional capacities of the prime minister, the play invites us to compare her revenge—the leveling down of the nation to this debased view of human nature—to Morgan's act of revenge on Jean. With his suicide, he pulls Jean down to his level of despair after she refuses to identify with his loneliness.

A partial answer to detective Langdon's second question, "Why did he do it here?"—that is, in front of Jean—emerges in a series of flashbacks leading up to the moment Morgan first sees Jean. As soon as Morgan finishes unpacking in his boardinghouse room facing the town square, he goes to the window with a gun to look for possible targets. A blind rage against the world in general fills him at this point. His plans clearly become more focused when we see him following Marcia from the British Library. He follows her home and then to a jumble sale where he watches her get change from Jean who supervises a stall. His eyes remain fixed on Jean. The stage directions underscore the importance of this moment: "He looks content. He has found what he is looking for" (60). A desire for human contact replaces the unfocused rage of a sniper. He senses in Jean a profound loneliness like his own. In the few hours he spent following Marcia, John saw that she was unsusceptible to loneliness or at least better equipped to deny it. Her manner at the library is crisp and professional. And her home life, as Morgan observes from the bushes of her lovely suburban home, is a bustle of activity with a husband and children to attend to.

Morgan's intuition that Jean was suffering from some deep emotional damage akin to his own is more accurate than he ever realizes. Immediately after his suicide the film flashes back to the happiest moments of her life, in 1953, when she was 19 (Joely Richardson as young Jean) and in love with Jim Mortimer, an airman scheduled to leave soon for the war in Malaya. This first series of flashbacks begins with them making love in a troop carrier and ends with her thinking aloud this touching entry in her diary before going to bed: "Never dreamt, never thought any such happiness possible" (24). In later flashbacks we see that her "lie of omission," for which she suffers deeply for the rest of her life, is her reticence to tell Jim that she needs him and that she doesn't want him to go off to Malaya for seven years. He does so and is murdered shortly thereafter in a gambling and opium den. In the following years she became a spinster and, in the words of Hare, "the classic repressed Englishwoman."[8]

Class differences contribute to the barriers between Jean and Jim in the early 1950's, while they are muted among the younger generation in the 1980's. In a flashback scene with young Marcia, Jean delicately explains that because she reads books she somehow is not allowed to express how she feels with her boyfriend. She is lower middle class and attends university, while Jim is working class. As an engine fitter he is essentially a mechanic for the air force. Class tensions arise in the tea scene when Jim and Jean announce to his parents their plans to marry eventually. In line with working-class tradition, Mr. Mortimer insists that the home, not the university, is the proper place for Jean while Jim is in Malaya. Jim leaves Jean to defend her university plans while he sits in conspicuous silence.

Yet in the scenes set in 1984 there is no indication that class differences might account for the barriers between Jean and John, Karen and John, Langdon and Chrissie. To do so would detract from the larger claim that a retreat into self creates the essential barrier between people in Thatcher's England. This implies that the essential barriers between people could be dismantled, not by getting rid of the class system as it is sustained and perpetuated by the educational system and the monarchy, but by getting people to feel more, and to express their feelings more honestly and directly. To paraphrase John Morgan, everybody needs to exhume the "simple feelings" buried deep within them. As in *Dreams of Leaving*, emotion per se is the source of moral authority with which to evaluate the present.

In *Knuckle* everybody really knows capitalism is bad, thus the portrayal of capitalist as liars. In *Wetherby* everybody deep down really knows what the true "simple feelings" are, thus the portrayal of Jean Travers in a state of deep emotional denial. Three weeks after the suicide, Langdon finally corners Jean into admitting a degree of responsibility for Morgan's death, thereby coming close to exposing her "lie of omission." Flashbacks uncover the mutual despair of Jean and John before her final confrontation with Langdon, yet curiosity about her responsibility keeps the fourth line of investigation alive. Her confession reveals the pivotal emotional lie in the play. The truth emerges reluctantly: In nearly every postsuicide scene—many of which occur by coincidence—someone asks Jean what she did to provoke him, only to be met with her silence.

After a day of investigation Langdon returns to Jean's house to ask a few questions. He manipulates the conversation to draw out of her an explanation about how she might have provoked him. He tells her that people who knew Morgan said he possessed "a blankness. A central disfiguring blankness." She seizes on this quality to justify a tenuous memory of him and thereby dissociate herself. She recalls taking his presence at the dinner party for granted. Langdon says he too had been at dinners where he did not know who everyone was, yet he traps Jean into pained silence when he says "though usually it's different if you're the hostess" (28). The only excuse she could offer is that Morgan crashed her party, but Langdon already knows this, and it wouldn't explain why Morgan killed himself in front of her. On a professional level Langdon's investigation ends here. He resigns himself to never knowing the real cause of the suicide.

Yet the question about her responsibility continues to torment Jean. While fixing breakfast for Jean, Marcia blurts out questions on everybody's mind: "why on earth did he choose to come and do it to you? . . . did you offend him in some way?" (35). Jean stops Marcia's insensitive flow of questions that cut so close to the truth with an answer that preserves the mystery: "I think it was more what we shared. . . . A feeling for solitude" (36). Marcia's conjecture that Jean somehow offended Morgan reappears in a later scene between Langdon and Chrissie. With the case still puzzling him, he muses aloud while taking a bath: "The problem is no crime has been committed." "Unless," responds Chrissie, "she did something to provoke him" (46). Between the suicide and the end of the film the audience is rarely allowed to forget the question of Jean's responsibility.

Langdon and Jean don't meet again for several weeks, yet he sets in motion a series of events that lead to his second confrontation with her silence. At Morgan's funeral in Derby, Langdon meets Karen Creasy, the girl who had vehemently rejected Morgan's appeal for contact. With the detective in him still active, Langdon suggests Karen visit Jean, thinking no doubt that she might shed some light on what really happened. Karen's intrusion into Jean's life, the result of Langdon's whim and Karen's "impulse" (45) to attend the funeral, turns out to be as disturbing to her as Morgan's suicide. Karen is the most frightening apotheosis in the play of Thatcher's policies that encourage people to withdraw into strictly private spheres of concern. She is an intellectual and emotional zombie who displays zest only when eating or watching television. She describes Morgan as "weird" and his suicide as "something silly" (44). She didn't like him because he talked too much about the film *Gandhi* after they saw it together, while she "really didn't think anything" (44). She complains, with complete innocence of the effect she has on people, about how Morgan pestered her until she had to ask his professor to ask him to stop watching her.

After this initial conversation, Karen never again volunteers to talk about Morgan. In fact, within hours she forgets about him. After dinner Jean asks her how long she knew him. Karen replies "who?" and has to be prompted before she realizes Jean is talking about John Morgan. They spend the next evening silently watching television together after Karen again resists talking about Morgan:

Jean: Karen, I feel there's a lot you'd like to tell me.

Karen: Not specially.

Jean: And sometimes you can't get it out.
(*There is a silence. Karen says nothing. Jean moves back, speaking very quietly, defeated.*)
Yes. If you like I'll watch television with you. (52)

Unable to spend a third evening watching TV with this vacant, affectless teenager, Jean escapes to Leeds where she encounters Langdon and Chrissie in a Chinese restaurant—by coincidence he assures her. She explains that she had to get away because Karen had begun to frighten her: "it's as if she's missing a faculty. . . . She has no curiosity" (55). Marcia's claim that men often fall for the vacant, distant type of woman comes to mind when Jean tells Langdon that she suspects Morgan became violently obsessed with Karen. Disturbing parallels exist between Jean and Karen as they do between Marcia and the younger generation. Although Jean realizes that she and Karen have had similar experiences with John, it is the dramatic irony of these scenes that she doesn't see her own repressed silences in Karen's refusal to talk.

The second confrontation between Langdon's questions and Jean's silence occurs directly after the coincidental meeting in the restaurant. He offers to ask Karen to leave so they return to Jean's house together. As they stand outside Karen's upstairs room, Jean decides, out of embarrassment, not to go through with the eviction. As Langdon turns to go, his eyes go to the trapdoor in the ceiling from where, he rightly assumes, Morgan fixed the tile. He seizes the opportunity to ask her what happened between them when they left the dinner party for a few minutes to repair the roof. She frowns, says nothing, then moves by him as she goes down stairs.

Several days later, Langdon's disturbing question returns to plague Jean in the form of a vehement accusation from Karen. The scene is a reception for teachers and parents after a school performance of Robert Bolt's *A Man for All Seasons*. Karen stands alone drinking wine when a parent, Mr. Varley, comes up to her and begins asking harmless questions such as "who are you?" and "what do you do?" (62). Karen immediately recoils from his curiosity, which provokes anger and more curiosity in Mr. Varley. He grabs her arm and repeats his questions as she drops her wine, trying to escape. The spectacle captures the attention of all present. When Jean suggests to her that she "drove Morgan crazy" by resisting such innocent curiosity, Karen flings back this accusative question: "tell me, since you're so clever, what did you do? . . . If it wasn't an accident, I'd love to know what you did" (66-67). Karen, the interrogated, becomes the interrogator and forces Jean to face her own silence on the matter.

Two events conspire to bring Langdon and Jean together for the third time and to her moment of confession. Roger Braithwaite told him that Jean changed from a skirt into slacks while fixing the tile with Morgan. Certainly not incriminating evidence, but enough to confirm Langdon's suspicions that Jean had somehow provoked Morgan. The chief impetus for the third encounter is Chrissie's unanticipated return to her husband, which completely devastates Langdon. Thus he approaches Jean, not as a detective seeking to pin down evidence of a crime, but as a shattered man seeking sympathy and the truth behind an emotional crime analogous to the one he has just suffered. He tells Jean that it undermined "my whole idea of myself. What I'm doing as a policeman" to discover he was the 'subplot' of the 'real story'" (72). The mysterious suicide and Chrissie's mysterious leave-taking had shaken his confidence in his ability to get at the truth at both a professional and personal level. The need to restore his confidence replaces idle curiosity as his motive for investigating the "real story" behind the suicide. The deeply buried emotional explanations for the suicide become accessible to Langdon only when he approaches Jean on an emotional level. Only by revealing the source of his heartbreak does he establish the trust and understanding necessary to elicit a similar emotional frankness.

Langdon's success upon moving into an emotional key illustrates one of the criteria by which we are invited to understand the characters in *Wetherby*: a character's blindness to the reality around him is directly proportional to his or her sensitivity to the emotional complexities of any given situation. An earlier scene between Chrissie and Langdon suggests that his reliance on logic blinded him to the "subplot" of their relationship. He asks her, "isn't it logical" for her to divorce Derek. If he had asked how she felt she wouldn't have been able to sidestep the issue so easily. Langdon's reference to logic clearly echoes Roger's claims about the value of logic to civilization in the immediately preceding scene from the dinner party. Roger is the fool in *Wetherby*, profoundly out of touch with the emotional levels of reality unearthed by the flashbacks. He dismisses his wife's arguments about racism because they are emotional and have "no basis in logic at all." He makes a little speech about logic and claims it "holds society together" and prevents people from killing each other. He believes that without the civilizing constraints of logic people would go around saying what they really feel and the result would be "barbarism" (48, 49). Dramatic ironies abound. As Roger extols the value of logic a young man sits in his midst who spent the day contemplating killing other people because of not enough emotion in his life. And the play as a whole claims people have entered into a new barbarism in the 1980's because they don't say what they truly feel.

Faced, then, with Langdon's dogged persistence and his newfound emotional sensitivity, Jean is, as the stage directions say, "trapped at last" (73). Her story is told with a series of crosscutting flashbacks that reveal the intimate connection in her mind between her emotional "lies of omission" to Morgan and to Jim 30 years before. Guilt fuses the memories: her refusal to speak her true feelings led indirectly to their deaths. In the tile-fixing scene, Morgan's words show a desperate need to establish contact with Jean on the basis of shared loneliness. He needs to feel that he is not the only one in his state of despair. As they lay on the floor after their frantic embrace, he says with increasing vehemence, between her denials: "You're in trouble. . . . You're lonely. You and I—we understand each other. . . . You've been here. Where I am" (87). At length she struggles free, saying, "I haven't. I'm sorry. I haven't been where you are. I have to change." His last words are, "You will," said with "terrifying ferocity" (87).

Killing himself in front of her the next day fulfills his threat. He must have known that his mysterious suicide would stand as a question and accusation in her life, forcing her to admit that she had been where he is. Reactivated memories of Jim Mortimer and repeated questioning about the suicide from Marcia, Langdon, and Karen succeed in pulling Jean back into a despair she denied existed. Jean very likely could have prevented Morgan's death if she had shared with him her feelings of despair—a supposition supported by the evidence that Karen's denial of contact helped drive him mad and that soon after arriving in Wetherby his search for contact replaced the plan to murder people randomly.

The confrontation between Jean and John repeats an analogous moment 30 years before. As we see in this flashback to their last few moments together before he boards the troop carrier, Jean could have stopped Jim from leaving for Malaya if she had expressed her true feelings. As he turns to leave he says: "Are you being true with me? If you've anything to say, speak it now." With tears in her eyes she shakes her head and simply says, "Nothing" (77). Repeated crosscutting between Jim's death—a young Malayan slashing his throat with a knife—and Morgan's suicide heavily underscore the guilt ridden connection in Jean's mind between the two moments of repressed silence.

The act of telling Langdon her story absolves Jean of guilt and releases her from the weight of the past. Their long tender embrace after she finishes her story is an emblem of this release as the stage directions indicate: "They rub their faces together, all the tension going out of them. . . . All the memories go, as they embrace" (89). Thus Jean's three-week nightmarish plunge into the past ends. The few remaining scenes of her teaching and with Stanley in a pub show her resolutely back into a normal round of activity. Confronting the mystery behind Langdon's two questions—never a mystery to Jean—brings no change in her life except a renewed awareness of the need for repression.

Langdon quits his job upon solving the mystery. In a brief sequence in his flat we see him calmly rip his CID (Criminal Investigation Department) card into little pieces. The process of discovering the real reasons for Morgan's suicide teaches him that his professional methods of investigation are woefully inadequate for discovering the "real story" behind the crimes he deals with every day. He experiences the closest thing to an anagnorisis in the film.

To underscore Jean's resumption of emotional retrenchment, the film ends as it begins, with her and Stanley sharing a bottle of wine in a pub. Their toast "to all our escapes" points to the only movement possible in a society going "in reverse." Reduction of consciousness is the common denominator of all the escapes in *Wetherby*. Survival in the 1980s demands it. The ending doesn't suggest that Jean's journey into her repressed past and her ensuing rediscovery of powerful emotions will lead her to start "worrying about other people's lives," to reinvoke Hare's criticism of Thatcher. However, by holding up the capacity to feel as the basis for a critical perspective on the 1980s under

Thatcher, Hare opens up intriguing contradictions that become more apparent in his work of the late 1980s.

It's clear that this film is intended to be an alarming portrait of the consequences of Margaret Thatcher's assault on public morality—an assault that has indeed dissolved some of the shared values between people and left them more alienated. However, it is not clear how Hare can credibly assault an ideology that celebrates individualism by suggesting that people should feel more. The problem here is that the Conservative Party had already claimed the private moral ground Hare chose to stand on in *Wetherby*. John Morgan kills himself because he believes people had buried their "simple feelings." These "simple feelings" operate as the basis for lost connectedness and public value, yet Thatcherism, as a self-consciously ideological movement that polarized political thinking, made it impossible for there to be a "simple" unconscious, inarticulated relationship between feeling and public value in the 1980s.

9

DISCOVERY OF THE SOUL
IN THE 1980s

It was in the seventeenth and eighteenth centuries that morality came generally to be understood as offering a solution to the problems posed by human egoism and that the content of morality came to be largely equated with altruism. For it was in that same period that men came to be thought of as in some dangerous measure egoistic by nature; and it is only once we think of mankind as by nature dangerously egoistic that altruism becomes at once socially necessary and yet apparently impossible and, if and when it occurs, inexplicable. On the traditional Aristotelian view such problems do not arise. For what education in the virtues teaches me is that my good as a man is one and the same as the good of those others with whom I am bound up in human community. There is no way of my pursuing my good which is necessarily antagonistic to you pursuing yours because the good is neither mine peculiarly nor yours peculiarly—goods are not private property.

—Alasdair MacIntyre, *After Virtue*, 1981

In the introductory remarks to her interview with David Hare conducted in the spring of 1989, Kathleen Tynan says that ever since seeing *Knuckle* in 1974 she has been drawn to the light, clever style and leftist views of his drama and film. Yet the true appeal, she says, "has more to do with recognizing a detective of the soul."[1] Hare may have handed her the phrase "detective of the soul" when he told her that his new film *Paris by Night* was about "what all my work is about. It's about the soul."[2] "Detective of the soul" aptly describes the essential unifying concern of *The Secret Rapture* (1988), the film *Strapless* (1989), and *Racing Demon* (1990). It may be said without exaggeration that all the characters in these three works can be divided up into two groups: the enlightened—those in touch with their soul, and the unenlightened—those who somehow suppress or deny their soul.

Although Hare uses the verbal trappings of Christian mysticism to express his sense of soul ("the secret rapture," the racing "demon," and "the immortal soul") it is actually fully humanized as in liberal theology and New Age thinking. "Soul" thus refers to immanent rather than transcendent spiritual powers. Despite this significant difference, soul functions much like a deity in these three works: it is a universal, spiritual power that serves as the ultimate moral authority. Acceptance or denial of this inner spiritual force results in various forms of regeneration or corruption, just as the consequence of accepting or denying God is salvation or damnation.

It is easy to distinguish between the "saved" and the "damned" or the "good" and "evil" in these works. Those with soul possess a sensitivity approaching clairvoyance regarding matters emotional and spiritual. The corollary of this sensitized state of mind in the soulful characters is often a lack of guile about the motives of people less innocent and altruistic. Those with soul also invariably display an extraordinary capacity for love, often expressed as sexual passion. The soulless or the "damned" display a corresponding demonology of characteristics: greed, materialism, emotional illiteracy, cynicism, an inability to love, and an obsession with logic, efficiency, and order.

Several dramatic strategies depend on this vision of polarized states of mind: (1) dramatic action consists of a clash between enlightened and unenlightened sensibilities in which those without soul feel implicitly criticized by the enlightened and therefore oppress them in various ways; (2) character development is defined as movement toward or away from soul, that is, toward greater or lesser emotional sensitivity; (3) with soul as the common ground of morality rather than soaring consensual ideals dramatic action becomes much more private than that of earlier works of the 1970s. Gone are the public settings and vast stretches of time found in *Plenty* and *Licking Hitler*. Action now consists primarily of a series of domestic tableaux dealing with death, marriage, birth, falling in and out of love, and illness. Hare selects such moments because they are capable of touching the deepest emotional and spiritual chords. A deficiency or abundance of sensitivity can be revealed in a character's response to such emotionally charged moments.

Each of these three recent works offers a variation on these dramatic strategies first fully established in *The Secret Rapture*. The title refers to the moment when a Catholic nun achieves spiritual union or marriage with Christ. To achieve this union was and still is the distinctive spiritual quest of the Carmelite order of nuns, the most famous of whom is Teresa de Avila of Spain (1515-1582). The analogous "rapture" in the play occurs offstage between Scenes Five and Six when Isobel Glass achieves spiritual union with her own soul while walking naked on a paradisial beach at Lanzarote. After this rapturous experience she remains in what appears to be a mystical trance, suffused with a heightened awareness of the spiritual power within her, until murdered by her ex-lover and business partner Irwin Posner, who had lost his soul out of greed several weeks before. In exchange for a doubled salary he betrayed his love for Isobel and pressured her to accept a takeover of their small graphics design firm in London.

The trajectories of Irwin and Isobel—the corruption of his soul, the sanctification of her soul—and the resulting antagonism between them characterizes the dynamic between the soulless and the soulful in these works of the late 1980s. Irwin kills Isobel, not out of unrequited love (he had by that time already demonstrated his inability to truly love), but because she comes to personify precisely what he had lost: soul. Thus his obsessive need, as Isobel tells him, "to be saved through another person."[3]

A similar dynamic exists between Isobel and her older sister Marion, who is the junior minister of the environment for the Tory government. Every encounter between them provokes in Marion a towering rage because Isobel's goodness and spirituality make her feel inadequate and guilty. As the play is chiefly about these two sisters, Marion is angry most of the time, until, as a direct consequence of mourning Isobel's death, she undergoes a spiritual regeneration and begins to understand for the first time in her life that people like Isobel make her angry because they confront her with the poverty of her own inner life. In the last scene she explains these self-discoveries to her husband Tom: "It's all obscure. It frightens me. What people want. Tom. It's frightened me ever since I was a child. My memory of childhood is of watching and always pretending. I don't have the right equipment. I can't interpret what people feel. I've stood at the side. Just watching. It's made me angry. I've been angry all my life. Because people's passions seem so out of control" (83).

In Marion's angry response to Isobel's goodness Hare believes he has grasped something essential about the nature of the current Tory government under Margaret Thatcher, its opposition and how they interact. In the Tynan interview he talks about the larger social implications of the Marion/Isobel dynamic as follows:

It's about people who are corrupted by the age. Because of that, they take certain attitudes to the good character. . . . Isobel is a woman who has certain values, but, I'm afraid, in the course of the evening she becomes less and less able to articulate them because of the effort of trying to swing round people who are so rigid in their way of thinking. That's really what the play is about. The play is a tragedy, and she has a fatal flaw. What is her fatal flaw? That she's a good person. People gang up on her because implicitly they feel criticized by her. That, I'm afraid, is the effect of the good on us nowadays.[4]

This statement reveals assumptions that I will explore more fully later. Yet I'll say at this point that the notion that good people have the power to induce guilt and rage in bad people verges on the sentimental. Furthermore, it would be far from clear how this struggle between good and bad sensibilities addresses the political realities of England in the 1980s in the way Hare intended it to, if Marion (the main person to "gang up on" Isobel) were not identified as a junior minister in the Tory government. She is clearly modeled after Mrs. Thatcher.

In the absence of any impersonal (that is, ideological or institutional) dimension to Marion's conservatism or Isobel's goodness it appears that two equations are operating here: emotional illiteracy equals conservative orthodoxy, and emotional sensitivity equals opposition to orthodoxy. With conservative beliefs and opposition to them reduced to states of mind, to personal dispositions, politics becomes a clash of sensibilities.

Hare uses the phrase "gang up" to describe the "orthodox" response to Isobel's goodness: "People gang-up on her because implicitly they feel criticized by her" he says.[5] In other words, Hare is saying in *The Secret Rapture* that the policies and behavior of those in the Tory government in the 1980s were partly motivated by guilt-induced anger at the spiritually enlightened forces of the opposition. The fact that Isobel and later Lionel in *Racing Demon* unintentionally mobilize the soulless powers against them—such mobilization being the central action of both plays—attests to the enormous power of their goodness, which is at the same time rendered powerless and impotent by the "ganging up." Isobel and Lionel cannot actually do anything with their goodness, aside from stirring up oppression.

I suggest that what we find here embedded at the heart of these works is the consoling fantasy of the weak and alienated, found in all sentimental literature, that flatters their sense of goodness and at the same time justifies their inability to act upon such goodness. Literature becomes sentimental when it celebrates goodness that has been rendered incapable of being acted upon, thus the familiar tag—"virtue in distress."[6] With his "ganging up" scenarios Hare revives the essentials of sentimental literature. In her defense of the sentimental in her book *Sentimental Modernism* (1991), Suzanne Clark is quite right when she says that modernist discourse is contemptuous of emotion, yet she simplifies antisentimentalism when she limits it to being part of the modernist attack on the emotional capacities of woman.[7] To be antisentimental, according to my use of the word, is to be suspicious of emotion when it remains passive and when its power and moral authority are overestimated.

In the long passage from the Tynan interview quoted above, Hare believes that a public, ideological dimension exists in this "ganging up" dynamic when he says that Isobel tries to express "certain values" and that people such as Marion are "corrupted by the age." There is room for skepticism here. First, it is difficult to see how Isobel expresses "certain values." She is the most passive and inarticulate leading character Hare has ever created. He revised the part for the New York production because many people had found her too passive, too good, too innocent. They wondered why goodness had to be so weak. In the revised version Hare gave her a few new lines such as "plainly," "I know," "of course," and "I know that," which make her more assertive, but do not help to clarify what values are expressed.[8] The only thing Isobel expresses is goodness, yet personal goodness alone is not a value in the public, ideological sense of the word. Goodness expressed as emotional sensitivity is an admirable personal attribute that cannot be automatically aligned with any particular political orientation. Personal goodness is just as likely to be found among Tory politicians as it is among Labour politicians.

As for Hare's claim that people like Marion have been "corrupted by the age," the word "corrupted" clearly refers to her greed and materialism, but how does the play give personal greed a public dimension implied by the phrase "the age"? In what sense has "the age" (that is, public values or historical and cultural forces) caused her to be greedy and materialistic, if, as she realizes while undergoing her regeneration in the last scene, she has been missing vital emotional and spiritual faculties ever since she was a child? How do we reconcile Marion's claim that she lacked vital emotional faculties since she was a child with Hare's observation that "the age" corrupted her? What is the source of her materialism?

I suggest that to understand how "the age" could corrupt Marion entails seeing that greed and "the age" have come to mean the same thing for Hare. That is, Hare no longer recognizes a distinction between certain emotional styles and the ideology that encourages the accumulation of personal wealth. This conflation of public and private spheres appears in an interview conducted by Gerard Raymond of *Theatre Week* in which Hare amplifies Marion's greed into a "governing principle": "'A sense of politics has nothing to do with preaching, polemics or ideology . . . it is about the effect that dominant beliefs of the day have on us.' In *The Secret Rapture* the governing principle, overriding all moral values, is the 'sanctification of greed.'"[9]

Can Isobel's goodness or Marion's greed be considered a value, a "governing principle," or a "dominant belief"? In an interview with Carol Homden of *Plays and Players* in 1988 Hare explains that recently he had been trying to define the source of reaction as "an emotional quality in the English": "Fifteen years ago I said in response to the theatre of the left, you can't write about politics without talking about the deep problems of reaction in this country. Why are the people so reactionary? I've gone on plugging about this; I've tried to define it more and more as an emotional quality in the English."[10] For those who view the emotional qualities of the English as the starting point rather than the end of inquiry into the problems of reaction in Britain, Hare's recent work focuses on only the tip of the iceberg. A distinguishing feature of his work written in the decade between *Plenty* and the trilogy (*The Absence of War*, *Racing Demon*, and *Murmuring Judges*—see Chapter 11) is the absence of attention to social, political, ideological, or institutional sources of reaction.

Aside from emotional differences, what establishes Marion as reactionary and Isobel as nonreactionary? The 1980s saw spectacular acts of individual greed which gave the decade a certain notoriety; however, greed is symptomatic of the neoliberal, free-market ideology of possessive individualism and not itself a belief or principle. In other words, the 1980s didn't become the decade of greed as a result of many discrete individuals suddenly becoming greedy or even from individuals in the Tory government (or the Reagan administration) who were fated to be greedy with congenitally defective characters.

All the essential ingredients of *The Secret Rapture* reappear reworked in *Strapless*, a feature film starring Bruno Gantz as Raymond Forbes and Blair Brown as Lillian Hempel. It premiered at the Toronto International Film Festival in September 1989. The film is about Lillian's achievement of spiritual enlightenment to which the title refers. Lillian, a 36-year-old American National Health Service doctor, achieves enlightenment or "straplessness" shortly before she models a strapless dress at a fashion show at the end of the film.[11] The catalyst for her enlightenment is love: the entire film is essentially one long courtship between Lillian and Raymond who, like Isobel, is soul personified. He carries the spiritual charge that touches Lillian's soul and transforms her, but only after she undergoes a long and painful process of self-discovery and self-acceptance.

When Raymond suddenly disappears without a trace after three months together, Lillian's subsequent painful adjustment consists of learning, as Isobel says in *The Secret Rapture*, that "the great thing is to love. If you're loved back then it's a bonus" (5). Lillian's initial rage and hurt pride give way to radiant happiness as she realizes that being in love with Raymond awakened dormant spiritual powers within her. The film concludes with Lillian spiritually "strapless": that is, fully alive to the abundant spiritual resources of her soul. Isobel is in a similar rapturous state before her death.

Hare says that he wrote about the Church of England in *Racing Demon* (which opened at the National Theatre in January 1990) "because the state of the church reflects the way things are generally in this country."[12] "The way things are" in church and country is characterized as a conflict between the emotionally sensitive and insensitive. *Racing Demon* is thus a remarkably close reworking of *The Secret Rapture*. Much like Marion, the Thatcherite "enterprising" bishops are presented as number crunching, emotionally illiterate bureaucrats who want to run the church efficiently like a business. Getting bums on seats is the sum total of success for them. Their enlightened counterparts are three vicars from a small parish in the South London diocese controlled by one of the bishops. These three vicars struggle to alleviate the suffering of their impoverished parishioners, primarily Jamaicans. True religion for them, like the true love of Lillian or the saintliness of Isobel, flows from the fullest acceptance of one's self or soul.

One of the central focuses of the play is the ongoing antagonism between Lionel Espy—the kindest, gentlest, and most sensitive of the three vicars—and Bishop Southwark who in the end manages to remove Lionel from his London diocese. During the course of the play Southwark accuses Lionel of nearly everything a vicar could be accused of—unenthusiastic performance of the litergy, lukewarm faith, incompetence, inefficiency—yet it becomes evident in their final confrontation that he doesn't like Lionel because his goodness makes him feel uneasy and inauthentic. Southwark's religious orthodoxy, like Marion's political orientation, turns out to be an unenlightened emotional condition.

The fact that both *Racing Demon* and *The Secret Rapture* are built around the dramatic action of soulless people "ganging up" on soulful people because they feel implicitly criticized by them indicates that this "ganging up" dynamic is crucial to Hare's thinking about "the way things are generally" in Britain between those sympathetic to Thatcherism and those opposed. In *Strapless* the "ganging up" dynamic doesn't appear, although the polarization between emotional literacy and illiteracy does in a series of contrasts between the pre and postenlightenment experience of Lillian.

How does Hare's sense that politics in England in the 1980s is essentially the "ganging up" of the soulless on the soulful fit into the trajectory of his playwrighting career? And what are the implications of appealing to the soul as the ultimate moral authority?

To anyone familiar with Hare's earlier successes (particularly *Knuckle*, *Teeth' n'Smiles*, *Licking Hitler*, and *Plenty*) it may come as a surprise that the soul now operates as the site of morality in these works of the middle to late 1980s. Even though Hare had begun to privatize morality as early as 1979 in *Dreams of Leaving*, his earlier work of the 1970s so firmly embraces national public ideals that it was some time before I understood the magnitude of the shift. The fact that a paradoxical humanist socialism has been the characteristic form of leftism in Britain for the past hundred years—beginning with William Morris, George Bernard Shaw, the Fabians, George Orwell, and later evident in the drama of John Osborne, early Edward Bond, Arnold Wesker—makes it easier to see how Hare's journey inward was not an unusual direction for him to take.

With his recent interest in the emotional dimension of reaction,[13] and his claim that his work is "about the soul,"[14] Hare would be the first to distinguish himself from socialists to the left of him who believe morality is not based on individuals be they good or evil, altruistic or egoistic, emotionally sensitive or insensitive. Perhaps the most trenchant criticism of the mainstream British humanist/socialist tradition comes from David Marquand, a former Labour MP, who says in *The Unprincipled Society* (1988): "Altruism is merely a special case of egoism. It is still freely chosen by the individual. And what the individual can freely choose he can freely unchoose."[15] Isobel's saintly goodness, Marion's and Lillian's regeneration, and Lionel's admirable charity work—all a function of emotional sensitivity—could be considered, in Marquand's words, "spasms of alruism" and therefore not capable of providing the basis for a public good.[16] Political and social thinking that stresses the public nature of morality claims that in order for such "spasms" to have a meaningful and consistent impact on society, they need to be orchestrated within a collective or consensual vision of public goods that are greater than and independent of the sum of individual interests and dispositions of character.

Many people would agree with Marquand that there is a distinction between character (personality) and political beliefs, that there is no direct and necessary correlation between any personal quality (goodness, emotional insensitivity, or the capacity for love) and any particular political orientation. Tories are just as likely to be kind, loving, good, sincere, and emotionally literate as anyone else in British society. Furthermore, good people can with utter sincerity pursue political policies with disastrous consequences for the country, just as bad people can pursue with utter insincerity political policies with positive consequences for the country. Hare's work of the late 1980s opens itself up to such observations because they reconstitute political issues into conflicting dispositions of character.

Can the vast changes brought about by the Tory government during the 1980s be reduced to emotional insensitivity and a massive case of bad temper caused by goodness? Will the National Health Service need to rely on love induced spiritual enlightenment for its survival? To what degree did the friction in the Church of England between the enterprising evangelical faction and the liberal faction deeply concerned about poverty in the inner cities result from a clash of personalities?

Hare's appeal to the soul appears to be a form of moral intuitionism. The belief that the discovery of what is right and wrong simply entails looking deeply enough into the soul depends on the assumption that within everyone a sealed off portion of human consciousness exists free of social and historical conditioning. However, any appeal to a universal spirit (whether it be called Brahman, the noosphere, the human heart, God, or soul) masks specific cultural and political viewpoints: in the case of Hare in the mid-1980s, those of a politically disoriented and weakened group of middle- and upper-class people who live predominantly in Southern England, and tend to work in the arts, the media, education, or one of the caring professions.

While positing the soul as the ultimate moral authority is suspect in the most cohesive of cultures, it is particularly so in the context of Britain in the 1980s: how can the soul provide the basis of opposition to a government that has explicitly and aggressively redefined morality as the possession of individuals? In what was by many accounts the most politically and morally polarized decade since before the war, Hare universalized the liberal values shared with the new right and then colonized an enlightened position within them. According to John Peter of *The Sunday Times*, the appearance but not the substance of opposition to Thatcherism—seen in Hare's work—was typical of a theatre establishment unaccustomed to facing stark political and moral choices. Peter says that it was the explicitness and bluntness of Thatcher's views that unnerved British theater in general in the 1980s and left it struggling to find a viable language of opposition: "Apart from some agit-prop-style plays by fringe groups, which you could simply call the theatre of discontent, British drama hasn't found a language to deal with the 1980s, when the issues are starker, politics tougher, and the moral choices more extreme."[17] Playwrights such as Hare were understandably reticent to embrace the stark alternative left to them by Thatcherism (collectivism) especially as they were accustomed to working within the framework of a vaguely leftist humanism in which the basis of morality had long been both individual and universal/national, yet rarely collective.

Before setting forth several historical explanations for Hare's discovery of the soul as well as his own sense of how his thinking evolved in the 1980s, I want to establish very clearly the precise nature of this shift by first contrasting briefly these works of the late 1980s with earlier work of the 1970s in which moral authority is firmly located in the public sphere, and then by explaining in greater detail how the site of moral authority gradually moves inward beginning with *Dreams of Leaving* (1980), *Saigon: Year of the Cat* (1983), and *A Map of the World* (1982), and culminating in *The Bay at Nice* and *Wrecked Eggs* (1986) which explicitly prepare for the full embrace of soul in *The Secret Rapture* (1988).

Hare's work of the 1980s (*The Secret Rapture, Strapless,* and *Racing Demon*) neatly inverts the following general statements about his work of the 1970s (*Knuckle, Teeth'n'Smiles, Licking Hitler* and *Plenty*) in which morality is assumed to be a public matter: (1) The central conflict is always between an individual, who occupies the moral high ground of the play by virtue of his or her public convictions, and various institutions (the City of London, Cambridge, the Secret Service, the country house way of life) that obstruct progressive social change. (2) No character is ever judged to be either morally reprehensible or admirable on the basis of personality or character; however, the "villains" tend to be kind, gracious, loving, and civilized people, while the idealists—Archie, Susan, Maggie—are invariably cruel, selfish, and emotionally disturbed in some way. (3) Ideals, political passions, and participation in transforming social experiences carry the spark of romantic love and moral enlightenment rather than qualities of soul.

In *Knuckle,* Patrick Delafield is a very good man on a personal level: "A very Christian man" his Scottish housekeeper calls him (79). His moral corruption stems not from any defect of character, but from his position as an investment banker in the City of London. His daughter Sarah occupies the moral high ground in the play with her rage at his profession, and maintains her integrity at the cost of being strident, pretentious and unhappy. Her boyfriend Max says she has an "emotional kind of conviction" (36), which he means as a criticism. Curly forfeits the chance of loving Jenny when he drops the investigation into the crimes of his father's bank: it's a lack of convictions about public morality, not a deficiency in his soul, that causes Jenny to reject him.

In *Teeth'n'Smiles* Maggie's realization that the revolution will never happen fuels her self-destruction. Like Sarah, she is deeply alienated from society, not from her soul. She ceases to love Arthur because he doesn't share her rage at unfulfilled ideals: he still naively believes in the revolution. As with Curly and Jenny, the source of their incompatibility is ideological rather than emotional.

In *Licking Hitler* Archie Maclean is often brutally insensitive to those around him, particularly to young Anna Seaton, yet we admire him for his convictions. He knows that he should be fighting to transform British society rather than helping to preserve it from Hitler. Anna gradually learns to love Archie for his ideals, certainly not for any personal goodness or emotional compatibility. In her letter to him, written 30 years later, she says, that she spent her life "trying to keep faith" with his "shame and anger" as she witnessed the "steady impoverishment of the people's ideals" and the "corrosive national habit of lying" (54). Anna's love becomes the expression of their shared view of how society should be, while in *Strapless* Lillian's love is a celebration of her own emotional rejuvenation.

Like Archie, Susan in *Plenty* commands respect and admiration for groping inarticulately toward a vision of what British society could be, despite her cruel treatment of her husband Raymond Brock. Those representative of forces opposed to her vision of how Britain should be—Sir Leonard Darwin, Sir Andrew Charleson, and Raymond Brock—are all decent men personally, even exemplary in Brock's case. Yet they contribute to the moral bankruptcy of postwar British society by supporting the imperialist and elitist imperatives of the Foreign Service.

Although morality ultimately remains public property in *Dreams of Leaving* (1980), the film takes the first large step in the process of privatization by giving love and emotional sensitivity (rather than participation in historical events charged with idealism) the power to raise a person's political consciousness. William's love for Caroline transforms him from a complete political and emotional neophyte into a morally scrupulous critic of the newspaper for which he writes. And Caroline's love for him gives her a sense of moral discrimination that forever frustrates her easy acceptance of a morally impoverished society.

Love also transforms Lillian in *Strapless* into a crusader to save the National Health Service, yet it leaves her radiantly happy, while it leaves William in a state of permanent despair and it drives Caroline mad. Love moves Lillian from unhappiness to happiness, while it moves William and Caroline from happiness to unhappiness. What accounts for these opposite trajectories? I suggest the explanation rests on this essential difference: in *Dreams* the public and private spheres are still interdependent; whereas in *Strapless* the connection has been fully severed. With the private sphere autonomous, that which can damage or sustain Lillian can only come from within. Before falling in love, Lillian is emotionally clamped down for strictly personal reasons. She is an overworked, 36-year-old, single, unloved, repressed physician. After falling in love she remains radiantly happy regardless of what happens in the public sphere with her fight against cuts to the National Health Service. In contrast, William and Caroline's initial happiness or blissful ignorance depends on their being oblivious to disturbing social realities. While living in a spiritually bankrupt society, their love cannot flourish into happiness, because that which is good and capable of sustaining their love is still public property. Consider another telling contrast: love fills William with new moral knowledge as if he had been an empty vessel, whereas Lillian starts off morally full so that love gives her the courage to act upon what she already knows is right.

As positive moral value begins to move inward for the first time in *Dreams of Leaving*, it is not surprising that traces of a corresponding demonology of privatized negative values begin to appear at the same time. Personal characteristics such as a penchant for logic and having no needs suddenly become indicators of spiritual turpitude instead of, as in earlier works, an affiliation with an institution or ideology responsible for regressive social conditions. For example, much to William's amazement and envy, his roommate Andrew "needs nothing just his work" (27). Needing nothing signifies an emotional blankness: Andrew's work consists of the spiritually inert task of writing a dictionary of sixteenth-century Arabic slang. One day Andrew announces that he is getting married to a woman he met only the week before who works in the same area of scholarship. The contrast suggests that Andrew doesn't possess the emotional equipment needed to experience moral enlightenment.

In subsequent plays admiration for the logical becomes more prominent in Hare's demonology of unenlightened personal qualities. In *Dreams of Leaving* it figures into one small episode in which Caroline happily tells William that she sells paintings logically according to size rather than quality. Logical describes the emotional style she aspires to generally, especially in her relationships with men.

Two years later Hare wrote *Saigon: Year of the Cat* (1983) in which morality resides for the first time solely in the individual. The opposition between logic and feeling becomes correspondingly more central to the action. The unifying objective of the film is to show how a logical frame of mind blinded the American ambassador and his top military advisors to the hopelessness of their hold on Saigon and South Vietnam. Their reliance on logic fatally delayed the evacuation process by several months, forcing them to abandon, in the mad haste of a two-day evacuation, a community of 40,000 to 50,000 dependent Vietnamese—former embassy employees, spies, IBM employees, favorite cooks, shirtmakers, and such. The scenes featuring Barbara Dean (a middle-aged English woman who works at a bank, played by Judi Dench), whose emotional sensitivity tunes her into the signs of Saigon's immanent fall to the North, provide an ongoing counterpoint to the emotional stupidity of the embassy officials locked into their logical strategies.

However, the logical versus emotional counter-pointing reveals more about Hare's interest in upgrading the individual as the site of morality than it does about the fall of Saigon. The actual Ambassador Graham Martin's inability to concede defeat had more to do with personal vanity, fervent patriotism, and strategic misinformation than with a logical emotional style.[18] But this is the least of the changes that serve Hare's intentions. Questions such as what was

American doing in Vietnam in the first place, and what was the tragedy of the war from the perspective of the majority of South Vietnamese don't come into focus as a consequence of defining morality in private rather than public terms.

The fall of Saigon appealed to Hare as subject matter for it offered him a way of giving individual emotional faculties a role of decisive moral importance. In the Introduction to *The Asian Plays* collection, he says: "As soon as I realized that the American Ambassador had been, literally, unable to imagine a US defeat, I was able to begin writing."[19] Moral responsibility for abandoning the dependent community of Vietnamese could thus be assigned exclusively to the failure of imagination in the Ambassador and two of his advisors.

However, Hare's exclusive focus on character short-circuits his awareness of highly pertinent cultural and political realities that might have entered into the picture had morality been viewed as public. Awareness of the experience of South Vietnam as a nation from about 1960 to 1974 would have prevented Hare from assuming that the abandonment of a small group of Vietnamese directly involved with and sympathetic to the Americans was a tragedy for all South Vietnam. The real tragedy of South Vietnam from a South Vietnamese perspective is that the Americans, over a 25-year period, gradually subverted indigenous political movements, and generally infantilized the nation until it was left corrupt and politically defenseless before North Vietnam. And furthermore, the dishonorable exit from Saigon was only a tiny episode of the Vietnam War that was started and sustained by religious, ideological, economic, and institutional imperatives that had little to do with the emotional faculties of the relatively few individuals who implemented them.

If studied in the clear bright retrospective light of later plays in which morality is more obviously private, *A Map of the World* (1982), with its implausible characterizations and multitude of tenuously linked topics, appears to possess a coherence and unity of purpose that would otherwise be difficult to detect. Although written after *Saigon: Year of the Cat*, which happily assumes the primacy of character over political beliefs, *A Map of the World* self-consciously and laboriously sets out to test the notion that personal motivations and desires determine one's political beliefs, that there is no such thing as public values and principles external to and independent of emotional characteristics.

Each of the three main characters—Stephen Andrews, Peggy Whitton, Victor Mehta—undergoes an enlightenment that consists of becoming disburdened of the delusion that what they believe is free and pure and independent of their personal biases, insecurities, jealousies, and desires. They learn, in the words of Henry in Tom Stoppard's *The Real Thing*, that "public postures have the configuration of private derangement."[20] Stoppard, a right-wing writer, uses this dubious insight to discredit the left-wing politics of young private Brodie; while Hare—a left-wing writer—uses it to personalize the "public postures" of all the main characters. *The Real Thing* claims that those who protest against the nuclear arms race do so to serve personal interests: to impress a beautiful woman, or to save one's cottage near a missile base. This is akin to the claim that Victor Mehta's right-wing views are a function of his emotional rigidity and "wretched fastidiousness," as Stephen calls it.

Consider the enlightenment of Stephen Andrews, who matures and discovers the personal underpinnings of his "public postures." The play is set in a hotel in Bombay, India. The occasion is a UNESCO conference on world poverty. Stephen attends as a journalist for a left-wing literary magazine in England. In a debate with Victor Mehta (a famous Indian novelist loosely patterned after V. S. Naipaul) he admits that loneliness plus jealousy of Mehta's successful philandering (Peggy broke a date with Stephen to have lunch with Mehta) motivated his ploy to humiliate Mehta by pressuring him to read before the conference delegates a self-censoring statement about the nature of fiction. Stephen says to those gathered at the scene of the debate: "If I've learnt anything in the last twenty four hours, it is that no argument is pure, it's always a compound. Partly the situation, partly temper, partly whim . . . sometimes just pulled out of the air and often from the worst motives. Peggy, no offense" (69).

He also suddenly gains the passion and confidence of his formerly "pure" or merely theoretical left-wing convictions while walking through the worst poverty of Bombay on the way to the Gateway of India. He becomes convinced that UNESCO's efforts to alleviate poverty deserve his idealistic commitment and must be believed in, despite the fact that bureaucratic waste and political maneuvering reduce the actual flow of rice to a trickle. The physical reality of the aid effort turns out to be less important than one's attitude toward it.

Stephen continues to describe his sudden transformation as "the act of suddenly deciding what I feel . . . no more apology. Hold to my beliefs." We idealists, he explains, "betray our instincts. We betray them because we're embarrassed, and we've lost our conviction that we can make what's best in us prevail" (73). Judging from Stephen's transformation, that country named Utopia (without which "a map of the world" "is not worth even glancing at" in Oscar Wilde's opinion quoted in the frontispiece), is actually a state of mind, an instinct to be nurtured. Emphasis has shifted decisively from the content of a belief to the passion, courage, and conviction with which one believes. Before his sudden conversion, Stephen was, according to Peggy Whitton, a "ragbag of opinions" who had, unlike the African delegate M'Bengue, "bought his principles" at the corner store at no personal cost. She says, "when he [M'Bengue] says 'principle,' we listen. It's at some cost. It's at some personal expense. But your principles have been bought in the store on the corner and cost you nothing" (45).

The primacy of feeling is also demonstrated in Stephen's attitudinal relationship to UNESCO after his conversion. Why does he immediately leave the UNESCO conference for the hinterland of India just after passionately reaffirming his commitment to the organization? Why leave his newfound passions hanging in the void without actually doing anything with them? The answer is that as emphasis shifts from ideological content to attitude, power transfers from the public to the private sphere, from the power of ideas and action to the power of a certain way of being. The power and impact of the newly transformed Stephen is considerable. By moving Mehta to write a novel of their encounter—the basis of a movie two scenes of which appear in a play presenting the original Bombay events—Stephen touches the feelings of millions of readers, and movie and theatre audiences. This entire process owes its existence to Mehta being moved emotionally by Stephen's death. As Mehta explains to the bumbling movie director Angelis, he was compelled to write the novel about Stephen and the UNESCO conference not because he was impressed with Stephen's political beliefs, but because of "an emotion I had" while traveling north by taxi to the site of the train accident that killed Stephen. "I was moved by what happened," he explains, and chose to stay away from the rest of the conference "in memory of Stephen" (78). The play concludes with Mehta and the actress playing Peggy exchanging small talk that turns reflective when he quietly muses about a truth the play has been working toward on every level: "This feeling, finally, that we may change things—this is at the center of everything we are. Lose that . . . lose that, lose everything" (82).

This is a double affirmation of the power of feeling. He admires the feeling one may change things (not Stephen's political beliefs about how to change things), and he gains this admiration through an emotional response to Stephen's death, not through anything Stephen does. Mehta learns a truth at the heart of every work since *Dreams of Leaving*: ideology and participation in public events no longer have the power to transform people and enlarge their political consciousness. Such power now belongs to emotion and a way of being.

Note how Stephen's pretransformation "pure" idealism stage is posited at the expense of deemphasizing and trivializing the power of public realities available to him in his "pure" stage. In contrast to Stephen, the African delegate M'Bengue is held up as an example of someone actually "involved" with efforts to alleviate poverty and whose principles were acquired at "some personal expense." Why couldn't the same be said of Stephen? Surely a journalist for a left-wing journal in England can be just as authentically "involved" with poverty and world hunger as any civil servant of an African country. (It is well known that corruption among government officials causes considerable poverty and starvation in many African countries.) Also, why should the spectacle of poverty in Bombay suddenly give Stephen an authentic emotional concern with poverty when he could walk through the poorest districts of any major British city and see poverty all the more grotesque for existing in a wealthy Western nation?

The assault on the public dimension is advanced in other ways. Hare tries to undermine the objectivity of political beliefs by invoking principles that are actually attitudes or opinions masquerading as principles. It is much easier to prove that no principles are free of subjectivity if the "principles" under discussion are not really principles, which, in the normal sense of the word, refer to public standards of conduct and morality. We are frequently reminded that Stephen is left-wing and that Victor Mehta is right-wing, which would naturally lead one to expect a genuinely political dimension to their arguments in which both claim to be arguing from the basis of "principle"—a word sprinkled liberally throughout their discussions. However, at no time do we see principles at stake that could be identified or even construed to be either left- or right-wing. For instance, a principle appears to be at stake when Mehta refuses to read the statement about the nature of fiction after discovering that Stephen wrote it. "That is the motive behind this fine display of principle" Mehta exclaims, immediately assuming, quite rightly, that jealousy motivated Stephen (38). When Peggy reprimands Stephen for his petty display of jealousy, he defends himself by saying "it's principle . . . certain things are important. Certain things are good" (45). Stephen's true motivation is obvious, and it is also clear that the purpose of the scene is to teach him that "no argument is pure" as he later professes to have learned, but what is the principle, left-wing or otherwise, repeatedly invoked here? What are these "things" that are "important" and "good"? What principle, political or otherwise, can be extracted from the following statement and the discussion surrounding it?: "Fiction, by its very nature, distorts and misrepresents reality, so in a way a man who stands before you as a writer of fiction, as I do today, is already some way towards admitting that as a historical witness he is unreliable" (36). As a statement strictly about the nature of fiction, it is not only problematic (fiction need not be factual to be true), but also devoid of political content.

Political principles could easily be at stake if Mehta's so-called unreliability as an historical witness of third-world issues were shown to be somehow symptomatic of right-wing views. Yet M'Bengue's condemnation of Western media misrepresentation is so sweeping and vague that it is impossible to determine just what it is that Mehta is being accused of, aside from making jokes at their expense. M'Bengue speaks of "struggles" and of "those who struggle" as if what he means is self-evident (40-41). Struggles to feed people? Build dams? Struggles against right-wing dictatorships? Struggles against socialist regimes? How is Mehta's comic discrediting of these unidentified "struggles" a function of his being right-wing? Hare leaves us in a guessing position regarding these questions because he is really interested in the emotional style rather than the ideological content or practice of being right-wing. In Mehta's case, being right-wing dwindles into cynicism, just as passionate idealism is the sole content of Stephen's socialism. When Elaine, an African-American delegate, urges Stephen to "argue it out" (47) with Mehta, "it" presumably refers to the principles Stephen has just claimed to be important. Yet the big central debate between Stephen and Mehta turns out to be a clash of attitudes toward the trickle of aid that gets through UNESCO: idealism versus cynicism.

Wetherby (1985) is Hare's last work that still contains traces of a public morality, yet only in the paradoxical sense that the content of public morality is exactly the same thing as the individual capacity to feel. In other words, Hare fully embraces subjectivity as the basis of morality, yet upgrades it into the sole universal/national currency and expects it to behave just like the soaring national ideals in *Licking Hitler* and *Plenty*. The clearest indication of the enhanced moral authority of subjectivity is that love is no longer merely the catalyst or handmaid of a new enlightened sense of public morality as it is for William in *Dreams of Leaving*. Falling in love with Jim Mortimer does not raise young Jean Travers's political consciousness; love simply endows her with a permanent emotional sensitivity. For the first time in Hare's work love is a good in itself and not because it leads to something else. Emotional literacy is the pinnacle of enlightenment, and thus the true and only gauge of moral value.

However, it is vital to note that Jean's discovery of a subjective source of moral authority does not lead to rejoicing as it does for the emotionally sensitized in *The Secret Rapture* and *Strapless*. This is because of the conflation of public and private morality. As women in love with absent men, Jean Travers and Lillian Hempel (*Strapless*) find themselves in identical positions; yet Jean's response is permanent repression, while Lillian's is radiant happiness. Why the radical difference? Because Lillian's love exists complete and independent of exterior reality within the charmed circle of her own soul, while Jean's love is incomplete without a corresponding expression of love in society. Thus Jean's repression, like that of Archie, Susan, and William, testifies to an alienation from a society no longer animated by any public values; however, the crucial step toward privatization of morality taken in *Wetherby* is that love, or emotional literacy in all its forms, is expected to be the essential bonding and cohering ingredient of society rather than the postwar socialist/consensual ideals.

John Morgan is the only person in the film *Wetherby* who displays an intellectual as well as an emotional grasp of the connection between social and emotional impoverishment, and he kills himself. He draws upon his research on the Norman village of the 13th century when he speaks of "goodness and anger and revenge and evil" in response to Stanley's observation that "when I find good . . . my first feeling is one of nostalgia. For something we've lost" (79). The implication that community fragments to the degree these honest old emotions are buried is conveyed in nearly every scene with images of loneliness, emotional dishonesty, and, in the case of Karen Creasy, total emotional withdrawal. Roger Braithwaite is John Morgan's counterpart. He believes logic "holds society together" and as such is clearly cut from the same mold as earlier "logical" characters (48): Caroline in *Dreams*, the ambassador in *Saigon*, Victor Mehta in *A Map*.

Wetherby is unique among Hare's transitional works for possessing a morality in which the public and private dimensions are exactly the same. It is private because emotional illiteracy is the only cause of social fragmentation, thus implying that the only solution is emotional rejuvenation throughout society. Private repression is not merely a metaphor for public loss, it is public loss. *Wetherby* advances this equation with shockingly powerful and disturbing emotional conviction, yet the question remains: how true is it? To what degree has social consciousness withered in England because of emotionally unenlightened individuals? Can the fracturing of society in the 1980s be attributed to the condition of Mrs. Thatcher's emotional faculties and of others like her? Stanley seems to think so when he says that she is "Taking some terrible revenge. For something. Some deep damage. Something inside" (78). While the emotional aptitude of those actively engaged in the political process is undoubtedly vital, is it as significant as suggested here and throughout the film? *Wetherby* shows that the loss of connectedness is felt very deeply, yet, unlike *Licking Hitler* or *Plenty*, this film doesn't offer a sense of the historical and political causes of this loss.

In the introduction to the screenplay of *Paris by Night* Hare says the story of Clara Paige (Charlotte Rampling) the Euro MP came to him "like a free gift, an afterbirth to compensate for all the labour of *Wetherby*."[21] I suggest that writing *Paris by Night* was a relatively effortless experience because it offered him a release from the terminal mode of writing about England that he had locked himself into in *Wetherby*. Terminal because if emotional sensitivity is the basis of community, and if one believes that England suffers from a progressive erosion of community, and furthermore, if one writes about such loss from the perspective of the emotionally sensitive, then further social fragmentation would have to be conveyed with ever more desperate modes of repression and escape. However, it is difficult to imagine a more desperate escape than John Morgan's suicide. Where would one go from here? Escalating the level of people's despair would be not only problematic (mass suicide?), but somewhat puzzling to the voting public who, in 1984, had handed Mrs. Thatcher her second victory, thus giving her good reason to think she should continue on the path that Hare felt was fragmenting the country.

Hare faced at least two strategies of moving beyond the terminal mode of *Wetherby*: shift his focus and write primarily about the emotionally insensitive (the Roger Braithwaites and Karen Creasys instead of the suicidal John Morgans); or sever emotional sensitivity from its onerous public role, that is, write of Stephen Andrews' idealism and newfound confidence without grafting on a left-wing ideological dimension, or write of Jean's repression and Morgan's yearning for goodness without making their sensitivity the only indicator of absent public values. With a fully privatized morality, Morgan would be self-sustaining. He would no longer need to look for goodness outside himself. Suicide would be unnecessary and incomprehensible if those good ancient values and simple feelings he misses could be found within his own soul.

Hare chose this second option (severing emotional sensitivity from its public role) in his plays of the late 1980s. However, in his next work, the film *Paris by*

Night (1988), he chose the first option of writing about the emotionally
insensitive. This film is a thriller that draws connections between individuals
with stunted emotional capacities and conservative politics. The personality
disorders and personal greed of Clara Paige, a Euro MP and Tory candidate for
the British Parliament, and the blatant vulgarities of Adam Gillvray, a leading
intellectual of the Tory Party, are established as the source of their conservative
views. The film leaves room for familiar skepticism. People became more self-
interested in England in the 1980s, but did they do so because of the personal
greed of Tory MPs and intellectuals? Does this film convincingly address the
phenomenon of conservative politics in the 1980s by claiming that a direct
correlation exists between Clara's belief in free-market ideology and her
propensity to mistreat her spouse and ignore her child? Margaret Thatcher, her
closest political mentor Sir Keith Joseph, other key Tory politicians, as well as
sympathetic intellectuals such as Ferdinand Mount (author of *The Subversive
Family* and possible model for Adam Gillvray), Roger Scruton (editor *of The
Salisbury Review*), and Milton Friedman may have inflicted irreparable damage
on the social fabric of Britain, yet one cannot therefore automatically assume
anything about their personal integrity or emotional capacities.

Anyone who reduces politics to a debate about human nature would never
pose a threat to Margaret Thatcher, who is absolutely convinced that her view
of human nature occupies the moral high ground. To impugn Thatcherism on
the level of human nature and character is to attack where the new right feels
very strong. The ongoing theme of Margaret Thatcher's speeches in *The
Revival of Britain* (1989), is that the cornerstone of morality must be, in her
words, "the great truth that self-regard is the root of regard for one's fellows."[22]
She believes the socialist view that self-interest is selfish and bad is actually
corrupt and debased for it presupposes a very low estimation of the natural
inclinations of mankind. Her effort to give people greater powers of choice (a
favorite word of hers derived from Milton Friedman) flows from her trust that
people will act in ways that do not harm their neighbors. Although social,
political, and economic developments in Britain did not produce much evidence
in the 1980s to justify such trust, Margaret Thatcher and other conservative
politicians should not therefore be considered personally corrupt. Many of those
who voted for Thatcher did so because they were moved by her sincerity and
unshakable sense of conviction.

However, both the right and the left would do well to contemplate seriously
these words of David Marquand who insists that politics should not be reduced
to a debate about human nature: "Of course, we are egoists. And, of course, we
are altruists. We are capable of appalling meanness, selfishness and greed. We
are also capable of up-lifting generosity, self-sacrifice and tenderness to others.
But the first do not make us, in some way, a- or non-social; and it is not
because of the second that we live in society."[23] The real point of controversy
between the left and the right should be about how best to structure the means

of bringing out the best in people and not about whether people are essentially good or bad. They are capable of being both.

Although marred by a personal line of attack on Tory ideology, *Paris by Night* is at least free of the sentimental fantasy (operating in *The Secret Rapture* and *Racing Demon*) that bad people "gang up" on good people out of guilt. This "ganging up" dynamic depends on soul which does not exist in *Paris by Night* perhaps because Hare was not yet ready to treat it as an independent moral authority. Having established the complete absence of any public good in *Wetherby*, he momentarily had nothing to replace it with. The fact that Clara remains impervious to guilt or remorse throughout the film is a sure sign of her soullessness. She remains static and beyond regeneration because her political orthodoxy, although personalized, is not yet defined as the denial of soul or aggression against those with soul. For example, although Clara and her husband Gerald (Michael Gambon) ruin Michael Swanton with a fraudulent sale of their overvalued mail-order business, they do so purely out of calculated self-interest rather than guilt-induced anger at him. Similarly, greed and a strong sense of self-preservation (rather than guilt) motivate Clara to deny Michael a much-needed loan and later to impulsively kill him.

A total absence of soul defines her villainy while, in contrast, a suppression of soul (the "human stuff" Hare also calls it) defines the villainy of Marion, Valentina in *The Bay at Nice*, and Tony the young evangelical curate in *Racing Demon*. And, likewise, the niceness of Michael Swanton, unlike the goodness and kindness of Isobel or Lionel, is not the expression of soul and therefore lacks the necessary moral dimension to induce guilt in the less sensitive. Swanton is simply less self-interested and greedy than Clara. Like Isobel and especially Lionel, he is weak and put upon, yet—and this is a crucial point—he does not possess their potent compensating spiritual powers.

Although in some ways a big belly laugh of a play, *Pravda* (1985) actually displays a highly perceptive grasp of the moral climate of Britain in the 1980s. In part because it is the product of a collaboration with Howard Brenton, who consistently maintains a strong focus on public as well as private realities in his work. Like Clara Paige and Adam Gillvray, Lambert Le Roux is a Hobbesian creature of self-interest and greed, yet his villainy never dwindles into emotional illiteracy or unkindness to his wife and children. His villainy is rather characterized in impersonal terms—as an allegorical figure representing the power of money. The result, according to some English reviewers of the National Theatre production, is a flat cartoonish character that pushes the play toward undergraduate-style agitprop.[24] This is largely true, yet one of the strengths of the play is that "Howard Hare" does not suggest that conservativism is objectionable because Tories are personally bad people.

By creating a character that embodies the power of money "Howard Hare" attacks the heart of the then current Tory ideology of free-market capitalism. It is a firm article of faith among the new generation of Conservatives led by Margaret Thatcher that the maximum public good can be achieved only if money is allowed to flow unrestricted wherever its can create maximum profits. For "Howard Hare" the consequences of this belief in action are plain to see on Fleet Street: newspaper proprietors are more than ever willing to cater to the lowest common denominator. If sex and violence sells, then by all means give it to them. Although never explicit, the clear implication of the satire is that something more than money should also inform decisions about the buying and selling of newspapers and their editorial policies. This something more would protect and nurture public values not served by an unregulated market.

Another strength of *Pravda* is that not only does it refrain from personalizing politics, it viciously lampoons those who do. In the broadest sense, *Pravda* is about the absence of a genuine political opposition in Britain. It offers a story with obvious parallels to British politics in the past decade: a power sweeps through the country, winning everything before it, not only by its own strength, but very much by the weakness of its opposition. This story indicates that Brenton and Hare together view recent political developments in Britain with a clearer eye than they do separately. Stuart Hall, one of the leading socialist intellectuals in England, agrees with their perception that the success of the new right is due in no small measure to the moral vacuum in which it operates: "Now the astonishing political fact that the people can be colonized by the right has in part to do with the fact that there is no alternative vision of what or who the people are."[25] A sure sign of the moral and ideological weakness of both the left and the paternalistic old High Tory establishment is that they were reduced to attacking Mrs. Thatcher personally. According to Andrew Gamble in *The Free Economy and the Strong State* 1988), the very term "Thatcherism" reflects the personalization of politics in the 1980s: "To term the program which the conservatives adopted in the 1970s 'Thatcherism' is to personalize it, and in doing so to distort its character by directing attention to what is least important about it—the peculiarities of style and belief that are associated with one particular leader."[26] Why wasn't there a "Churchillism" or a "Heathism"? If Hare's recent work is indicative of general trends in British society, the need to attack one's political opponents personally increases to the degree one lacks a clear and viable alternative. Having moved onto the same liberal ground as the conservatives, Hare strives to maintain a distinctive moral position on the basis of enlightened individualism by staking out an exclusive claim on the soul.

Much of the satire in *Pravda* is directed at the personal line of attack later evident in *The Secret Rapture* and *Racing Demon*. Like the Tory government's opposition that has "Thatcher on the brain," Le Roux's opposition has "Le Roux on the brain." Thus the spectacle of all the dispossessed planning to buy a newspaper from which to launch a attack on Le Roux's character. One of them exclaims, "At last, the chance to get back at the bastard. We'd have twenty-four pages! We could fill them every day with stories about what a shit he is."[27] Convinced that they are acting in the national interest, they proceed to fill their paper with stories of Le Roux's personal corruption such as how he abused his first wife and once shot a man in the leg over some minor dispute.

Their entire smear campaign turns out to be the first stage of Le Roux's successful sting operation. He fed them false stories about himself through his seemingly disaffected assistant Eaton Sylvester. Before serving his ex-editor Andrew May with a writ of libel (which bankrupts their newspaper through legal costs as planned) Le Roux tells him, "you are all weak because you do not know what you believe" (114). "So much easier to believe that I was a criminal" (116). If they knew what they believed they would fight Le Roux with ideas as Andrew May's left-wing wife Rebecca urges them to.

Leaving aside the valid criticism that Rebecca reinforces the stereotype of a female character confined to being the nagging morally uplifting sidekick of a more interesting male character, one's attitude toward her seems to reflect one's attitude toward the political opposition in Britain. Those reviewers who agree that the opposition is nearly dead find her advice redundant—of course they lack ideas; those who think the opposition very much alive find the play unbelievably one-sided and believe it is a weakness of the play that her ideas are not brought to bear. Brenton's own opinion is that "to have Lambert Le Roux defeated or in any way successfully opposed would be sentimental and false."[28]

Brenton and Hare claim that *Pravda* is an indivisible creative effort; nevertheless, it is possible to speculate with some confidence about their individual contributions in light of their different assumptions about morality and social change. By the time of the collaboration in 1985, Hare had already personalized his critique of conservative ideology in *A Map of the World* and *Paris by Night*, which suggests that Brenton may be responsible for the satire on the personal mode of attack on Le Roux, which entails, of course, the impersonal characterization of Le Roux as well as the implication (perhaps needlessly articulated by Rebecca) that the opposition should fight Le Roux with ideas. In any case, the assumption that morality must have a public dimension prevails.

Although the 1980s made Brenton much less sanguine about the prospects of a socialist transformation of society, he continued to believe in the revolution. He just took a much longer view of change than he did in the 1960s and 1970s. Like Hare, Brenton believes there is a reactionary and progressive personality or view of human nature, yet he does not separate character from political practice as demonstrated by his use of the words "optimism" and "despair" which bear Gramsci's influence and appear frequently in his recent plays, articles, and interviews. For Brenton, optimism about the essential goodness of mankind is inseparable from a revolutionary socialist practice pursued no matter how unpromising the prospects for change are.

He is very much describing his own tough-minded idealism when he explains why translating *The Life of Galileo* by Bertolt Brecht cheered him up: "That angry but circumspect, tough, but sly attitude which Gramsci called 'pessimism of the intellect: optimism of the will' shines in the text."[29] The truth is betrayed during the entire play until the very end when Andrea manages to smuggle Galileo's book across the border: this single covert action allows for the slim margin of hope that Brenton seizes upon. On the other hand, to despair is to believe, in the words of Severan, the self-proclaimed reactionary in *Greenland* (1988), that "in the end we are all selfish, self-obsessed, with a dark heart. Human nature? It is evil and it will out."[30] This pessimistic view of human nature is for Brenton the basis of reactionary ideology.

Although a clear public dimension exists in nearly all Brenton's works, I would suggest that insofar as he aligns a particular ideology with a particular view of human nature, he won't likely pose much of a threat to the right. The new breed of conservative firmly believes that their view of human nature is morally superior to that of the left: they are simply no longer susceptible to the left's claim to the moral high ground on such terms. According to Stuart Hall, the supreme moral confidence of the new right has made it "not simply a worthy opponent of the left, but in some deeper way its nemesis, the force that is capable in this historical moment of unhinging it from below."[31]

Brenton stops short of sentimentalism, for he expresses his optimistic view of human nature in political practice and theory: character alone never becomes the indicator of moral worth as it does in Hare's work of the late 1980s. Most of Brenton's plays in the 1980s—like Hare's—are about survival in exile, in dark times of reaction. His strategy of survival is always essentially the same: remain optimistic and actually do what you can to assist the transformation of society, which in *Sleeping Policeman* (1983) means discussing the installation of sleeping policeman (speed bumps) in a Peckham ward meeting as the socialist councilor Dinah does. By celebrating what he considers optimistic actions rather than simply an optimistic view of human nature, Brenton avoids overestimating the power of feeling and sensibility.

However, there is perhaps a way that Brenton's desperation to find an antidote for despair and a consolation for powerlessness in reactionary times arguably injects a measure of unreality into his defiantly optimistic scenarios. In an article aptly entitled "A Crazy Optimism" he explains how translating George Buchner's play *Danton's Death* reaffirmed his conviction that the revolution is a gradual never-ending process, that change is "organic" rather than "conjunctural," as Gramsci would say. Brenton admires the line "the lava of the Revolution flows," which he notes appears twice in the play. He adds: "For Buchner the play was what the world was going to be like, the Revolution was never going to go away. History has proved him right, of course. Asked, 'What was the outcome of the French Revolution?' Mao Tse-Tung replied, 'It is too soon to know.'"[32] The image of a never ending flow of lava contains Brenton's somewhat unreal consolation: to think of the revolution as a slow inexorable process confers enormous long-range power and efficacy on the small seemingly isolated futile acts of individuals who keep the "optimistic" faith. The unreality of this consolation is the absolute confidence that the socialist revolution marches steadily forward, despite all setbacks and detours: there is a big difference between Brenton's claim that "history has proved him right, of course" and Mao's "it is too soon to know."

The danger of embracing this determinism is that it can be so comforting that it can turn Brenton's normally tough optimism into the chirpy, self-satisfied attitude of Palace, a character in *Greenland*, whose description of how utopia was achieved (the second half of the play is Brenton's vision of utopia set 700 years in the future) is a celebration of the "ordinary life": "Just life after life lived through as best they could be lived. Ordinary life triumphed and made an extraordinary world."[33] Brenton has created an unusual form of sentimentalism here: the overestimation of the power of ordinary actions as opposed to feeling.

Hare's next two plays, *The Bay at Nice* and *Wrecked Eggs* (1986), deliberately and explicitly reaffirm a private basis of morality in such a self-conscious way that there is room to suspect that *Pravda's* lampoon of the left's personalized attack on Le Roux made him feel he needed to reassess and reaffirm his thinking about the soul.

The Bay at Nice and *Wrecked Eggs* are more static and wordy than any previous plays with the possible exception of *A Map of the World*. Both plays feature two or three characters debating a variety of topics unified by Hare's effort to put to rest any remaining doubts about the validity of a character/soul-based morality. Observing that Hare sometimes seems to be debating with himself in his work, Kathleen Tynan asked Hare to comment on these two plays. He tells her that they are more or less private pieces in which he is working out obstacles to his growing up: "I cared very little about whether the public came to see these plays. We put them on because I couldn't grow up unless I worked out some things I felt."[34]

I think partly of *Pravda* when he says he had "various things" to "sort out" because these two plays refute *Pravda's* key assumptions about morality in two ways: first, in *Pravda* the opposition gathered around Fruit-Norton is condemned for the poverty of its ideas and action, while in *The Bay at Nice* and *Wrecked Eggs* opposition to prevailing orthodoxies is not even possible. The Communist Party of Russia in *The Bay at Nice* and the American way of life in *Wrecked Eggs* are presented as monolithic, all-powerful, rigid orthodoxies against which viable opposition is laughable and absurd. If it is impossible for oppositional forces to act on the basis of ideas and convictions, then naturally they cannot be blamed for failing to do so. If the Fruit-Norton gang were placed against the orthodoxies of Soviet Russia and the United States as presented in these two plays, they would be justified in retreating into private life to cultivate their sensibilities, their characters, and their capacities for love, which is precisely what the unorthodox oppositional figures (Sophia in *The Bay* and Grace and Loelia in *Wrecked Eggs*) do in these plays.

Second, as another possible rebuttal to *Pravda*, much of the energy of these plays is devoted to proving that what the so-called orthodox characters are like (their character and personality) is more important and a truer measure of their moral turpitude than what they may do or believe. In other words, these plays imply that Fruit-Norton and his gang of dispossessed are fully justified in attacking Le Roux personally because character is the true source of good and evil. Taken together these two strategies of undermining public ethical criteria provide a sentimental solution to powerlessness before alienating "orthodoxies": the solution places a high value on feelings and sensibility (goodness, capacity for love, etc.), while ensuring at the same time that nothing can actually be done, that feeling cannot be translated into action.

Both plays are ostensibly debates between the claims of public and private morality; yet the debates are not genuine debates because we are never allowed to judge public values in action or in theory. Instead, what we see is the process of self-denial on the part of the unenlightened characters, and self-acceptance on the part of the enlightened characters. For instance, in *The Bay at Nice* Valentina's advocacy of public criteria of morality is transparently the projection of a life-long habit of self-denial. She is clearly the prototype of Marion in *The Secret Rapture* whose conservativism is really a symptom of defective emotional faculties. Both women lack "human stuff" as Hare terms it.[35]

A Map of the World also foregrounds the emotional style rather than the content or action of Stephen and Mehta's left- and right-wing views; the difference being that in these two later plays Hare sets out to exorcise the hold of public values altogether, whereas in *A Map* Stephen's socialist values are valid if he holds them with the right kind of passion and attitude.

The central question in *The Bay at Nice* is should Valentina's 36-year-old daughter Sophia abandon her two young children and her husband Grigor, a successful and ambitious Communist Party member and headmaster of a school, for Peter Linitsky, a 63-year-old sanitation worker and divorcee who describes himself as "seriously disturbed"? What would appear to be the obvious answer is obviously wrong because the real choice is between a soulless, loveless life of dutiful self-denial with Grigor within the suffocating grasp of the Commununist Party and a loving, self-reaffirming and fulfilling life with Peter without, of course, Communist Party membership.

The distinction between the enlightened and the unenlightened in *The Bay at Nice* is not quite so apparent as it is in *The Secret Rapture* and *Racing Demon* because Sophia's decision to leave her young children and dutiful husband for an elderly nearly senile sanitation worker is not an obviously good and virtuous thing to do, unlike Isobel's dutiful attendance on her sick father or Lionel's social work in the inner city of London. Making the soulful option appear unappealing may be Hare's way of testing its value.

The Bay at Nice is Hare's first work in which the self or soul exists as an independent moral force, as an end in itself. Sophia's escape into private life—

"the only hope now is to live your life in private" she says—is precisely that: she embraces nothing but herself and her love for Peter.[36] She takes no ideological baggage as Stephen does in *A Map of the World*.

The Bay at Nice is more a justification for rather than a test of the moral authority of soul. Although Valentina vehemently opposes Sophia's intention to divorce Grigor, her own wasted life provides the best argument for Sophia to go ahead with the divorce. All her arguments against the divorce—she invokes discipline, duty to others, responsibility, self-sacrifice—sound as if they could flow from a belief in communist collective ideology (why, after all, is the Communist Party invoked so often in this play?), yet it becomes progressively clearer that her arguments are a function of her harsh self-denying character. Sophia is well aware of the private source of her mother's harsh opinions and wins the argument by forcing her to admit as much in front of Peter with details from her suppressed past. Valentina reluctantly explains that after giving birth to Sophia in Paris in the 1920s she suddenly decided it was time to end her bohemian art student life, become a responsible parent, and return to Russia where she lived a lonely miserable unhappy life. Peter finds it a puzzling story. Asked why she didn't return to Paris, she says it would have been "cowardly" (39) and that she would have been unhappy anyway. Ideology had nothing to do with her decision to return or stay: "I wasn't a communist. I know what has happened since. I'm still not a communist. How could I be? But I made a decision" (40).

The final image of Valentina is of a repressed, willful, obstinate woman who decided to stick—"people should stick" (27) she says at one point—to her decision for the sake of sticking it out as a sort of perverse character-building exercise. She sounds very much like Clara, Marion, or Mehta when she says, "I just get on with it. I know what life is. And what it cannot be" (27). What is arguably new about Valentina in terms of Hare's demonology is her repression of soul. She is a very spirited woman who has maimed herself. She is thus more like Marion (who possesses emotional sensitivity that can be awakened as revealed in the last scene) than Clara or Mehta.

Political orthodoxy is also reconstituted as soullessness in the figure of the young curator who attends to Valentina as she judges the authenticity of the Matisse painting—thus the title *The Bay at Nice*. We learn only three things about him: he is a Communist Party member, he is eager for advancement in his career, and he has no imagination and no sensitivity to the emotionally expressive qualities of the art he deals with everyday. When Valentina says, "painting is ultimately to do with the quality of feeling" he replies, "I can't tell. I'm an Academician. My heart is in the catalogue" (14). The soullessness-equals-the-party equation is underscored when Valentina guesses correctly (as if one needed to guess) that Peter Linitsky is not a Communist Party member. Naturally he isn't because (leaving aside the telltale signs of his low status and near senility) he, like Sophia, has the courage to act on the basis of feeling.

Loving Sophia is an "adventure" he says, that, although painful and frightening, "uncovers feelings I didn't know I had" (35).

With Russia divided into the soulful and the soulless, it is not surprising that, as in his three works of the late 1980s, an antagonism develops between these two types. Why is the play set in a museum? Valentina and Sophia could easily have had their discussion in Valentina's apartment, in a park, or just about anywhere with a measure of privacy. The answer I suggest is because the museum situation allows Hare to demonstrate the threat Valentina's spiritual capacities pose to the party. As the young curator explains, she was asked to authenticate the Matisse because "it was felt you understand his spirit" (12). Valentina smiles knowingly when he tells her that they felt this, not the scientific experts employed by the party at the ministry. The meeting is thus covert and conducted at some risk, for as the curator explains further: "Professor Satayev expressely forbade your being asked. He was against it. He authenticated the painting, he insists. By scientific methods" (12). The party's power and rational expertise stops where Valentina's begins—at the emotional level. Having been a student of Matisse in Paris, Valentina understands his "handwriting" or "spirit" as she later explains to Peter (33). She is able to bring to bear a knowledge that is purely intuitive and emotional. By forbidding the museum from seeking her advice the party displays their fear and ignorance of this inner dimension. And by setting one solitary person against the vast anonymous bureaucracy of the party, Hare emphasizes Valentina's power—she can mobilize the hostility of highly placed officials of the state—while at the same time underscoring her vulnerability and impotence. The entire dramatic situations of *The Secret Rapture* and *Racing Demon* are essentially variations on the ganging-up dynamic between Valentina and the Communist Party in these brief moments concerned with the Matisse painting.

Wrecked Eggs is a more obvious test of a private basis for morality than *The Bay at Nice* because the question—is what people do more important than what they are like?—is the subject of explicit debate. "Test" may not be the word, for Hare's heart is not in the "do" end of the argument, which is thus rarely a viable contender. *Wrecked Eggs* is set in a clapboard cottage in upstate New York and has three characters: Robbie Baker, a young lawyer, his wife Loelia, a tennis coach, and their guest Grace, a press agent from Manhattan and a tennis student of Loelia's. They have gathered, at Robbie's request, to "celebrate" the impending demise of his marriage to Loelia. He felt that by ritualizing and formalizing the event he could minimize the emotional trauma. The three characters tiptoe around the topic of divorce—an excellent pretext for them to talk about anything else such as things Hare wants to "sort out"—until it resurfaces at the end in a way that confirms that what people are like is more important than what they do.

The play consists of their prebarbecue conversation in which Grace emerges as a heretic vis-à-vis American culture, which Robbie staunchly defends. She confesses to being disgusted with her job, has no idea how much she earns, and envies Robbie and Loelia for their ability to find comfort in material possessions (a beautiful cottage, a pickup truck, a satellite dish, etc.) all of which puzzles and upsets Robbie. He thinks one's attitude toward work is irrelevant. "If you make money, your job is a success. It's as simple as that" (67). And "things" he says, "are surely . . . in a way they're what you work for" (71).

However, their central point of contention expresses explicitly a concern about the basis of morality. Grace explains that her job as a publicity agent makes her feel helpless and angry because professional duty forces her to attend to what her clients are like, their personalities, rather than to the morality of their actions. Her current client, a property developer, happens to be destroying 12 blocks on the West Side of New York to make room for high-rise apartment buildings. She finds it appalling that the public doesn't really care if the developer destroys an old established community as long as he has an interesting personality: "He's an asshole, but. What is he like? What is he like? is the only question. The question is never 'Is this right or wrong? (*She shakes her head, suddenly vehement.*) It's not, 'Shall we do this?' 'Should this be done?' No, it's 'Do we like the guy who's doing this?' 'Is he a nice guy?' Not even nice, is he good copy? Then, hell, let him do what he wants" (77). Is a person's personality more important than what they do? is the central question of *Wrecked Eggs*, which is sorted out in favor of personality and character. The temptation to view this play as a rebuttal to *Pravda* is strong here because *Pravda* asks precisely the same question of Lambert Le Roux in a situation similar to that of Grace's developer, and demonstrates, with its vicious lampoon of the opposition's personal attack on him, that what Le Roux actually does is far more important than what he is like.

Despite the less than-promising-claims of personality (both Robbie and the developer appear deficient in personality; Loelia wants to divorce Robbie because he can't be himself—of which more will be said later), *Wrecked Eggs* systematically undermines in a variety of ways the notion that what someone does is more important than what they are like. First, both Grace and Robbie agree that there is nothing anybody can actually do to stop greedy developers from destroying the city. So the question is therefore rhetorical from the start. Grace's yearning for some public standard appears as a sort of peculiar nostalgia. Robbie thinks "it's kind of pointless" to complain (77). "There's nothing you can do. That's how people see things" he says (77). Grace agrees. "I feel helpless" is her explanation for her habit of writing letters to newspapers under the pseudonym Amelia Grant to protest about things like exercise fantasy videos, unemployment among blacks, and greedy developers. The implication being that if Robbie and Grace don't judge themselves on the basis of what they do or don't do (action being impossible, they both agree) how can they or anybody judge the property developer for what he does or doesn't do?

Second, and more obviously, Robbie and Grace never face her question of whether the developer's destruction of 12 blocks on the West Side of New York is right or wrong. It is an excellent question for it entails a genuine confrontation between public and private assumptions about morality. The question asks are there any values (aesthetic, cultural, political, environmental) shared by the people living in those soon-to-be destroyed blocks? And should such values supersede any individual's desire to displace all of them for apartment towers and a handsome profit?

However, Robbie sidesteps these questions about the morality of the developer's actions and Grace proves to be too dimwitted and half-hearted to keep him on track. Robbie's position is that "What's he like? is the most important question" (78). He explains: "Like, say, when you fall in love, it's not because of what the other person does. Or else, you know, Mother Teresa would be the most propositioned woman on the planet. Because what she does is unbeatable. But that's got nothing to do with what draws people to people" (78). Robbie is largely right in this case. Personality, rather than what people do, usually draws people together. But then in her initial question Grace never suggests otherwise. What draws people to people is not the issue. All Robbie has done is emphatically restate what Grace has already noted with dismay, rather than confront her question "is this right or wrong." Is destroying 12 city blocks for redevelopment morally unbeatable? not will destroying 12 city blocks for redevelopment make people fall in love with or like the developer? is her question.

Robbie's second argument is equally flawed. He draws on his experience as a lawyer to claim that "nobody's interested in what people do. I'm a lawyer, for instance. I watch juries. You think they're judging the case? No, of course not. They're deciding if they like and therefore trust the defendant. They're judging the person" (78). Grace stammers, "*begins to get flustered*" [stage directions] (78), agrees, then confesses that she is dating the developer's son. Again, the point being that if she can't actually do anything on the basis of public criteria of what is good, how can she expect anyone else to. Undermining her credibility is clearly meant to undermine her initial question. Whereas she should have pointed out to Robbie (her relationship with the developer's son notwithstanding) that people are rarely, if ever, put on trial for their personalities, that the entire legal process begins because someone is highly interested in what someone else has actually done or is alleged to have done. The legal system would be a farce if laws (expressing public values) were not brought to bear.

The third assault on the notion that people should be judged by what they do recapitulates and elaborates these early argumentative skirmishes between Robbie and Grace by further stressing the impossibility of actually doing anything to change the way things are and by claiming that those who do not realize this are seriously deluded. Apparently Grace's mention of her pseudonym and her nostalgia for a morality based on what people actually do trigger in Robbie childhood memories of his father that were so painful that he changed his name from Dvorak to Baker to dissociate himself. When Grace discovers Robbie's true identity as the son of Bill Dvorak the famous spy, she expresses admiration for his father: "He seemed principled . . . he believed the two sides should be equal" (86). And she is surprised that his trivial betrayal of giving operational details of nuclear submarines to the Russians led to such a notorious trial. In other words, she is puzzled as to why he changed his name. Robbie's response explains his aversion to judging people according to what they do or believe:

I disliked him as a person. That's my objection. I don't care what he did, as you'd say. . . . His contempt was astonishing. He'd walk down a street and say, these people have no culture. . . . He'd analyze a problem, come to what he called a logical conclusion. He always had some expert rationale. That's why he did what he did. Because he alone understood. He claimed to understand the need to defuse the cold war better than anyone. And that's about as dumb as you can get. (86-87)

Robbie's description of his father's character is a reminder of just how narrow and ubiquitous Hare's demonology is in his transitional plays. Starting with Caroline and Stievel in *Dreams of Leaving* (in which Hare begins to privatize and personalize evil) every villain or unenlightened person is described as either logical (Caroline, Stievel, Braithwaite in *Wetherby*, the American ambassador and his close advisors in *Saigon: Year of the Cat*), or snobbish, arrogant, and superior (Mehta in *A Map of the World*, and to some degree Valentina in *The Bay at Nice*). What is distinctly new here in *Wrecked Eggs* is the use of this familiar demonology to discredit a certain kind of public moral action usually associated with leftist political action (instead of the right-wing posture of Mehta).

Contrary to Robbie's claim ("I don't care what he did, as you'd say"), what Bill Dvorak actually did is vitally important to both Robbie and Hare. Robbie is not attacking arrogance per se, but arrogance as a function of a particular public moral perspective. If his father had been an exemplary civil servant who just happened to be an arrogant, logical-minded man within the confines of his own home, Robbie may have still disliked him, but he would not have changed his name as a result. And such a private story would not have been of any interest to Hare. The act of betraying your country, like actively protesting against greedy developers, is an act of moral arrogance (as opposed to arrogance per se, as a function of the personality, of say, a man who believes himself superior for reading certain books). The point is that Bill claimed to know what is right and wrong in society, in the public sphere. And it is precisely this public moral perspective that Robbie attacks in his father, despite his claims to the contrary.

Hare's eagerness to discredit Bill Dvorak's public moral action can be measured by how his act of spying is presented as totally futile and ridiculous. In recalling the trial, Grace says, "the things that he told—operational details of nuclear submarines they were hardly critical" (86). Why not a betrayal at a very high level that sets the American military establishment back several years? The extreme triviality of the information passed to the Russians underscores the impossibility of Bill achieving anything and therefore effectively shifts our attention from the act itself to Bill's mental state—his personality. One is invited to conclude that only an arrogant, deluded crackpot could believe that such a trivial gesture would help diffuse the cold war.

Loelia's condescending admiration for Bill Dvorak further adds to the impression of a cranky, slightly deranged man with defective reality-testing equipment. She likes his "fuck you all" attitude and married Robby thinking she would get—"like father, like son"—an unconventional man (90). Yet she tells Grace, as if it were needless to say, that Bill was "absurd," a "joke" for thinking he could do something: "He thought he could do something. That isn't sinister, it's completely ridiculous" (90). Grace agrees. Leaving aside Hare's misreading of American culture and politics (the status quo is not an absolutely immovable monolith), in what moral space can one operate if acting on one's sense of right and wrong in the public sphere is "completely ridiculous"? The answer should be clear in light of the process of privatization I have traced from *Dreams of Leaving*. The contribution to this process in *Wrecked Eggs* (aside from rendering public moral action "completely ridiculous") is found in the closing episode of the play which works out the final parameters of the soul-based morality that is taken for granted in subsequent works.

The subject of divorce resurfaces after Robby reluctantly discloses painful childhood memories that led him to assume a new identity. While he is out doing some last-minute shopping, Loelia tells Grace that she is leaving Robbie because she is exhausted from living "with a man whose whole life is an attempt to pretend to be someone else" (90). "Robbie can't be himself" (91). And moreover, having been born in Milton, Nebraska, and told that she would be happy, Loelia feels she has the right to be happy (92).

Grace's response to this silly right-to-be-happy theory is not out of character considering her heretical views on the American obsession with success, money, and fantasy (as Amelia Grant she writes letters to newspapers attacking "the idea that everyone can have what they want" [75]). Grace urges Loelia to stick with the marriage because, as she explains: "I hate this idea that we're all just sensation. . . . 'I feel good, I don't feel good.' As if we were nothing except what we happen to be feeling at the moment" (92,93). With great urgency (because Robbie's car can be heard) Loelia asks for advice. In the following exchange Grace suggests a course of "action" that, in sharp contrast to Bill Dvorak's public moral act, takes place within the confines of Loelia's head:

Grace: I'm just saying you have certain qualities I envy. Qualities which aren't just . . . momentary.

Loelia: Like what?

Grace: Loyalty. Courage. Perseverance.
(*There is a pause.*)
If you don't use them, you're going to feel lousy.

(*Loelia looks at her from across the room, moved. Then with sudden violence.*)

Loelia: Fuck you, Grace, you've ruined my weekend. (93)

At that instant Robbie walks in. Loelia follows him into the kitchen and then returns to announce, "I'm staying till Tuesday" (94) (instead of Monday as planned). The play ends with Grace's question: "a.m. or p.m.?" The answer, I think, is clear.

The more enduring qualities—the "something more" than momentary sensation—that Grace advises Loelia to draw upon are "Loyalty. Courage. Perseverance." The remedy thus lies in adopting a certain attitude—a remedy in every way antithetical to Bill Dvorak's morally arrogant action. Instead of changing her behavior or asking Robbie to modify his (he becomes irrelevant to the solution at this point), Loelia simply has to focus on herself and undergo an inner transformation.

Between Bill Dvorak's global arena of moral action (fighting the cold war) and "just sensation" Hare presents character or the soul (presumably the source of loyalty and courage) as the narrow high ground on which individuals can negotiate a moral stance without being arrogant, ridiculous, and impotent on the one side or merely "sensational" on the other.

Loyalty, courage, and perseverance are admirable qualities to draw upon in many situations, however, I suggest their appeal is eroded somewhat in this context because the distinction between them and "just sensation" is not worked out convincingly: the contrasted qualities end up looking more similar than dissimilar. First, to label Loelia's "angry" and "confused" (92) feelings and her decision to end her marriage "just sensation" trivializes her experience of ten bad years of marriage. Why call a decision that took ten years to arrive at momentary and sensational? Is "just sensation" a valid way to categorize her response to her experience? Loelia's complicity in this trivialization appears contrived with her fatuous claim to have the right to be happy. One gets the impression that Leolia is being jacked around to suit shifting and momentary purposes. Earlier in the play she needs to be genuinely angry and hurt to create a marriage dilemma to solve, yet in this discussion with Grace she turns into a flaky woman to justify Grace's character-building homilies posing as an antidote to fleeting, self-indulgent whims.

And finally Grace tells Loelia that if she doesn't use her qualities of loyalty and courage, "you're going to feel lousy," which implies that feeling good is the ultimate objective. If so, we are back in the "I feel good, I don't feel good" sensationalism Grace has just described. What is it that makes the feeling good from staying with Robbie less sensational and momentary than the feeling "lousy" from leaving Robbie? Both are variations on feeling. The play closes with a dilemma framed to allow only private character solutions. Earlier questions of public morality can no longer be engaged. Hare was ready to write *The Secret Rapture*.

In this sense *Wrecked Eggs* was a preparation for *The Secret Rapture*. However, of the two companion pieces, *The Bay at Nice* has proven to be the more fruitful model for the later works which present variations on Sophia's retreat into private concerns set against the spiritual wasteland of the Soviet Communist Party with its soulless bureaucratic drones such as Sophia's husband Grigor and the young museum curator—both prototypes for Marion as well as the bishops in *Racing Demon*.

It would seem that emotional sensitivity (Sophia's choice of love rather than duty, and Loelia's loyalty and courage) would be more appropriate as opposition to the self-denying bureaucratic collectivism of the former Soviet Union than to the orthodoxy of America where individualism thrives, where self denial is not the national pathology. In the Tynan interview Hare says that in *Wrecked Eggs*, "life in Russia is contrasted with life in America, where people, although theoretically free, lead lives as rigid as the lives in Russia."[37] However, what these two plays demonstrate, along with the later work, is that the historical and political dimensions of rigidity or orthodoxy have been reconstituted as traits of character. With the prevailing individualist ethos of America transformed into a combination of crass materialism and emotional repression in the form of Robby, Loelia's acceptance of enduring qualities in herself (loyalty and courage) can appear to be opposed to the "rigid" way of life in America of which Hare speaks. With the rigid orthodoxy of the former Soviet Union and of Britain in the 1980s conceived in emotional terms, it becomes possible for characters with identical emotional reflexes—Marion in *The Secret Rapture*, and Grigor and Valentina in *The Bay at Nice*—to be representative of radically different political ideologies in different countries.

10

DISCOVERY OF THE SOUL
IN HISTORICAL CONTEXT

> If we British at this moment have a Way of Life, then I know no more
> about it than a housewife in Kamchatka. The only pronouncement I
> could make with any confidence about our Way of Life is that at present
> it seems to me to be invisible in the stewpot. From the West we look
> Red, from the East we look Blue. We are revolutionaries who have not
> swept away anything. We are Tories loudly denouncing taxes and
> regulations chiefly invented by Tory Ministers. We are Socialists busy
> creating peers and cheering pretty princesses. . . . We are a Socialist-
> Monarchy that is really the last monument of Liberalism.
> —J. B. Priestley, *New Statesman*, 1949

Having charted the progressive privatization of morality from *Dreams of
Leaving* (1980) to *Racing Demon* (1990), I am ready to explore the historical
dimensions of this process, to suggest how the shift is symptomatic of specific
cultural and political developments in Britain during the past 25 years. The
election of Margaret Thatcher as prime minister in 1979 created a crisis for
Hare and many others on the left because her government was the first to
openly assault the consensual ideals which form the unspoken assumed basis of
morality in his work in the 1970s.

From 1945 to 1979 the Conservative and Labour Parties shared a commitment to social equality and full employment (the legacy of W. H. Beveridge and
J. M. Keynes, respectively). These admirable public ideals sustained the welfare
state and extensive government control over industry and finance. This consensus started to come apart in the late 1960s and early 1970s when it became
clear to many people on both the right and left that the welfare state was
serving the country rather badly, and that sluggish economic growth was
making it very difficult to remain committed to either full employment or the

welfare state. In 1970 the Conservative government under Edward Heath was the first to jettison commitment to full employment with its Seldson Park Program that curbed union powers and allowed inefficient companies to close. The Labour governments under Harold Wilson and James Callaghan continued Heath's policies while remaining theoretically committed to full employment.

Meanwhile the consensus came under increased attack from the ideological fringes of both parties. From the far left came Tony Benn, whose participation in a sit-in with the workers and shop stewards at the Upper Clyde Shipbuilders yard in 1971 radicalized him and convinced him that the essence of socialism is workers' control. With this perspective he went on to blame both the overcentralized state bureaucracies and the revisionist wing of the Labour Party for betraying true socialist ideals with highly undemocratic, hierarchical, nonparticipatory forms of government. Although radical at the time, by the late 1980s Benn's ideas had finally started to infiltrate Labour Party strategies to regain popular support. Benn thinks the ascendant "modernizers" in the Labour Party led by Neil Kinnock and Tony Blair have moved the party even closer to the conservatives in their economic policies and attitudes toward privatization, yet many in the Labour Party now agree with Benn that the party and national electoral systems need to be more democratic and that reform of essential state institutions should be considered.[1]

From the far right came Margaret Thatcher and Keith Joseph. Both had converted to neoliberal, free-market ideas by 1974. They spent the rest of the 1970s convincing conservatives that the consensual ideals of social equality and full employment were highly undesirable as well as impossible to implement. Their theory of Britain's decline features the valiant forces of free enterprise gradually losing the fight against wasteful, undemocratic state bureaucracies. They accused the dominant paternalistic wing of their party (later rechristened "wets" by Thatcher) of betraying the true principles of conservativism with their complicity in the socialist consensus.

After Thatcher's election in 1979 the illusion of consensus, fostered by Callaghan to the end, was completely destroyed. The election of a government that brazenly denied the claims of equality—the most sacred of consensual ideals—presented Hare with a fundamental challenge, for he had devoted much of his playwrighting career to exposing the wealth, privilege, and cynicism of institutions (the City, Cambridge, the Foreign Service) that obstructed greater social equality and justice. Recall that in *Knuckle* it is only against the authority of widely held values that one could portray a banker confessing that capitalism had corrupted him morally. The extraction of this confession from Patrick reenacts the relationship between the Labour and Conservative Parties from 1945 until the late 1970s: Labour could always, from its position as moral guardian of the consensus, force the right to admit that capitalism was a nasty beast that had to be contained safely within socialist parameters.

In 1975 Hare told Catherine Itzin and Simon Trussler that *Knuckle* "is an almost obscenely constructive play": "It says something about it being impossible to live within this system without doing yourself moral damage. It's a play about knowing, about the fact that there are no excuses, and the fact that people who are damaged by the system know themselves to have been damaged, and are not ignorant of what they've done to themselves. And that is a large claim."[2] In Thatcher's Britain in the 1980s it would have been a wildly improbable fantasy to claim that the exuberant stockbrokers and bankers of the City "know themselves to have been damaged" morally by capitalism. In the 1980s people like Patrick became immune to guilt about capitalism.

The polarization of British politics, with both the far left and the ascendant new right deserting the middle ground, left Hare stranded on uncertain moral ground without a clear sense of who his audience was. He needed to redefine the moral underpinnings of his work. One can gauge his profound sense of impotence and alienation by the fact that, with the exception of *Wetherby* and the coauthored play *Pravda*, he stopped writing about England from 1979 to 1984. As he told Benedict Nightingale in 1982, even living in England had become very trying: "England breaks my heart. I find it almost impossible to live here. My irritation is so great that I spend a lot of time abroad."[3]

My argument, in short, is that the breakup of the postwar consensus propelled Hare to discover and colonize the soul as his new basis of morality. He decided social revitalization would come from individuals fully accepting the good within themselves rather than from believing and acting upon public ideals. However, no real distinction exists between a soul based morality and the neoliberalism of the new right that Hare found so irritating. Both define moral value as an individual possession.

Evidence suggests that Hare's own personal growth and transformation during the 1980s led to his belief that the conflict between regressive and progressive forces in Britain today is essentially a clash between the emotionally sensitive and insensitive. From numerous articles and interviews one can assemble a personal narrative of his development in which an arrogant, moralizing, condescending, rationalistic, ill-tempered, flashy, smartass young man of the 1970s grew up and matured in the 1980s into a sensitive man in touch with his spiritual and emotional needs and capacities.

Having noted Hare's greater emphasis on emotion in his recent works, Michael Bloom writes in the November 1989 issue of *American Theatre*: "He wonders if his early plays were 'too densely intellectualized,' and hopes his newer work will be more emotionally satisfying. When I ask why he thinks the recent plays and films—*The Bay at Nice*, *The Secret Rapture* and *Strapless*—are more intimate in scale and subject, he answers: 'Possibly I'm growing up.' He declines to elaborate and switches from the personal to the aesthetic."[4] The phrase "grow-up" also appears in his explanation to Kathleen Tynan of why he wrote *The Bay at Nice* and *Wrecked Eggs*: "I couldn't grow up unless I worked out some things I felt."[5] It's evident from the same interview that "growing up" entails getting in touch with the emotions. In the following passage Hare agrees with Tynan that his work continues to improve and believes this is because he had learned over many years to, as he says, "understand my emotions." He continues: "I remember Max [Stafford-Clark of the Royal Court] saying something which has absolutely haunted me. 'The problem with you, David, is that you want to be entertaining every moment.' What he was effectively saying is that my gift is very flashy. It's taken me a long time to express myself rather than let my gift run me."[6]

According to a *Newsweek* interview, "growing up" means not being a "smartass" and avoiding political ideology of any kind which Hare considers propaganda: "I'm bored by propaganda, either from the left or right. But goodness makes me weep. I see Isobel that way. So I said, Why don't I write about goodness? Why be smartass?"[7]

Hare told Benedict Nightingale he wrote the part of Isobel with the actress Blair Brown in mind for she "could convey goodness, without being pious, or sanctimonious or obnoxious."[8] "Sanctimonious" and "obnoxious" are words Hare would also use to describe his former self-righteous self and the anguished characters of his early work. As he says to Nightingale: "People seem to feel my plays are full of characters torturing themselves about how to live, instead of just getting on with it. And when they hate my work, they hate it because they think I'm somehow claiming to know how to live better than them."[9]

In these testimonies of personal growth Hare redefines his former political beliefs and assumptions about public moral values as a variety of attitudes and emotional states, which is precisely what he does to public values in the transitional plays of the early 1980s. In *A Map of the World* Stephen's pretentious, ill-tempered political posturing is presented as a projection of jealousy, loneliness, and immaturity. When Stephen announces, "I've grown up here" in the central debate scene with Mehta, Hare appears to be in the process of exorcising his own past as well (69). Bill Dvorak, the arrogant spy in *Wrecked Eggs,* could also be an earlier version of himself he is eager to put to rest. Robbie's condemnation of his father—"he claimed to understand the need to defuse the cold war better than anyone"—echoes Hare's assessment of his former immature attitude in the Nightingale article (86-87).

In this "growing up" narrative the shift from a public to a private basis of morality is reconstituted as an inevitable, more or less involuntary, biological process of maturation rather than a self-aware participation in a historical process. In this way the narrative provides a way to escape history and ignore the individualistic basis of the new right political and moral agenda and therefore avoid recognition of how in essential ways he had "grown into" what he protests against.

This biological "growing up" narrative describes how Hare negotiated his postconsensus soul-based morality with the necessary illusion of living in an ideological no-man's land. A vital question remains: Why didn't he pursue what would seem to be—for someone who thinks of himself as a socialist writer—a more likely response to the breakup of the consensus and embrace smaller less monolithic public values? After all, the move from a national perspective to the soul is a gargantuan step. Surely some intermediate level of community or collective enterprise could be found with which to identify. Why the all-or-none approach in which the postwar national consensus is first endorsed totally and then totally abandoned?

I suggest that the answer can be found in the undemocratic, hierarchical, nonparticipatory way the postwar consensus was sustained almost from its inception. The consensus as administered encouraged individualistic support of collective ideals and thus sowed the seeds for Hare's inward-turning solution. The consensual ideals gained national appeal from the genuinely revolutionary upheavals in British society during the Second World War when military success demanded that on the home front rigid class and gender barriers be suspended, that talent be the measure of one's value, and that power be decentralized to secure full participation.

However, soon after the war, with socialist ideals enshrined in a wide variety of legislation and welfare state institutions, powerful, long-entrenched traditions of Fabian and Tory paternalism reasserted themselves, joined hands, and turned socialism into something that was managed by bureaucrats and politicians from the top. Socialism thus became something that was done to and for the people, not with or by the people. This meant that while collectivist ideals were allowed to flourish in theory on a national level, they never really developed into a lived reality for the vast majority of people who were treated as atomistic objects of charity by a nanny state.

As many historians and intellectuals from both the left and right have argued, collectivism became statism partly because the Labour Party—which should have fostered popular democratic practices from the bottom up—jealously guarded their authority and suppressed any attempts to set up alternate or competing forms of participation in the form of workers' control, self-management, and smaller collective organizations.[10] In the hands of the power-hogging state bureaucrats and party officials, the consensus became a destructive national myth that inhibited and co-opted smaller collectives for the sake of the single big one that soared above petty class, political, and regional differences. So the consensus became by definition a vision of public collective morality that could only be embraced individually. Smaller group struggles for change presumed alternate grounds of public value, and, more important, threatened the centralized authority of the state which both parties were equally eager to uphold.

The difference between consensual and nonconsensual modes of radicalism becomes clear when contrasting Howard Brenton's and David Hare's drama of the 1970s. Hare advocates change within the parameters of the consensus, which for Brenton is the chief obstacle to more radical change. Starting with *Knuckle,* Hare's works of the 1970s are about the failure of solitary, classless, nonpartisan individuals to bring about change within some national institution; whereas Brenton's plays of the same period are about the failure of marginalized leftist groups struggling to change society from outside mainstream political and cultural institutions.

For example, Brenton's *Magnificence* (1973) begins with a group of activists conducting a squatting demonstration in an abandoned flat in London and ends with the assassination of a cabinet minister. The antimainstream orientation of the group is underscored by the presence of Veronica, an outsider who joined the group on her two-week vacation from the BBC. Will says to her: "Can tell you work for the BBC, 'cos of the way you go on about ordinary people.'"[11] Veronica belongs to that loosely defined group of middle-browed, idealistic professionals Michael Frayn describes in his brilliant essay "Festival" (about the Festival of Britain) as the "gentle herbivores"—the Sunday school teachers, media and arts people, welfare state bureaucrats—who like to plan and orchestrate things (like the Festival of Britain) for the ordinary people.[12] If the ordinary people initiate their own good causes, people like Veronica descend, as Will says, "like a plague of locusts . . . chomp, chomp. Adventure playgrounds, free contraceptive clinics, schoolroom abortion service, chomp chomp."[13]

Similarly, the revolutionary zeal of the group of young communist working class strikers in the potato chip factory in Brenton's *Weapons of Happiness* (1976), although obviously futile, is clearly meant to look admirable and heroic next to the mature, moderate positions of those around them like Hicks, their Labour Party representative. He urges them to express their discontent in a reasonable manner within proper union channels. "See," he says, "the best you can hope for in this world is to nudge. Give it a bit of a nudge."[14] Hicks's "nudge" approach to social change is the way of the consensus with the Labour Party gently propelling the nation forward as properly directed and managed by the right people at the top.

Having never endorsed moderate consensual means of social change, Brenton didn't need to reassess his dramatic strategies and moral assumptions when the consensus collapsed. He continued to write of collective, grass-roots activism, although with even less optimism than before in *Sleeping Policemen* (1983), and *Greenland* (1988). His plays, like those of other more radical socialist playwrights in Britain—Caryl Churchill, Edward Bond, David Edgar, John McGrath—often celebrate the marginalized and futile efforts of those trying to establish some sort of smaller collective solidarity on the basis of political beliefs, social class, or gender. What is unusual about the two Brenton plays I've discussed is that they make explicit what is generally implicit in the work of these playwrights: that the monolithic collectivity of the consensus and smaller collective enterprises are mutually exclusive and antagonistic. Brenton's squatters and young strikers can exist only at the fringes of the great middle ground claimed by the consensus.

In Hare's early work, the sense that the consensus excludes other levels of solidarity persists in the defense of the middle ground against diversionary tactics from the fringes, from those who cling to partisan political viewpoints, and their social class. From *Knuckle* to *Plenty* Hare defines the moral idealism of his central characters (Jenny, Sarah, Maggie, Archie, and Susan) as soaring above any less-than-national basis of solidarity. Although the despair and anger of these characters is cranked up to a very high pitch, the fact that such anguished feelings of loss are refracted through solitary individuals stripped of all but national allegiances positions Hare as a radical voice firmly within consensual parameters.

In *Plenty* it is very telling that soon after confronting the national moral bankruptcy exposed by the Suez crisis, Susan retreats in despair in the last scenes of the play and tries to recreate in absolute solitude her experience as a secret agent during the war—the only time in her life she felt truly at one with the national purpose. The play ends with the paradoxical spectacle of Susan trying to recapture the purity of a public vision of morality while wandering about the Midlands alone, stripped of money, friends, husband, and home. In these last scenes the most naked individuality is yoked to a public morality at its most abstract and general. No intermediate levels of solidarity exist between Susan and her soaring national ideals.

To return to the question, Why didn't Hare renegotiate his public morality on some less monolithic collective basis after the consensus broke up?, personal and historical reasons can be proposed. It is not surprising that Hare, who has spent nearly his entire life within establishment institutions with selfconsciously national moral, educational, and cultural mandates (the Church of England-affiliated school Lansing College, Jesus College Cambridge, the Royal Court Theatre, the Royal National Theatre) conceives of moral value according to the deeply entrenched paternalistic structures and public service ethos that dominates British society. From 1974 forward all his work set in England features individuals allegiant to a central absolute authority (soaring consensual ideals or the soul). He thus replicates patterns of thinking and feeling about morality and authority that exist at the heart of British political and cultural life.

Having used the words "individualistic," "abstract," and "universal" to describe Hare's former consensus-based morality, I suggest that he instinctively worked out a soul-based morality in the 1980s because it brought him very close to where he started. The soul, like the consensus, is individually embraced and universal. The essential ingredients persist: he has simply given public moral value a new name, milder manners, and a private habitation. In this sense, the soul is very much a resuscitation of the consensus.

As the assumed universal moral perspective of everyone, both the soul and the consensus exert enormous power and authority that belie the passivity with which they are held and sustained. In *Knuckle* a capitalist banker can actually be brought to confess to being corrupted by the system because it is assumed that he knows, like everyone else, that soaring above exists the true standard of right and wrong. Likewise, in *The Secret Rapture* Marion, a junior minister in the Tory government, can be moved to confess that she is emotionally illiterate because she knows, like everyone else, that buried deep within her soul exists the true standard of good and evil. The crucial distinction being that the consensus did in fact exercise considerable moral authority over many people in England for about 30 years after the Second World War, whereas the soul could not have plausibly operated as the assumed possession of everyone in the polarized 1980s.

The continuities between Hare's pre and postconsensus writing indicate that the seeds of his thinking about moral value in the 1980s were sown during the consensus which encouraged a solitary, passive, instinctual engagement with national ideals. What I want to do now is further historicize his moral stance of the 1980s and 1990s by suggesting how it is typical of a centrist response to the centrifugal fragmenting force of Thatcherism that manifested itself in traditional political form in 1981 with the appearance of the SDP-Liberal Alliance, which drew upon roughly a quarter of voters who wanted to bolster the shaken middle ground. The Alliance was more willing than the new neoliberal right to endorse institutional solutions to Britain's political, economic, and social problems, and more willing than Labour to facilitate wealth creation by individuals. The emergence of the Alliance, dedicated to holding the middle ground with ultimately liberal rather than collectivist assumptions, parallels the shift in Hare's work from a public to a private basis of morality.

Hare's retreat to the soul is a somewhat rarefied variation on the attitudes and values of a relatively small, yet highly influential, group of people who still dominate the universities, the Church of England, the subsidized arts establishment, and welfare state bureaucracies. This group vehemently opposes Thatcherism, and, yet, having always had one foot planted solidly on the same liberal ideological ground, they are able to offer little in the way of an alternative except a more caring and kinder version of the new right's individualistic market-driven vision of society. Like Hare, these people, who tend to gravitate to the center of British political and cultural life, invested heavily in the egalitarian reformist ideals of the consensus while remaining largely oblivious to the elitist, undemocratic, paternalistic manner in which such ideals were administered. They found social democracy highly congenial in theory, not in practice.

The Alliance did become interested in structural reforms that would have enhanced the practice of democracy, yet such interest appears to have been motivated primarily by the need to secure power for the party. Electoral reform became increasingly important to the Alliance as they repeatedly failed—because of the "first past the post" election system—to turn their considerable voter support into corresponding power in Parliament. In the 1987 election the Conservatives won 376 seats with 42.3% of the vote, while the Alliance won 22 seats with 22.6% of the vote.[15] In *A United Kingdom* (1986) David Owen, one of the founders of the Alliance, argues that proportional representation is essential for national unity and prosperity: "Our greatest weakness is the absence of a constitutional structure that creates and fosters the necessary consensus. To halt our economic decline we must halt our political decline. Proportional representation can provide the key to building a new consensus."[16]

It is not surprising that the new right did not have much respect for those who vociferously attacked "Thatcherism" without being able to articulate a clear ideological alternative. In the mid-1980s they seized upon the phrase "chattering classes" to express their scorn. In the December 3, 1989, issue of the *Manchester Guardian Weekly* Alan Watkins (the *Observer*'s political columnist) discusses the chattering classes phenomenon: the origin of the phrase, who belongs to the "CCs," and why the phrase became "part of the language." He believes the phrase was first used in his presence sometime in late 1984 by his neighbor Frank Johnson, who had stopped by for a visit from his adjacent Islington apartment. Johnson subsequently used the phrase in his parliamentary sketches for the *Daily Telegraph*. Watkins adopted it and claims to have soon popularized it with frequent use in his political column. Originally conceived to describe opinion formers of vaguely leftist leanings—"journalists, television people, media folk generally"—the right quickly found the phrase a very useful term of abuse for those in the left establishment it considered "far removed from the nitty gritty political realities of today." Watkins could be describing the concerns of leftist theatre in the 1980s when he lists the "alleged concerns" of the chattering classes from the perspective of the leading London newspapers:

With the aid of computer technology it is possible to trace the alleged concerns of the CCs. *The Times* thinks they rabbit on about official secrecy; why Mrs. Thatcher is ghastly and/or a Philistine; the awfulness of traffic jams and the need for consensus in British politics. *The Sunday Telegraph* believes they have nothing better to chat about than public spending priorities and why the Falklands War was wrong. *The Sunday Times* thinks they witter about materialism, the state of British cinema and (again) the awfulness of Mrs. T. These are clearly mere footnotes to the mainstream concerns of modern society. Which leads to the third implication about the Chattering Classes: They are ever so slightly pathetic.[17]

To "witter" about "the awfulness of Mrs. T"—that is, to personalize politics as Hare has done—is the reflex of those unsure of an ideological basis from which to criticize the Conservatives.

According to a *Sunday Times* columnist Watkins quotes, "hatred of Mrs. Thatcher seems to have become obsessively implanted in the minds of the chattering classes and provides their principal source of conversation." Although interested in defining the chattering classes phenomenon rather than explaining why they are obsessed with Mrs. Thatcher, Watkins quotes three questions aired in the *Guardian* (April 1988) that point to the answer: "Why have so many of the chattering classes succumbed to the embrace of the new right? Why do so many of those who still oppose its politics half-accept the assumptions which underlie them? Why do quite clever people fall for the mixture of obsolete economics, pop history and primitive psychology which provides the intellectual cladding for those assumptions?"[18] The answers to these questions can be traced, as I have already suggested, to the debilitating legacy of the consensus which was an expression of deeply embedded undemocratic political traditions and the ever-resilient class system that served to inoculate certain professional classes of socialist-minded people from collective and truly democratic practices, thereby disarming them before someone who finally called their bluff. Having never been committed to socialism or social democracy in practice, the former guardians of the consensus were left with nothing with which to fight the Conservatives except their patrician paternalistic style and temperament.

To help the chattering classes recognize the weakness of their opposition was one of the objectives of Andrew Neil (editor of *The Sunday Times* after 1983) throughout the 1980s. In an interview with Geoff Mulgan of *Marxism Today* (March 1990) he bluntly calls them intellectually bankrupt and laments their influence:

Mulgen: Can I ask about the 'chattering classes'? Why are they so important a part of your demonology?

Neil: Well, they are important only in the sense that what they believe has a disproportionate influence in the country. They are still dominant in the media and among opinion-formers, and their values are still dominant. I think they have a baleful effect on Britain—partly because they are intellectually bankrupt now. . . . They have done no work in the 1980s at all to try to rebuild a credible left-wing analysis of a modern society. They are intellectually lazy.[19]

Although Andrew Neil ascribes more importance and influence to the chattering classes than Alan Watkins does, neither suggests that anyone on the right feels morally inadequate or guilty in relation to them. From the perspective of the new right, Hare's "ganging up" scenario with conservative forces attacking good people out of guilt appears to have little bearing on reality.

For a right-wing perspective on the "ganging up" scenario, consider the response of Roger Scruton to what he calls the "liberal intelligensia." He is the editor of the conservative journal *The Salisbury Review* and the chief guru of the Conservative Philosophy Group. In an essay entitled "The Left Establish-ment," which appeared in the December 1988 issue of *The Salisbury Review*, he investigates several theoretical explanations (Marxist, "the indoctrination theory" as applied by David Marsland to sociology, and the "public choice" theory of James Buchanan) to account for the power and influence of "the left establishment" he sees entrenched in the universities, the schools, the Church of England, and the media.

Instead of feeling threatened or challenged by "the left establishment" Scruton is puzzled about the source of the strength of this influential group he finds bereft of the underpinnings normally associated with political establishments such as popular support and a set of ideological beliefs:

In the days of McCarthyism it was hardly puzzling that universities, schools and publications tended to manifest the same fears and bigotries as the surrounding world: such a fact does not cry out for special explanation. But when a seemingly immovable left-wing consensus emerges in the intellectual world at the very moment when the people as a whole are turning their backs on left-wing ways of thinking, we are faced with an interesting and in some ways surprising occurrence. We discover, for the first time in our history, a full-scale left-establishment, at the very moment when the much sought-after constituency of the left—the industrial proletariat—has finally disappeared, not only from the real world, but also from the popular imagination. Moreover, not only is the tide of popular opinion retreating from socialist ideas—at least from those which seem to legitimize the control of society by the state—these ideas are no longer put forward in a spirit of conviction even by those who claim to believe them. The only strength that attaches to them, is that of opposition to their enemy, whose evil, however, is so great as to endow them with a constantly renewable motivating power. The case provides, I believe, a novel challenge to theories of ideology. How is this growth of a "left establishment" to be explained, and what does it indicate about the social conditions of the "capitalist" world?[20]

Scruton finds the stubborn pockets of leftist resistance "interesting," "surprising," and a "novel challenge to theories of ideology."

While Scruton's scornful condescension toward the left is a typical attitude of the new right, his analysis suggests that he may not be quite up to the "novel challenge" of identifying the source of "strength" of the left. He is oddly silent about social class and the profoundly elitist ethos that pervades British political culture, which gives his discussion a peculiar unreality. To claim, as he does above, that a "left-wing consensus" "emerged" as a "growth" "at the very moment when people as a whole" turned from socialist ways of thinking (that is, when Margaret Thatcher came to power in 1979) is to ignore realities central to British society: that the "left-wing consensus" that persists into the 1980s and 1990s without the normal trappings that attend politically influential groups is the powerful remnant of the bureaucratic and intellectual elite (comprised of old-style Tories as well as socialist-minded people) of a certain class and/or sensibility that ruled the country during the postwar period and before. They did not suddenly "emerge" in the 1980s. It is the enduring continuities, not the recent disjunctions, that best illuminate the "surprising" and "interesting" behavior of the "left-wing consensus" Scruton investigates. Perhaps his silence about class reveals an understandable sensitivity on the part of some on the new right to the snobbism of the old establishment reflected, for example, in John Mortimer's unflattering portrait of Leslie Titmuss, the vulgar new right Tory minister with working-class origins in *Paradise Postponed* (1985) and *Titmuss Regained* (1990).

In contrast, Andrew Neil, with his Scottish Presbyterian background and thus less implicated in the English class system, assesses the "left establishment" with a clearer eye as the "dominant all pervasive elite that this country still has, which has dragged us down for most of this century."[21] With an eye on old establishment structures and class continuities behind the ideologically mute "left establishment," it is clear to Neil how the Church of England can oppose the new right: "It's always been to some extent the old Tory party at prayer and now it is the Chattering Class party at prayer."[22] Whereas Scruton remains puzzled about why, in his words, "all reports issuing from the Church of England (and especially those from its Board of Social Responsibility) have been of socialist persuasion" while noting at the same time that the church contains "far more Tories than socialists or social democrats among its congregation."[23]

In several interviews, Hare says that two experiences inspired *The Secret Rapture*: being close to a friend while she coped with the grief of her father's death, and an unsettling experience during a weekend at a country house in England in 1987 shortly after Margaret Thatcher was reelected. What he says of this experience is worth noting, for it would be difficult to conceive of a moment more emblematic of his response to Thatcherism in his work on the 1980s and early 1990s. In his review of *The Secret Rapture*, Benedict Nightingale sets the stage for Hare's anecdote as follows. "Over dinner he found himself talking to a celebrated novelist, who seemed mainly interested in money."

He asked me what I did with my earnings and I said I put them in the bank, and the whole table roared with laughter at my naiveté. It turned out that before he began to write each morning he spent an hour going through his portfolio. He said, you'd have to be very stupid not to have doubled your money this past year. And I thought this is something new in English life. Anyone who simply plies their trade without thinking about cash is thought to be a fool, an idiot.[24]

In the other slightly different version given to Michael Bloom of *American Theatre* magazine, Hare says more about his response to the general hilarity caused by his "naiveté": "The assumption that everyone will make as much money as they can and spend a lot of time doing it is new in England. The feelings of total inadequacy I had for not being part of this interested me, and I gave them to Isobel. And I'm proud to say, even having written the play, I still have no investments."[25]

Now consider this description of dinner guests laughing at Hare's naiveté about financial matters in light of his "ganging up" theory set forth several paragraphs later in the same Nightingale interview/review: "'I've noticed that goodness tends to make people shifty, and make those with bad consciences feel judged even when they're not being judged at all,' says Mr. Hare. 'It doesn't have to do anything to make itself hated. It just has to exist to cause chaos.'"[26]

Does Hare's "ganging up" theory apply to his own experience? Was the laughter of the other guests the "shifty" guilty reflex of people with "bad consciences" feeling they were being judged by someone's goodness? Perhaps it was. Or could it be that honest surprise prompted their laughter? Many people recognize that putting money in a bank is not a an optimal way to invest, especially if the amount is substantial. And it's not clear how putting money in the bank could be considered ethically superior to investing it in the stock market, when banks earn profits from investing individual deposits in ways some people find objectionable enough to opt for socially sensitive investment options. There doesn't appear to be much room for Hare to feel superior in this situation. I suggest that the distinction between him and the investing novelist is a matter of sensibility and personality: Hare is not the sort of person to spend much time thinking about how to invest his money. His sense of being different (and perhaps better—"I still have no investments" he is "proud" to say) rests on personal taste and breeding rather than on ethically superior actions or principles.

Hare's belief that he was up against unenlightened individuals, rather than an ideologically induced surge of investing, is conveyed in his surprised observation that "thinking about cash" is, as he says, "something new in English life" as if values had mysteriously shifted among people in general, making them more materialistic and eager to invest. However, personal investing is not new in England. And furthermore, it was the Tory government's decision to revoke foreign exchange controls in October 1979, five months after the election, that caused levels of personal investment to rise sharply in the 1980s. After 1978, annual private investment overseas rose from £4,600 million to roughly £10,600 million in 1983.[27]

Set against this episode from Hare's weekend in the country, his recent plays—especially *The Secret Rapture* and *Racing Demon*—appear to be revenge fantasies of the alienated which feature his brief moment of embarrassment amid amused dinner companions transmogrified into a scenario in which the spiritually and emotionally unenlightened gang up on saints whose spiritual powers are so awesome that all they have to do is exist to cause chaos and alarm. It is a dream of consolation in which one can only truly invest in one's self and all the dividends appear to be spiritual.

11

THE TRILOGY: THE REFRESHING
OF BRITISH INSTITUTIONS

Stephen: It is natural for you to think that money governs England; but you must allow me to think I know better.

Undershaft: And what does govern England, pray?

Stephen: Character, father, character.

Undershaft: Whose character? Yours or mine?

Stephen: Neither yours nor mine, father, but the best elements in the English national character.
—George Bernard Shaw, *Major Barbara*, 1907

To Govern Is to Serve.
—Slogan of Tory Party Conference in 1984

With the publication of *The Absence of War* in 1993, David Hare's trilogy about English institutions (Parliament in *The Absence of War*, the Church of England in *Racing Demon* 1990, and the judiciary in *Murmuring Judges* 1992) was complete. Whatever one may think of these plays (*Racing Demon* turned out to be a critical and popular success. It won four awards as Best Play of the Year, including the Olivier Award, and throughout a period of nearly five years was performed 257 times on all three National Theatre stages and on tour), Hare should be applauded for writing about British institutions when there is serious and widespread concern about their health.

Ever since the constitutional settlement of 1688, upon which the present British form of government is based, discontent with British institutions has existed at the fringe of British political and cultural life. The most remarkable development in the past decade is that such discontent has moved close to the heart of British political discourse. Trying to understand the reasons for the economic and social decline of their country has been the postwar British obsession. What distinguishes the constitutional reform movement of the late 1980s and early 1990s more than anything else is its resolute focus on the undemocratic nature of power invested in the core state institutions, rather than on the failings of the people who run them or the inadequacies of the various ideologies and policies that they have been called upon to implement. Now that the achievements of Margaret Thatcher's years in power can begin to be assessed, there is a growing conviction that the decline of Britain is ideology and political party proof. The Scottish journalist Neal Ascherson was one of the first to voice this conviction when he said in 1985 that the "fundamental misjudgment about this country" was the view that "Britain has the finest institutions in the world, but they find it hard to function properly just at the moment, because our economy doesn't work. The truth is the exact opposite. The reason that Britain's economy doesn't work is that British institutions are in terminal decay."[1]

Two years later, another journalist, Robert Chesshyre returned to Britain from a three-year stay in the United States and, alarmed at the deterioration of quality of life in Britain and the "depth and complexity of the national malaise," decided to travel around the country on a pulse-taking survey and publish his discoveries in a book. He discovered that "there is limited faith in the responsiveness of Government—national or local. I was frequently told, as I researched this book, that 'it does not matter which lot get in.'"[2]

Many increasingly believe that the only way Britain will become a more prosperous and democratic society is through a major overhaul of its institutions, which is to say, through constitutional reform. In 1985 polls revealed that 46% of the public wanted a Bill of Rights and 55% thought their institutions worked well.[3] In 1993 the MORI (Market and Opinion Research International) "State of the Nation" polls for the Rowntree Reform Trust revealed that 79% of the public wanted a Bill of Rights and that "fewer than one in ten have any faith in the ability of existing institutions to protect our rights."[4]

Although many thousands of people involved in a wide range of activities contributed to this sea change in public opinion, I want to mention some of the most notable voices and milestones in the reform movement since it began gaining momentum in the mid-1980s. One of the more articulate and persuasive early voices was that of Neal Ascherson, who regularly drew attention to the dilapidated state of British institutions in his weekly column in *The Observer* during 1985. In 1988 his essays were published in the book *Games with Shadows*. In 1988 Tom Nairn's influential book *The Enchanted Glass* appeared. He explores the complex historical reasons for Britain's "enchantment" with the monarchy and the other feudal structures of the British state. In the December 2, 1988, issue of *New Statesman & Society,* a small group of people with a wide range of political views and backgrounds launched

Charter 88, an organization committed to reforming all core British institutions, and introducing a Bill of Rights and a written constitution.[5] As Stuart Weir (editor of *New Stateman & Society* and one of the founding members of Charter 88) explains, the title "Charter 88" was selected as a reaction against celebrations of the Glorious Revolution in 1688: "In 1988, the Establishment celebrated the Tercentenary of the Glorious Revolution and the complacent (and contradictory) myth of the infinitely stable and 'flexible' political regime it created. As editor of NSS, I wanted to dramatize the magazine's argument that the immune system of the body politic had failed and our politics were consequently riddled with anti-democratic and authoritarian viruses."[6]

Since December 1988, nearly every issue of *New Statesman & Society* has contained an article or two exploring the institutional weaknesses of some aspect of the British state. In July 1990, Charter 88 sponsored Britain's first constitutional convention since Tom Paine fled to France.[7] In May 1994, Charter 88 cosponsored with Rupert Murdoch's *The Times* a conference about the monarchy. A year later the papers presented appeared in the book *Power and the Throne,* edited by Anthony Barnett. By 1994 Charter 88 had 50,000 signatories. In 1989 Stephen Haseler published *The Battle for Britain* in which he describes realignments in British politics with the battle lines drawn between old paternalistic forces committed to the corporatist status quo and the coalition of forces committed to institutional reform. These new lines run through rather than between the traditional political parties. In 1988 the leader of the Labour Party, Neil Kinnock, called those involved with Charter 88 "wankers and whingers."[8] The next year Roy Hattersley, a leading member of Kinnock's shadow cabinet, announced that the Labour Party would draw up its own Charter of Rights, which became public in 1992. In 1990 Margaret Thatcher in her Aspen Address proposed to draw up a Magna Carta for Europe. It is noteworthy that she used the word "entrench"—a key Charter 88 word—that signals a willingness to depart from the unwritten and therefore unentrenched constitutional status quo.[9] In July 1990, Robert MacLennan, a Liberal Democrat MP, launched his party's draft of a written constitution.[10] In 1991 the right-of-center Institute of Economic Affairs published a collection of academic essays, representing a wide spectrum of political views, that reassess the strengths and weaknesses of Britain's unwritten constitutional framework.[11] At the Labour Party Conference in 1993 the dominant concern was the political and social rights of individuals. Neil Kinnock, no longer party leader, became a signatory of Charter 88 at this conference.[12]

In two books that appeared in the early 1990s (*Wake Up Britain: A Latter-Day Pamphlet,* 1994, by Paul Johnson, an ardent Thatcher supporter; and *Common Sense A New Constitution for Britain* (1993) by Tony Benn and Andrew Hood, both on the far left of the Labour Party) the authors agree that discontent with the lack of democracy in Britain has reached truly disturbing levels. They agree that for democracy to work "the people" must be consulted.

Johnson believes most of the institutions are basically sound and that they could work as they are supposed to if all the unelected lobbies, pressure groups, and single-issue fanatics were removed and a Swiss-like system of direct consultation set up to reconnect the people with their government; while Benn and Hood believe more direct consultation can be achieved only by entrenching the rights and powers of citizens within a written constitution and a Bill of Rights. In the second half of the book they offer a detailed draft of both. You know something new is afoot in British politics when those at the opposite ends of the political spectrum such as Johnson and Benn agree about more than they disagree.[13]

In the introduction to *Asking Around* (his account of how he conducted research for the plays), Hare comments on the timeliness of his trilogy: "A friend of mine remarked that it was my special good fortune to have completed a trilogy about British institutions at precisely that moment when British institutions were finally admitted to be in a state of collapse."[14] Many were admitting collapse well before 1993, yet few would contest Hare's good fortune of having addressed the issue at about the time it became a truly national concern.

If there is a consensus in Britain in the 1990s it is that its institutions are in a state of crisis. Some detailed basic information about the nature of this crisis and its history needs to be conveyed before one can begin to understand what Hare is saying about the crisis in the trilogy. These three plays are very much of their time—the late 1980s and early 1990s. They are Hare's response to events and issues of the past decade that will likely transform political and cultural attitudes in Britain in the 1990s more than Thatcherism did in the 1980s. The present crisis in Britain's institutions is partly a legacy of Thatcherism (so familiarity with her policies and ideology is helpful) but, more important, it signals departures from Thatcherism.

To discuss the British institutions is really to discuss the British constitution. Unlike the United States, Canada, or European countries, Britain does not have a written constitution or a Bill of Rights. Although unwritten and thus tricky to define in any precise manner, the British nevertheless possess a powerful constitution. It consists, to put it as plainly as possible, of the traditional conventional practices and unspoken rules, as they have evolved during the past 300 years, that define the prerogatives of and relationships between the institutions that comprise the British state—both houses of Parliament, the monarchy, the Church of England, and the judiciary. Within this ancient feudal arrangement the individual is not a citizen with specific rights and powers, but rather a subject allegiant to the absolute sovereign power of the Crown in Parliament. When William and Mary of Orange were installed as king and queen by the constitutional arrangement of 1688, real power shifted to both houses of Parliament, yet the absolute nature of sovereign power remained intact. In the years since 1688, as the power of the monarchy and the House of Lords diminished to the point that the role of both institutions has became largely symbolic, absolute sovereignty came to reside entirely in the House of Commons.

In 1959 Conservative MP Christopher Hollis claimed that parliamentary government had "been replaced by what can be described as alternating party dictatorship": "Our modern system of highly centralized Cabinet Government is now buttressed by a party system which limits the elector to choosing between the Cabinet; which, most serious of all, is rapidly transferring both debate and decision from the publicity of the floor of the Commons to the secrecy of the party caucus in the committee room upstairs or the party headquarters outside."[15]   A great deal has been said about how Margaret Thatcher emasculated the cabinet and turned the Tory Party into an extension of her will. There is no doubt that she further concentrated the power of the executive, yet those who want sweeping constitutional reforms realize that the real problem is not Margaret Thatcher, or indeed any individuals in government. Thatcher simply manipulated brilliantly the sovereign authority of an institution in which the secretive autocratic unaccountable exercise of power is entirely natural. As some reformers have noted, Margaret Thatcher was actually their best ally for she repeatedly demonstrated how the British state lends itself to functioning without the oxygen of democracy.[16]

People discovered that there was nothing anyone could do to stop the conservatives from putting into effect deeply unpopular legislation to abolish the Greater London Council (GLC—the elected city government of London) and other municipal councils, introduce a poll tax, undermine civil liberties by enhancing police powers, and strengthen the Official Secrets Act (which made it even more obvious that very little difference existed between the "national interest" and the desires of the political party that happened to be in power). People also discovered that their role in the political process was almost nonexistent, confined to the right to vote every four or five years. The rest of the time they must—in order for the system to work—assume a posture of deference to authority from above. That is, they must trust that through the decency and benevolence of their rulers justice and fairness will prevail in society.

Among reformers, frustration with this "culture of deference" (Stephen Haseler's phrase) runs very high, as is clear from this statement of Anthony Barnett, who is the chairman of Charter 88: "The unwritten constitution we have inherited is so much hot air. People are fed up with being told that they should be impressed by the mystifications of the arcane rules of clubland, especially when they are told this by patrician voices supposedly speaking on their behalf."[17] Barnett wrote this in December 1988 when Charter 88 was launched. Events since then indicate that frustration has risen steadily among a broad coalition of reformers as well as the general public.

It is likely that constitutional reform would have remained a marginal political issue if Margaret Thatcher's abuse of parliamentary power were the only evidence that the British are governed by a secretive, paternalistic, unaccountable state in which power is concentrated in a handful of antique institutions that expect deference and trust from a passive public. Many forces, ideas, and events converged in the late 1980s and early 1990s that eroded people's confidence in their institutions.

Before he discusses more compelling reasons for reform, Frank Vibert, deputy director of the Institute of Economic Affairs, offers a cynical one that arguably explains the motivations of some reformers, particularly MPs in the Liberal Democrat and Labour Parties. "One reason for the rise in interest is purely political. The longevity and commitment to policy reform of the present Conservative administration is resented by those in political disagreement with the agenda. Constitutional reform is seen as a way to fight political battles by other means. From this perspective, it is an agenda for those who are out of power—an agenda for the losers in the political process."[18]

Not surprisingly the Liberal Democrats—the biggest losers in the political process—have long been advocates of electoral reform. As for the Labour Party, there is plenty of room to distrust its belated interest in constitutional reform as long as it continues to conduct its own affairs in an undemocratic manner. In the eight years (1984-1992) he was leader, Neil Kinnock turned the party into a rigid top down party machine that mimicked the party he was supposed to oppose.[19] Also, as the party most likely to win in a general election against the Tories, Labour has been understandably reluctant to change a system that would give them so much unchecked power. Knowing this, the reformers have never tried to work within the Labour Party or any party. They are interested in changing the nature of political institutions rather than exercising power within them.

Perhaps the most potent pressure to reform British institutions comes from the widespread conviction that Thatcher's free-market enterprise ideas should be applied to the socially rigid way that access to all leading cultural and political institutions is still largely limited to the "right sort of people." The most glaring contradiction in Thatcher's policies was that while she was eager to apply the principles of public choice to the marketplace and the financial and business arena, she was considerably less willing to apply such principles to the hierarchical elitist institutions that effectively monopolize cultural and political power. She introduced the principles of public choice to various institutions (grammar schools, the health service, nationalized businesses and utilities, public housing), yet she stopped short of applying them to the core state institutions, for she derived too much pleasure from exercising their sovereign authority. Thus she was considerably less radical than many people think.

For the last 150 years the British ruling class—whether Conservative wet or dry, Socialist, Liberal Democratic, Fabian, Keynesian, or Monetarist—has been much more interested in redistributing material wealth than cultural wealth and power. The ruling class managed to deflect attention from its own privileged positions for such a long time, partly because the prosperity of England gave them sufficient wealth to redistribute and partly because most of them sincerely believed they were exercising their political and cultural power on behalf of the nation as a noble, disinterested public service.

According to Andrew Gamble in *The Free Economy and the Strong State*, "public choice" theory (selectively applied by Thatcherism) offers the first powerful challenge to traditional British assumptions about the role and nature of their institutions:

The contribution of public choice as a new intellectual discipline to the development of the New Right was that it provided powerful theoretical arguments against any notion that public bodies were disinterested and enlightened, while private individuals and companies were self-interested and rapacious. Public choice theorists started with the assumption that politicians and bureaucrats had their own interests which they pursued with the utmost vigour. The difference between private and public bodies was not that one had a special relationship to the public interest denied the other, but that the pursuit of self-interest by private bodies was qualified by the existence of a framework of rules and by competition. These constraints did not exist for public bodies.[20]

In the more straightforward words of Stephen Haseler, by the late 1980s, "the notion that a public interest—separate from the rhetoric to secure some private interest or aggregation of private interests—actually existed, was increasingly being challenged."[21] Haseler believes the real battle in Britain in the 1990s will be between those who believe in such a thing as a public interest and those who don't.

Thatcher's skepticism of the "public service" ethos may well turn out to be her most potent legacy if the current constitutional reform movement is able to nurture such skepticism in the cultural as well as the economic sphere. The sad fact is that Britain remains one of the most hierarchical and socially stratified and rigid societies in the world. Reformers provide a focus for the growing conviction that Britain will continue to become a poorer, angrier, and more fragmented country unless it learns how to unlock the potential of the people who find themselves born into the wrong class or region and therefore find it difficult to participate in the educational, professional, political, and economic opportunities of their society.

This is the analysis of L.A. Siedentop, who believes that the issue of equal freedom of access to cultural opportunities should be addressed, for it goes to the very heart of the debate about Britain's decline: "Instead of concerning itself with equal access to the marketplace, or with the notion of equality of opportunity, the government has placed its emphasis on fiscal and monetary policy joined to widespread 'privatizing.' All of this is justified in the name of a truncated version of liberalism which, as has often been suggested, bears some resemblance to mid-nineteenth-century notions of laissez—faire."[22] Siedentop further argues that a fully developed and modern democratic liberalism that opens individual access to cultural markets, as opposed to the "truncated version" limited to questions of monetary policy, has never had a chance to develop because of a centuries-old aversion on the part of Britain's ruling class to a theoretical, doctrinaire conception of democracy. The rights of individuals have never been formulated and this, in essence, is the key to the longevity and power of the patrician style of government. "British society," he says, "has for several centuries sought unity in manners rather than ideas. It has, de facto, discouraged discussion of what Marxists would call ideology, preferring to rely on shared manners or civility as the cement of society. 'Decency' and 'common sense' have been the undoctrinaire watchwords. It has sought consensus in a mode of proceeding rather than a set of basic beliefs, in manners rather than constitutional doctrine" (900). According to Siedentop, two debilitating consequences—of crucial importance to reformers—followed from the British habit of conflating the true anatomy of power with a certain style and manner:

First, such a conspicuous elite or "establishment" in turn influenced the nature of personal ambitions, creating a strong attraction to status rather than power or wealth. "Being someone" rather than "doing something" became uppermost, with sad results for innovation and competition. But if that was the sad consequence for those who continued to aspire, the even sadder result was that very many able people from working-class and lower middle-class backgrounds came to feel intrinsically unable to aspire—excluded from the full competition because they were not "the right sort." (900)

Siedentop concludes his article with a warning that unless the British create a new, more open society, they "will condemn themselves to a listless, static and resentful social condition" (900).

In his book *The Enchanted Glass*, Tom Nairn was quite right to call Siedentop's analysis "acute."[23] Siedentop's ideas and those of others like him have taken root and flourished in the past ten years and become the most common point of reference among reformers who invariably demonstrate a well-developed awareness of how the "public service" ethos with its overvaluation of decency and compassion actually serves the interests of those doing the "serving." They argue that, more than anything else, rulership according to caste rather than ability stifles the aspirations and prospects of most of Britain's population. They argue that the only way to rid the country of its culture of deference and paternalism is to reform any institutions that nurture and perpetuate them, thus their renewed scrutiny in the early 1990s on the monarchy and the House of Lords.

Here is a sample of the opinions (published in *Power and the Throne,* 1994) of those who participated in the conference about the monarchy in May 1993, which was sponsored by Charter 88 and *The Times*, owned by Rupert Murdoch.

Christopher Hitchens (writer in residence with *Vanity Fair* and author of *Blood, Class, and Nostalgia*) in his essay "The People and the Monarchy" thinks Britain now needs the honesty of Walter Bagehot (author of *The English Constitution,* 1867) regarding the interests served by the monarchy:

What I miss most in discussion of the British monarchy is any unembarrassed engagement with the interests served by it: not the role it plays, or the symbolism it exerts but the interests served by monarchy and by monarchism, not by just the Royal Family in its contingent form. . . . I think that people understand instinctively that the monarchy serves not the Conservative Party but the conservative interest. Walter Bagehot understood this quite unhypocritically and was plain enough to say so in ringing prose. He saw the Crown as an additional insurance policy against the claimant noise of the men and women of no property.[24]

In her essay "Do You Believe in Fairies?" Sue Townsend (author of the *Adrian Mole* series and more recently *The Queen and I* which has been turned into a play) announces that she is from the working class and has stopped believing in royalty. A recent experience of working among the deplorable conditions of a council estate had given her a vivid appreciation of how the class system stunts lives: "It is a dangerous state of affairs and it is a result of our terrible class system, which strangles people, wastes their lives and wastes their talents. I have to say that I see the Royal Family at the apex of this class system. . . . By debating the monarchy, we're breaking the last taboo, and it's time we did. I'm sick of this British timidity about institutions."[25]

According to Billy Bragg (a rock singer who came to prominence with his debut album *Life's a Riot*) in his essay "England Made Me Too," the monarchy needs to be reformed, not because of the embarrassing antics of the younger royals in recent years, but because it helps underwrite the privileges and powers of a self-serving ruling class:

Queen Elizabeth is the last of her kind not because of the shortcomings of certain members of her family, but because of the way in which those who govern us have exploited our loyalty to the Queen for their own ends. When it comes to the crunch, and despite her best efforts she does not belong to us, she belongs to them. She is not the Queen of England. She is the Queen of the Establishment. Her role in the unwritten constitution serves to legitimize its continued existence, its traditions and its goals. As we move towards integration with Europe, the challenge is not whether we should tear down the tacky remnants of the divine right of kings. It is to bring to an end the divine right of Etonians and their cronies to run this country of ours for themselves.[26]

If the opinions of Caroline Ellis (age 25) in her essay "A Right Little Royalist" (she is Charter 88's Political Officer and one of the editors of Charter 88's *Debating the Constitution,* 1993) are any indication, a generation gap is forming around the issue of constitutional reform. She interviewed her friends and found that most of them were republicans, regardless of their background. She herself grew up in a family that overdosed on the monarchy. Of her education she says "at the public school I attended from age thirteen, monarchy, state religion, snobbery and militarism all seemed to fuse into one."[27] She cites greater understanding of the structure of power in society as the prime reason people of her age have become republicans: "Who knows what makes little royalists into republicans? . . . For most of us antimonarchist stirrings formed part of a wider appreciation of the structures of power and the way that unwritten, archaic rules and institutions keep us subjects."[28] For her friend Ian, age 25, the generation gap is a matter of changes in attitudes toward authority and institutions: "Is he (Ian) prepared to humour those who, like his parents, place a lot of store on heritage and the monarchy as reflecting our national character? No! I really do think the monarchy affects our political culture. If ministers didn't have the Royal Prerogatives to hide behind, we might be able to make them more accountable. Of course we need other constitutional reforms."[29]

Rachid, a young black man who attended the Monarchy Conference, disagreed with a speaker who urged blacks to seek the support of the monarchy for their concerns:

The monarchy is at the pinnacle of an essentially autocratic system. One of the saddest things to me is that many working class people in this country have little idea of where power is or how it is exercised. Politicians collude in this ignorance. The monarchy deflects attention away from issues of power and distributive justice towards the soap opera of the institution itself. The monarchy underpins a system of haves and have-nots: not just in the economic or materialist sense, in a broader sense. I come from a world of have-nots. At school I was only dimly aware that other kids had parents who belonged to the professions, we had no contact whatsoever. People say "it's a small world." It's not. It's a very large world, it's just that a small clique populates all our institutions.[30]

The cultural divide between the haves and have-nots that Rachid criticizes is the primary focus of Hilary Wainwright's essay "Across to London." (She is a member of the Charter 88 Council and her latest book is *Arguments for a New Left: Answering the Free Market Right*.) Deriving inspiration from Tom Paine, who believed that political and cultural equality were inseparable, Wainwright says, "In the evolution of representative democracy in Britain, these two components of the radical republican tradition became separated. The goal of cultural revolution has been marginalized. Reformers from the English middle and upper classes, unchallenged by deferential leaders of labour, have found it easier to campaign for political and even economic equality than to shed cultural attitudes of superiority."[31] By encouraging experimentation and change in the economic sphere while tolerating the status quo in the cultural, Thatcher proved to be only the latest variation in this bifurcated radicalism or "truncated liberalism" as Siedentop calls it.

If popular support for constitutional reform continues to grow as it has in the past decade, Britain may experience the first real break with a centuries-long paternalist style of government. However, no reformer sounds rosy-cheeked about their prospects. Richard Holme (Lord Holme of Cheltenham, Liberal Democrat life Peer, cofounder of Charter 88, and author of *The People's Kingdom*) expresses a common feeling when he says that, "the last enemy of constitutional reform is perhaps the most deadly. Paternalism is the English disease, and it rages through the whole system of government."[32]

There are at least six other reasons why pressure to reform British institutions has escalated rapidly in the past decade. First, membership in the

European Community (EC) in which power is shared and decentralized threatens to erode the sovereign authority of the British Crown in Parliament. Thatcher's desire to hold onto such power was one reason her relationship with the community was so fractious. As David Marquand says in his analysis of Britain's ambivalence toward the EC, "the British political tradition, however, has no place for power-sharing. To the British, or at least to the English, power is by its very nature unsharable."[33] Also, as citizens of the EC, the British can lay claim to rights already entrenched by articles of the European Convention. The feeling among some reformers, fed by national pride, is that the British shouldn't have to depend on foreigners to provide them written rights and a constitution.

Second, the media have become more hostile to establishment values and institutions. Telegraph Newspapers, under the ownership of the Canadian Conrad Black since 1985, tends toward a promonetarist, anti-big government line at odds with the public service sector. Since the late 1980s *The Sun, News of the World,* and *The Times,* owned by the Australian Rupert Murdoch, have dispensed with the deference (to put it mildly) traditionally displayed in media coverage of the Royal Family.

This leads to a third reason. In the mid-1980s the Royal Family enjoyed a resurgence of popularity because of their displays of concern for the poor. The left, needing all the help it could get, seized upon the monarchy as source of moral opposition to Thatcherism.[34] Since then respect for the monarchy has reached an historic low. The monarchy has been at similar lows before, but according to Andrew Morton (author of *Diana: Her True Story*), "we are now at a turning point."[35] The mystique of the monarchy has been shattered and Morton contends that the younger royals, not the media, are primarily responsible. After the divorces, affairs, and embarrassing revelations about the private lives of the younger royals, it didn't help when Charles and Diana decided to conduct their quarrels through the media, already worked up into a feeding frenzy. The public mood has been ugly ever since the Windsor Castle fire, when it was discovered that the taxpayers would foot the bill for the repairs of the home of the richest woman in the country. Institutional/constitutional underpinnings have also been eroded. Charles's separation from Diana in December 1993 raised questions about his suitability as future head of the Church of England. And as England binds itself closer to the European Community, the Queen's role as head of the Commonwealth looks more and more irrelevant and anachronistic.

Fourth, Britain is a more multiethnic, multireligious society than it was in the 1950s, 1960s, and 1970s. Ethnic minorities with their own cultural and political traditions have never really developed an emotional bond with British institutions, which is essential for the requisite spirit of deference and respect. Pressure to disestablish the Church of England increases as it becomes more obvious that it is a minority religion among minority religions.

Fifth, the revolutionary events in Eastern Europe in the late 1980s renewed interest in studying the relationship between economic performance and forms of government.

Sixth, feelings of alienation in non-English parts of the United Kingdom are as strong as ever. Devolution in Wales and especially Scotland is an issue that won't go away. As these parts of the United Kingdom continue to nurture their own traditions and identity, the question of what will remain particularly English becomes more of an issue. What is the content and basis of a strictly English identity? British institutions may have served the empire well, but will they continue to satisfy the needs of a medium-sized European country heading into the 21st century?

As all the reasons canvassed so far indicate, there are specific pressures for each institution to reform, yet it is impossible for reform to proceed piecemeal for the elements all hang together, interdependent and mutually supporting. Parliament can't be reformed without redefining the nature and role of sovereign monarchical authority that underwrites it. The House of Lords can't be reformed without abolishing the hereditary principle in government, which would entail reforming the monarchy and vice versa. Disestablishment of the Church of England would entail altering the present role of the Crown as head of the Church of England. If a Bill of Rights and written constitution were introduced, the judiciary would have to be reformed. One reason Labour politicians, among others, oppose a Bill of Rights is that the judiciary would be solely responsible for interpreting the law and they simply don't trust the judiciary as presently constituted. The judges are considered too conservative and out of touch to defend the new rights and freedoms. Labour MP Conor Gearty says, "What that involves is the transfer of a great deal of power from the executive to the courts. There's a very serious question about the extent to which the courts are equipped to determine the balance in a way which preserves freedoms. Looking into the judicial record I became convinced that the English judiciary were not equipped for that task."[36]

In 1987 Lord McCluskey, in his Reith lectures, was more blunt in his opposition to giving judges a Bill of Rights to interpret: "Why it should be supposed that elderly lawyers with cautious and backward-looking habits of thought are qualified to overrule the judgments of democratically elected legislators . . . I do not profess to understand."[37]

British commentators who have thought carefully about the nature of their constitution have come up with a variety of images to describe the relationship between the people and the institutions that govern them. In *Games with Shadows* Neil Ascherson thinks of the British "nation" as a sacred grove the people can reverence but never enter. The druids of Westminster tend the grove and protect the hallowed relics of absolute sovereignty from violation that "would bring the oak trees crashing to the ground—no doubt leading to crop failure, plague and Roman invasion as well."[38]

In *The Enchanted Glass* (1988) Tom Nairn uses two images: an enchanted mirror and, like Orwell before him, a family. In his Foreword Nairn says that when the British look into the mirror "a gilded image is reflected back, made up of sonorous past achievement, enviable stability, and the painted folklore of their Parliament and Monarchy."[39] Later he compares Britain to a family that is "still managed almost entirely by familial custom—that is, by conventions established, 'commented' upon and incessantly and footlingly modified, rather than by script and principle. This management remains in the hands of an essentially hereditary elite whose chief attribute is knowing how to manage: their 'secret' is knowing this secret."[40]

Now, nearly a decade later, many of the children have grown up and are looking for a suitable retirement home for the family elders as they lay plans for building a republic. Disenchantment with the gilded image in the mirror is so widespread that the British people are actually beginning to see a vision of themselves reflected back in which they are the center of the story as possessors of ultimate political authority. As for the sacred grove, druidic security has been breached and none of the oaks have fallen. If and when the sovereign authority of the relics can be transferred to the people, the grove will become a public park and the relics placed in the Victoria and Albert Museum.

As a result of the current debate about constitutional reform the battle lines in British politics have shifted so that now the patrician High Tories—the "wets"—find themselves joining ranks with the old style paternalist socialists (Trade Unionists, Fabians, public sector professionals in universities, the BBC, and the arts establishments) who wish to retain, as much as possible, the corporatist welfare state institutions that flourished during the postwar consensus. Both groups believe the core British institutions, despite all their problems, are essentially sound and should not be replaced or abolished. The opposing alliance consists of Tory "drys," advocates of the social-market economy within the Liberal Democrat faction, modernisers within Labour, and the growing coalition of nonaligned forces committed to constitutional reform. Those in this alliance believe that British institutions are in a serious state of disrepair and are committed to radically changing some if not all of them. Some (most notably Margaret Thatcher) have feet planted in both camps, yet generally the lines hold and they will firm up if constitutional reform becomes the defining issue of British politics in the late 1990s and early 21st century.

Where can David Hare's trilogy be positioned in this larger realignment in British politics and more specifically within the debate about constitutional reform that has exploded onto center stage in the past ten years? He says he is pleased to have written these three plays about British institutions when, as he says, "British institutions were finally admitted to be in a state of collapse."[41] What is his sense of the causes of their collapse and what does he think ought to be done about it?

The basic question is, should British institutions be reformed with minor adjustments, or should they be abolished and reconstituted under the authority of a written constitution and a Bill of Rights? Few straddle the fence on this question, Hare is no exception. Much can be gleaned from perhaps Hare's most candid and explicit statement regarding his intentions. It appears at the end of the Introduction to *Asking Around* and was written in May 1993:

I realized the country was passing through a distinctive period in its history in which a government hell-bent on action was determined to suspect the motives of anyone who brought news of what life was actually like on the street. It had become an article of faith among the ideologues at Number Ten that professionals were incapable of representing anything but their own interests. What was under attack from above was not just the prosperity of all those whose job it was to help other people, but the idea of professionalism itself. Here in this book you may hear the stray voices of individuals, most of them unfashionable, who, in a way which is often humorous or exasperated, have nevertheless tried to go on making institutions work. It is to their efforts that *Asking Around* is dedicated. The one thing I have learnt and understood from five years' study is that British society needs not to abolish its institutions, but to refresh them. For, if not through institutions, how do we express the common good?[42]

This passage reveals that Hare assumes—as he usually does—an enlightened position within the status quo (now defended by the range of forces described above—High Tory "wets," public-sector professionals, journalists, artists, civil servants, etc.). He believes British institutions need to be "refreshed," not "abolished": that is, not radically altered and restructured under a written constitution. He dedicates *Asking Around* to the individuals who continue to try to make institutions work despite "attacks" on them from the "ideologues at Number Ten". The only people Hare talked to in his five years of research (according to *Asking Around*) were employed in the three institutions he writes about or in some related or dependent profession. It's not surprising that such people would not be in favor of abolishing the institutions that employ them: the subject of radical reform never arises. It appears, judging from who Hare does and does not talk to and what they do and do not discuss, that his essential attitudes about the role and value of British institutions were pretty much in place before he started his research.

The Introduction concludes with a question that I consider more revealing and significant than anything else he says in *Asking Around*: "For, if not through institutions, how do we express the common good?"[43] This question addresses a profound truth about British politics and culture. For centuries the values and identity of the British people have been bound up in an unwritten mystical pact with their institutions. Hare's question contains a continuity and a departure in his statements about his work. The continuity is that he has long been interested in seeking out the "common ground" or "good," a proclivity he became more and more aware of throughout the 1980s as is evident in many of his essays and interviews.

For example, in his essay "Looking Foolish" (1990) (published in his volume of essays *Writing Left-Handed*. 1991) he says that one of the "distinctive virtues of real plays" is the ability to evoke a sense of a "common ground" of feeling and thought: "they show us that feelings which we had thought private turn out to be common ground with others."[44] Several pages later, he returns to this theme with the claim that theatre is one of the few remaining forums where people can discover what views "they do or do not hold in common": "The theatre remains, in its ideal form, one of the few places where people of dissimilar views and backgrounds may come together and, in their shared response to what they see, find what they do and do not hold in common."[45]

What is it that Hare believes his audiences can discover they hold in common? What beliefs, feelings, and values inhabit this common ground that he frequently talks about? Until he wrote the trilogy, Hare never identified in any precise way the content of the common ground he tries to evoke in his work. As he explains in the essay "Looking Foolish," a writer seeks "the truth" which he believes can't be defined in terms of a cause or a narrow point of view. He establishes a clear distinction between politics and theatre, politicians and writers, pushing through a cause and seeking "the truth": "One side wants to serve what it calls the cause, the other what it likes to call the truth. Writers, absolutists by nature, can't help wanting to get things absolutely right. The politician's case against the right will be that the absolute and utter truth is fine in principle, but it doesn't always help in getting the job done."[46] A little later he further emphasizes that theater should evoke a truth beyond a "special point of view":

On all writers—left and right, comic and serious, commercial and uncommercial—there is only one overriding and continuous pressure, and that is to make us show things as being simpler than they are. Interest groups will always be waiting, whether they are political, religious or aesthetic, none of them really interested in the work itself, but only in ambushing it for the signals they decide it gives off towards their special point of view. But a play is not a speech. A play is not a message. Least of all is a play a point of view.[47]

In previous chapters I argue that the basis of Hare's "truth," "common ground," or moral vision that he wants to position in a space above the narrow views, causes, and demands of interest groups and politicians behaves in an absolute, universal/national, and above-the-political-fray manner precisely because Britain's highly contralized, top-heavy political and cultural institutions encourage this conception of power, authority, morality, or "the truth." This argument appears strengthened in light of the trilogy.

With the added perspective on the trajectory of Hare's work that the trilogy provides, I suggest that throughout the 1970s and 1980s Hare didn't feel he needed to reveal the nature of the "common ground." Heroines such as Jenny, Susan, and Isobel could remain inarticulate about the nature of their soaring national ideals or of their goodness because the institutions and cultural and political traditions underpinning them were never really threatened. Well, now they are as the debate about constitutional reform moves closer and closer to the center stage of British politics. Suddenly the silent, apolitical, mysterious center—the common ground—toward which Hare has gravitated all his career, has to speak and defend itself.

With his question at the end of the introduction to *Asking Around*—"For, if not through institutions, how do we express the common good?"—Hare, for the first time (this is the point of departure in how he thinks of his objectives and role as a playwright), identifies the basis of "the truth" and the "common ground." Instead of residing in vague national consensual ideals forged during the war or in something as amorphous as the soul, the "common ground" or "good" now inheres in something very concrete and specific: British institutions, the Church of England, Parliament, and so on. It is entirely fitting that a playwright who seeks to express common truths apart from politics and narrow points of view should in the 1990s come to the defense of British institutions, the prime incubators of the ethos of disinterested public service. In the trilogy, how do institutions express the common good? What is the common good? And how does Hare think they need to be refreshed? These are the questions that guide my exploration of the three plays.

Hare's effort to find and defend a common "good" or "ground" in Britain in the 1990s has become somewhat tricky, for he demonstrates the impossibility of establishing a common ground in the process of trying to defend it. When he says (at the end of the Introduction to *Asking Around*), "the one thing I have learnt and understood from five years' study is that British society needs not to abolish its institutions, but to refresh them," I wonder what the word "abolish" is doing in this sentence? In the five years (from July 1987 to July 1992) that Hare spent talking to judges, barristers, detectives, police officers, bureaucrats, politicians, bishops, vicars, Labour Party press officers, strategists working for Neil Kinnock's election committee, and others, he never asks anybody about whether British institutions should be abolished. In fact, the subject of abolishing or even of reforming them is never dealt with in the 250-page account of his research or in any of the three plays. Hare does ask a civil servant about "constitutional proprieties" in "The Law" section of *Asking Around*,[48] and in *Murmuring Judges* the home secretary agrees with a judge about preserving "the framework of the constitution,"[49] yet neither reference occurs in the context of a discussion about abolishing or reforming British institutions.

So who is talking about "abolishing" British institutions? Margaret Thatcher? In the Introduction to *Asking Around* Hare singles out the "ideologues at Number Ten" as the source of the "attack" on institutions and the "idea of professionalism itself." This is partly true. In ways already discussed, Thatcherism (with its abuse of parliamentary power, free-market ideology, and skepticism of disinterested public service) was one of many sources of pressure on institutions, yet she never attempted to "abolish" (aside from the GLC) or radically reform any of them, especially the three Hare chose to write about.

Consider the Church of England, subject of *Racing Demon*. In the early 1980s the conservatives tilted at the Church of England when prominent bishops criticized the Falklands War. In the mid-1980s relations turned chilly again when the Church published a study (*Faith in the City,* 1985) about growing urban poverty and suggested the policies of the current government were largely responsible. Aside from these instances, the government has pursued a hands off policy. Insofar as radical reform of an abolishing kind (which can only mean disestablishment) is an issue for the Church of England (and it has become one in the last decade), it is the agenda of two groups that overlap to some degree: the coalition of constitutional reformers (due to concerns about Prince Charles as future head of the Church, growing religious pluralism in Britain, and the realization that the Church, in its established form as the official state church, remains one of the linchpins in the antiquated constitutional framework), and clergymen within the Church itself. According to James Fenton (the distinguished poet, novelist, and journalist) 38% of the synod (the central administrative council) advocates disestablishment.[50]

As for the judiciary, subject of *Murmuring Judges*, the Conservatives largely ignored it until 1989 when they suggested that solicitors and barristers merge their legal functions. To suggest merger is well short of a call for abolition, yet it was perhaps the most serious threat to any of the three institutions Hare writes about that can be traced to Thatcher. In Britain judges are invariably (according to custom) recruited from a relatively small pool of barristers. Regardless of the motives of the Conservatives, about which there has been some debate, such a measure would have opened up the upper ranks of the judiciary to a much bigger recruitment base (with the additional solicitors who vastly outnumber barristers) thus helping to ensure that the backgrounds and attitudes of the judges would be more in tune with the public they serve. Although the Conservatives dropped the issue after stiff opposition from judges and barristers, constitutional reformers keep the issue of judicial reform alive for they believe—along with some Labour MPs—that a written constitution and Bill of Rights would change very little if left to be interpreted by a judiciary that remained as elitist and backward-looking as it is now. In Act One, Scene Two of *Murmuring Judges* the issue of merger is raised as something that will threaten the freedom of the judiciary (6). The implications, the causes, the nature of freedoms lost remain unexplored. The issue never surfaces again in the play.

As for abolishing Parliament, Margaret Thatcher opposed any reform that would have weakened the sovereign authority of Parliament which she was so fond of exercising. Also, the idea of abolishing Parliament isn't even hinted at in *The Absence of War* or *Asking Around.*

So, to return to my question, how is it that Hare could learn from five years of study that "British society needs not to abolish its institutions" if neither Thatcher (the only antagonist he identifies) nor anyone else Hare spoke to during those five years expressed a desire to abolish them? The trilogy and

Hare's account of his five years of research in *Asking Around* have a air of unreality about them. The absence of any reference to the ideas of constitutional reformers is conspicuous, yet he is clearly aware of their radical agenda and responds to it, for they are the only people in Britain talking about abolishing British institutions. In the current British context the word "abolish" when applied to British institutions effectively means "constitutional reform," for it is always used in conjunction with some plan for reform. For the first time in Hare's work, the strain of holding onto a sense of commonality in Britain clearly shows. How common is the "common ground" in plays about British institutions that exclude any reference to a wide swath of public opinion supportive of the most radical and innovative political movement in Britain since the Second World War that is concerned specifically with British institutions?

The central conflict in each of the three plays is framed in such a way that structural change—constitutional reform—is eliminated from the agenda. Of all the pressures being brought to bear on British institutions, Hare focuses on one: the enterprise free-market values of the conservatives under Thatcher. And he reduces these values to a vulgar materialistic sensibility bereft of an ideological dimension and characterized by a familiar demonology of personal characteristics (seen before in Tom French, the born-again businessman in *The Secret Rapture* 1988, and Robbie Baker in *Wrecked Eggs,* 1986): a zealous appreciation for the logical rational and qualitative, a tendency to reduce life to neat simplistic formulas, a cluelessness about the emotional dimension of their relationships, ambitiousness, a hell-bent desire for action rather than reflection, a powerful need for power.

Of all the antidotes being suggested as cures for what ails British institutions, Hare offers one: that the good, honest, decent people working in them be allowed to follow the promptings of their passions and instincts. British institutions need to be refreshed from within with good people providing heartfelt service.

In *Racing Demon*, the young combustible curate Tony Ferris epitomizes the new mercantile, rationalizing forces that threaten to turn the Church into one of Thatcher's enterprise zones. Tony is easily the most offensive character Hare has created so far. To tidy up his image for the hierarchy and streamline his life for saving souls, Tony jettisons his nonbelieving girlfriend in a scene in which he reeks of bad faith and insincerity. His evangelical zeal for preaching the gospel appears to be his way of compensating for low self-esteem and feelings of powerlessness stemming from his socially disadvantaged background. He is grammar school, the rest are Oxbridge. His style is gauche, a mixture of servility and manic bluster. His counterpart and immediate superior is Lionel Espy, a gentle serene man who conceives of his role in his south London district as helping the poor, not telling them about Christ, about whom he has no firm convictions. Morality and conventional religious spirituality have very little to do with each other as far as Lionel is concerned. Tony's criticism of

Lionel's pastoral style precipitates the conflict between Lionel and the Bishop of Southwark, who by the end of the play manages to demote Lionel to another church.

The sharp contrast between the pastoral styles and objectives of Tony and Lionel emerge in the scenes dealing with Stella, a poor young black woman with an abusive husband. She visits Lionel seeking solace from her husband, who won't tolerate her crying over an abortion he forced her to have. Lionel listens, sympathizes, offers a brief prayer, then sends her on her way after he takes her hand and offers his friendship: "I don't know if God'll help you. But now you do have a friend. You have me. This house is always open. Whenever you're lonely."[51] Tony, having overheard the last portion of the visit, is disturbed and as the other members of the four-member team arrive for a meeting he continues to press Lionel about why he didn't tell Stella about Jesus and invite her to Church. Lionel's response is to tell a story about watching a black female preacher in a bus queue who couldn't resist telling those around her about Christ their Savior. He admired her style, for as he says, "as long as you do it from the heart, in a way which is unforced and that suits you, then there's no problem" (19). He looks at Tony who, according to the stage directions, "*frowns, uncomprehending*" (19).

It becomes crashingly clear in subsequent scenes that doing "it from the heart" is not part of Tony's emotional vocabulary. He is a numbers man obsessed with filling the churches. His zealousness runs amock several days later when he visits Stella at her home, sees her scalded face, and insists on seeing her husband whom he suspects is responsible. Against her vehement wishes, he remains and lies in wait for her husband. His mission to demonstrate to Stella that "Jesus has your interests at heart" ends with an argument and a fist-fight with her husband (26). Tony's grotesque interference destroys Stella's life, perhaps irredeemably. In her last scene she delivers a soliloquy while cleaning Lionel's church for £2.50 an hour. Tony had apparently taken the case to court for she says she will refuse to press charges against her husband. She just wants him back and regrets that because of Tony an essentially good man turned into a scared and dangerous one (71-72).

The scenes with Stella are the only ones in which priests are seen acting in a professional capacity with the public, so it is to these scenes one should look for evidence of how the Church of England might be refreshed and how it represents a "common good." Lionel has failed in his personal life (his children don't respect him; his wife suffers from years of neglect), yet his heartfelt ministry to Stella stands out as the only possible source of renewal for the Church, especially in contrast to the ridiculous figure of Tony and the ambitious and treacherous Bishops.

While the conflict between materialism and the heart (passion and instinct) is confined within the institution in *Racing Demon* and worked out in terms of clashes of style and sensibility (how could the government open the C of E to the competition of the marketplace even if it wanted to?), there is lurking at the margins of *Murmuring Judges* the threat of a government-enforced merger of the legal functions of solicitors and barristers. This external threat is the focus of part of Act One Scene Two in which we learn that Irina Platt, a young black female lawyer, has raised £1million in just four days from barristers and judges eager to defend their freedom with the expertise of an expensive public relations firm. She works for Sir Peter Edgecombe QC, who characterizes the government plan as an attempt to apply the rules of the marketplace to the bar: "For years the bar has simply been there. We have existed. Without any need to justify ourselves. And now suddenly, bingo! No longer taken for granted. We are no longer exempt. We must take our case to the marketplace, not just for ourselves, but on behalf of everyone who values professional life" (7). After this early point in the play, the subject of merger is never raised again, although the marketplace does make an appearance later at a dinner in Lincoln's Inn personified in the form of the Home Secretary Kevin Cumberland who—it is tellingly revealed—was an accountant before entering public office.

Hare's real interest in *Murmuring Judges* lies with a story very much like the Lionel-Stella-Tony one: two professionals clash over how justice should be administered and in the process a distinction emerges between true (done from the heart) and false (not done from the heart) justice. Most of the play is concerned with the miscarriage of justice in the case of Gerard McKinnon, a young Irishman sentenced to five years in prison for driving the truck in a robbery. Two reasons are given to explain why he received such a harsh sentence for a minor first offense: despite solid evidence proving his role in the robbery, he denied any involvement, and his being Irish is a liability.

It appears obvious to Irina, who assists Sir Peter Edgecombe defend Gerard, that Gerard had been forced to lie, that for some reason he had been blackmailed into pleading not guilty. Like Isobel and Lionel, Irina occupies the moral high ground by virtue of her unerring instincts and her heightened capacity to feel. To confirm her feelings about why Gerard lied, she visits him in prison and begins to sound him out on a "proposition" that she describes as "purely my own. I haven't run it by Sir Peter":

Irina: If you were just the driver. The question is, of course, why you denied the whole thing. Perhaps if you'd pleaded guilty. . . . Did you ever consider that?
(*Gerard waits.*)

Gerard: It's hard.

Irina: Why is it hard?
(*Gerard doesn't answer.*)
You mean because of the others?
(*Gerard doesn't look at her.*)
Perhaps you should talk to me first about them.
(*Gerard shifts a little.*)

Gerard: I really can't say

Irina: You see, my feeling is, this is just instinct, while I watched you, I thought you were in fear. And so you'd probably done what they asked you. (35-36)

A few minutes later Gerard confirms what his discomfort betrays in this exchange: that "they" (his partners in crime) had indeed blackmailed him into lying. Armed with Gerard's testimony, Irina urges Sir Peter to appeal the case, which he reluctantly agrees to do, but only for what he says are sentimental reasons: Gerard has a wife and two very young children, one with Down's syndrome. Sir Peter refuses to believe Gerard had been blackmailed into lying. He thinks Gerard's revelation to Irina is just another manipulative lie. "I do know the type," Sir Peter says, "he's fighting like a rat" (83-84).

When Irina asks Sir Peter "how do you know?" he invokes his well-honed ability to judge people instinctively: "After a while, you have certain skills. It's not even conscious. It becomes animal. It's a gut instinct. Here. (*He points to his heart.*) I'd say, if anything, it's the crucial ability. You're asked to walk every day through a minefield of lies. If nothing else, you do develop a certain forensic capacity for knowing when someone is telling the truth" (84).

Neither Sir Peter nor Irina ever gain access to concrete evidence that would validate or disprove Gerard's word, yet both are equally convinced they know the truth. Sir Peter knows Gerard is lying, and Irina knows Gerard is not lying. Who is right? This question is the central crux that leads to the real substance of Hare's sense of how the judicial system could be refreshed. The central objective of the play is to demonstrate that Irina's instincts are right and the source of true justice and that Sir Peter's instincts telling him Gerard is lying are merely the typical prejudices that an upper-class lawyer would have toward a poor young uneducated Irishman involved in petty crime.

In a separate plot of the play involving the local police department, it is revealed (to the audience, not to Irina) that the detective responsible for arresting Gerard and his two accomplices had set them up in a way (the details of which are not clear to me or to any of the London reviewers in the *London Theatre Record*) that led to the blackmailing of Gerard. Also, Gerard is brutally beaten by several other convicts, which strengthens Irina's conviction that blackmail is involved. With this evidence from the subplot already established by the time Irina and Sir Peter have their climactic confrontation, we, the audience, know that Irina's instincts are right, and we are clearly meant to agree with her when she tells Sir Peter that his instincts are mere prejudice:

Irina: I will tell you. These judgments, these "judgments" you make all the time, these judgments which seem to be graven in stone, they have only the status of prejudice.

Sir Peter: I'm sorry. That is really not true.

(*Irina has wandered away, fired up now.*)

. . . It seems so obvious to an outsider. Do you really not know? All this behaviour, the honours, the huge sums of money, the buildings, the absurd dressing-up. They do have a purpose. It's anesthetic. It's to render you incapable of imagining life the other way

round.
(*Sir Peter shifts, uncomfortable.*) (84-85)

Although Hare's portrait of the judiciary, and particularly his characterization of Sir Peter, did not strike most London reviewers as new, it rings true. Prejudice has played an unfortunate role in English courts during the past 30 years. Think of the Guildford Four, the Birmingham Six, and the Maguires.

Although somewhat problematic (it's not clear how Irina can criticize Sir Peter for instinctively feeling his way to a legal judgment when she herself became convinced that Gerard was telling the truth through her feelings and instincts), Hare's prescription for an ailing judiciary is clear: the judiciary, like the Church of England, needs more professionals who serve the public from the heart. *Murmuring Judges* suggests that the judiciary, like the Church of England, is capable of being refreshed from within with people like Irina Platt. In the end she convinces Sir Peter to submit at least a plea of clemency for Gerard before the judge who reduces the sentence by six months. This episode demonstrates that the judiciary is still flexible and capable of minor change.

However, I suggest that in the entire trilogy Hare is nowhere more obviously responding to the radical agenda of those calling for constitutional reform than in his portrayal of the judiciary as eager to hire people like Irina Platt, a black female commonwealth scholar from Antigua, and her young colleague Woody Pearson, a cockney. Sir Peter says, upon introducing Irina to Judge Cuddeford: "We all felt she is exactly the very kind of person the Bar is now most eager to attract" (5). If the Bar and other British institutions were in reality in the habit of recruiting cockneys and black women then there would be no reform movement in Britain today and thus no reason for Hare to perceive that British institutions are in a state of collapse and in need of refreshing.

Reformers are convinced that Britain will never become a prosperous and unified country until it rids itself of the viruses of paternalistic rulership by those with the right sort of social pedigree. Britain's problems, they contend, are ultimately cultural not economic. At some level Hare recognizes this viewpoint and responds in a curiously contradictory way noted before: the main concern of the play is to expose how Sir Peter's prejudices against the Irish results in a miscarriage of justice, yet Sir Peter's prejudice oddly does not extend to blacks and cockneys. Prejudice is and is not a problem in the judiciary. Hare enters into a polemic with reformers without acknowledging their existence or concerns.

In *The Absence of War* (1993) Hare is concerned not with parliament and its strengths and weaknesses as an institution, but with the issue of why the Labour Party continues to lose to the Tories in general elections, in this case its fourth in a row on April 9, 1992, when Neil Kinnock lost to John Major. As the title suggests, the play portrays a Labour Party defeated more by itself than by the Conservatives, because it lost confidence in its most effective ideological weapons and forgot how to use them.

The play focuses strictly on the activities of the small circle of advisers and minders who run the four- or five-month election campaign for their leader George Jones, a character based on Neil Kinnock. Attention is quickly drawn to the nature of Labour's rusty weapons in Scene Two, when the newly hired publicity advisor—a young woman named Lindsay Fontaine—asks George's chief minder, Andrew Buchan, why George's wit and engaging personality fail to come across to the public: "You meet George, you think: 'this man is dynamite.' So you ask the next question. Why on earth does this never quite come across?"[52] The rest of the play focuses on Lindsay's question and provides a straightforward point of view: the dynamism of the "fantastically impressive" (4) Labour Party leader never quite comes across to the public because his wit, gaiety, and, most important, his passion have been smothered by his small circle of political advisers and minders obsessed with following tightly controlled, rational, risk-free campaign strategies. Except for Lindsay, what they fear most of all is George's tendency to ramble and garble the finer points of party policy. They brief him rigorously and make him stick to his lines and prepared speeches. To ensure that they all speak with one voice they wear "bleepers" (a pager with digital display), so if the spokesman for finance gives a statement on television about the state of the pound, they all know immediately what he said and can use the same words.

The familiar conflict between materialistic rational forces versus passion and instinct reappears as a struggle between Lindsay, who wants to free George from his verbal straitjacket, and the political advisers led by Oliver Dix, who want to keep him tightly laced up. What is for Oliver Dix incoherent rambling, is for Lindsay speaking from the heart. Dix, Lindsay George, and the rest of the characters agree that they cannot hope to dislodge the Tory lead in opinion polls regarding their ability to manage the economy, yet the play suggests that Labour continues to lose because the vulgar materialist spirit of the Tories has infected the Labour Party in the form of brainy emotionally deficient people like Oliver Dix who have prevented it from playing to its strengths—the caring issues, health, education, welfare provision—thus robbing it of a distinctive message.

After a disastrous TV interview in which George waffles on Labour's tax policy, Lindsay preempts Oliver's authority as chief adviser and calls an emergency strategy meeting in which she argues that letting George free to speak from the heart is the only way to recover momentum in the campaign:

Underneath George is always bloody furious. He's angry. And who can blame him?
(*George watches, giving nothing away.*)
Everything in him wants to let rip.
(*Andrew looks to George, but Lindsay goes straight on.*)
The public aren't stupid. They know he's been programmed. It's not hard to work out why this man's ratings are low. The public see only one thing when they look at him, and that's six rolls of sticky tape wrapped around his mouth. (91)

Overriding Andrew's objection that "a certain grayness" (91) is well worth the price for appearing to be good managers, Lindsay argues that it's the Labour Party's obsession with their enemy the Tory Party that "robs George of what he does best . . . (*She nods.*) George became leader because of a quality he had. That quality came from his passion" (92). Bryden Thomas MP, the campaign chairman, agrees. He urges George to draw upon his roots and speak like he did before he became leader:

Bryden: What we want is to hear the George we once knew. (*Now Bryden opens his briefcase and takes a volume from it. He puts it down on the table in front of them. George frowns, puzzled.*) All your major speeches before you were Leader.

George: Yes?

Bryden: When you first started, I often heard you, you write nothing down . . .

George: Yes, that [sic] right. (*He smiles.*) My father . . . my own father taught me. He said to me: speak, just speak from the heart.

Bryden: And you did. (93)

In the next scene we are given a glimpse of what George's heart would say if it were allowed to speak freely when he gives a speech at a rally in Manchester. He starts out strong without notes, falters, then in desperation pulls out a prepared speech. While extemporizing from the heart he describes a socialism that "is to do with helping people"—precisely the public service done from the heart that Irina enacts with Gerard and Lionel with Stella:

It is said to me: there is no longer hope in our future. No sense of potential. No sense of possibility. In our own lifetime, a whole generation has been effectively abandoned and dispossessed. They have been told to fend for themselves.
(*He pauses a moment, then thunders.*)
Comrades, my socialism is the socialism that says these people must not be let go. (*There is applause. You can see him use the moment to regroup.*) My socialism is . . . it is concrete. It is real. It is to do with helping people. (95)

As the play repeatedly indicates, George's vision of renewal, of moving forward, entails reclaiming roots and moving back to the way things were in the 1950s, 1960s, and 1970s when social welfare institutions, unions, and the nationalized businesses and services defined the common ground and when relatively few people disputed their paternalistic role of "helping people." Early in the play, while in a reflective mood, George laments the loss of the unions which used to hold people together with common values. Everything is so clear-cut for the Tories he says. They all rally behind "one objective. Which everyone knows. And is loyal to. (*He smiles and sits back.*) Money's a simple master in that way. But our master is different. And causes more argument. Our master is justice" (18). The current dilemma of the Labour Party George goes on to explain, is that, "justice has no organizations. It has no schools. It did have once. They were called unions. But the communities that produced them have gone. The industries have gone. So now justice recruits from the great deracinated masses. The people from nowhere. Who have nothing in common" (18).

Another character who keeps faith with George's postwar welfare-state vision of justice is Vera Klein, an elderly nearly deaf woman, clearly one of the pioneers of the Labour movement. She is invited to join party leaders on stage when they officially launch their campaign before the media. As activity swirls around her, she has a brief soliloquy: "The most exciting words of my life? 'Common ownership.' To hold things in common, this was our aim. This single phrase produced a thrill in me, like grasping a thin electric wire. Another phrase: 'moral imperative.' This was the language of after the war" (50). When party leaders file on stage and forget to include her, the implication is obvious.

George's speeches provide a simple and stark definition of the paternalistic "public service" ethos that the constitutional reformers believe is the root cause of Britain's decline. For reformers nothing is more corrosive than the belief that people are left "abandoned," "dispossessed," "deracinated," "from nowhere," and "have nothing in common" without the help of professionals in British institutions. It has been over 20 years since a common reference point existed in Britain about how best to secure hope and justice for people. According to reformers, people now want a greater role in defining and controlling the means of nurturing hope and justice rather than having them extended to them from professionals in institutions, no matter how decent and well-meaning. Also, people are not as forlorn and deracinated as George claims. They are not "nothing" outside British institutions. Perhaps the greatest implausibility of the trilogy (aside from the relationship between Tony Ferris and Francis Parnell in *Racing Demon*) is that a young distressed black woman in south London would seek the help of a white Anglican priest instead of turning to one of the many non-Church of England black churches flourishing in London.

All my analysis and evidence leads to the conclusion that Hare's central objective in the trilogy is to reenchant the relationship between the British and their institutions. The traditional British constitution is really an unwritten agreement that the people will trust in the decency and benevolence of their rulers. And it is therefore absolutely essential for the legitimacy of the rulers that they be allowed to serve, or at least be perceived to serve, otherwise the game is up. For centuries the discourse of service has effectively shifted attention from the elitist ethos and structure of the institutions to the personalities and character of those doing the "serving," and Hare would like to keep it that way.

The center of each play features a good decent individual providing—or talking of providing in George's case—heartfelt service to the common people. "Helping people" is the self-legitimating mantra of the ruling/managing class in Britain from the monarchy to the public-sector bureaucrats and professionals in the BBC, the Church of England, and the subsidized arts institutions. Hare displays none of the skepticism that, for instance, Kenneth Leech (an Anglican clergyman) directed at the Church of England at the time it was first touted as a moral voice against Thatcherism in the mid-1980s:

In assessing the Church of England and its political role, we must ask not only "what does it say?" but whose interests does it represent? When we have listened to all the radical rhetoric, where does the Church of England stand within the class structure? The recent report [*Faith in the City*, 1985] accepts what all social historians have shown, that the Church of England has never been part of working class culture or life. While the church has shown great concern about the conditions of the poor, the unemployed, the homeless, and so on, its character as part of the upper and middle class, as part of the establishment, is very clear. And there is no evidence that the official spokespersons of the church have any desire to change the system; rather they wish it to function in a more caring and compassionate way.[53]

Hare's trilogy demonstrates the truth of Stephen Haseler's claim that the very act of defending British institutions is actually liable to erode their authority: "The 'power of traditions' either means something to people or it doesn't. It cannot be inculcated, except perhaps in totalitarian regimes, and then only for a while. A 'ruling class' either exists and is obeyed; or it dies. It cannot have proponents."[54] British institutions can be believed in, deferred to, but not defended because to defend them is to destroy their magic and reveal the poverty of their basis of legitimacy. As evidence of such poverty, Haseler cites a defense of traditional authority by the late High Tory journalist David Watt of *The Times* that is remarkably similar to David Hare's: "Our class system is dying . . . only a very large, rich country can maintain stability and efficiency without some kind of elite, preferably as open as possible to talent, but still confident of its abilities and legitimacy. One of our problems is that our elite has lost that confidence, and many of those who have pulled and are pulling it down have neither the real self-confidence nor the instinctive feel to take its place."[55] In the trilogy, as in all Hare's work since the mid-1980s, society is divided into those who possess "real self-confidence" and "instinctive feel" and those who don't. While Watt doesn't define what these qualities are or explain why some have them and others don't, Hare begins to do so in small ways in the trilogy for the first time.

Soul—the moral authority of Isobel in *The Secret Rapture*—now possesses a more identifiable social style and pedigree. In *The Secret Rapture* the antagonists—Isobel and Marion—can be sisters, while the antagonists in *Racing Demon*—Tony and Lionel—couldn't be brothers because social class and educational background are now used to distinguish those with "real self-confidence" and "instinctive feel" from those without these qualities. Those helping people—trying to make institutions work—possess the right sort of background (or, like George, with a working-class background, and Irina, they have embraced the public service ethos), while those who pose a threat to established, traditional ways of doing things are portrayed as vulgar with the wrong sort of background.

Tony went to grammar school and clearly feels uncomfortable and gauche around his three colleagues, Lionel, Harry, and Streaky, who went to public school and Cambridge. It is pointed out that Lionel comes from one of the distinquished clerical families, his grandfather was dean of St. Paul's. No one with an Oxbridge education or an upper-middle-class background in England would become an accountant, Kevin Cumberland's profession before he became home secretary. And the name Kevin vaguely suggests a lower-class background: in British slang it is the "Kevins and Sharons" versus the "Hooray Henrys." In *The Absence of War* Oliver Dix's admiration for logical textbook management strategies appears to be a function of his lack of a refining liberal education (19). Shakespeare is pointedly foreign territory to him (18). When the ultimate basis for the political and moral legitimacy of the governing class is revealed by those defending it to be "instinctive feel," decent manners, and the right sort of background, then the game may be nearly up for British institutions, because these are precisely the reasons reformers are convinced they have to be radically reformed.

Several critics have expressed reservations about *Racing Demon* because Lionel, despite his goodness and decency, is a defeated man on both personal and professional levels who thus fails to be an effective agent for social change.[56] They are quite right. Much the same could be said of Lionel's counterparts in *Murmuring Judges* and *The Absence of War*. Irina, despite all her efforts, manages to have Gerard's five-year sentence reduced by only six months. And George loses yet another election and nearly forgets how to speak from the heart in the process. I suggest that the weaknesses of these three characters are fully intended as a testimony to the strength of what Hare characterizes as the powerful forces of materialism that undermine their efforts and the institutions they are a part of. However, the crucial point is that Hare is not interested in advocating social change in these three plays. Rather, he has openly become a conserver and refresher of the status quo.

These plays demonstrate that in Britain in the 1990s one can oppose Thatcher from the left and still be to some degree a reactionary. It's an irony Hare is partly aware of when he says in *Asking Around*: "She made conservatives of us all. We all found ourselves defending institutions which previously we would have had no time for, because those institutions were better than barbarism."[57] The greatest obstacle to constitutional reform in Britain is the widespread fear that the status quo is better than "barbarism." The words of Hilaire Belloc are appropriate here: "Children hold on tight to Nurse, for fear of finding something worse." The novelist Fay Weldon uses them to describe her own fears of abolishing the monarchy, although she knows it has to be done.[58]

12

HEADING HOME AND *SKYLIGHT:* COMING TO THE DEFENSE OF NOTHING

> The one significant fact about the Establishment is that it represents nothing in the national life. It has its roots in no class and no interest; it responds to no deep-seated national instinct. It is this rootlessness which is seen by its defenders as it main virtue, and by its opponents as its most depressing fault. Its defenders have, of course, found a euphemism for this rootlessness: they call it disinterestedness. It must be disinterested, they argue, precisely because it represents nothing. . . . Nothing, of course, could be more seductive. The representation of nothing can only be replaced by the representation of something; by the representation of specific interests, which may mean conflicting interests, or of real ideas, which may mean conflicting ideas. How much more simple, how much more civilizing, to avoid painful decisions, to represent nothing, to be nothing. . . . The whole point about the Establishment is that it represents no interests; and its claim to disinterestedness may, in this sense, be readily accepted.
> —Henry Fairlie from his essay "The B.B.C." in *The Establishment,*
> 1959

In the film *Heading Home* (1991) Irwin Posner's experience in *The Secret Rapture* reappears amplified and reworked into another parable about the spiritual decline of England after the Second World War. That is, Hare returns to the historical terrain of *Licking Hitler* and *Plenty*, yet with his privatized assumptions of the 1980s and 1990s.

Recall that in *The Secret Rapture* Irwin experiences a spiritual fall when he is seduced away from the true love of Isobel by the material blandishments of Marion, who offers to double his salary. He falls from a spiritual to a debased material realm and kills Isobel then himself when he realizes that he will never be able to recapture the love of Isobel. *Heading Home* consists of the sad memories of Janetta Wheatland (the Irwin-like figure played by Joely Richardson), a 63-year-old widowed librarian who has spent her life feeling exiled (thus one meaning of the title) from a perfect love she betrayed when she was an innocent 23-year-old living in London in 1947. She made a trip to London in the winter of 1946/47 to meet Charlie, a poet who worked for the BBC. She met instead another poet, Leonard Meophan (Stephen Dillane), with whom she soon fell in love. It was a perfect love with a good, emotionally enlightened man cut from the same mold as Isobel. Janetta recalls making love to Leonard in a Hotel on the south coast of England: "I do remember I'd never felt closer to anyone. I felt I was wholly alive. I was free."[1] The war was a transformative experience for Leonard as it was for Susan Traherne in *Plenty* and Archie Maclean in *Licking Hitler*, yet instead of burning with the scarcely suppressed rage of these characters, Leonard displays the same knowing quiet serenity seen in Isobel.

As Leonard explains to Janetta, the war enabled him to see beyond the surface of the physical world to a more real dimension: "Before the war I was brought up, I was trained to be brilliant. Like the rest of my family. I played cricket, I would have a proper career. Running the country. It was simple, I was English. I thought the real world was real" (25). He became a poet to keep faith with this vision of something beyond the "real world," which entails being a certain undefined way. His serenity suggests that his happiness does not depend, as it does for Susan and Archie, on engaging in fulfilling activity in the public arena. Before giving a reading of his poetry, Leonard says that as a poet he derives his strength, not from doing, but from seeing things clearly and missing nothing:

People claim poetry doesn't do anything. The say, what does it get done? (*He moves forward and starts to cross the room.*) Isn't it weak to sit around thinking and writing when there's been so much destruction in the world? (*He pauses a second.*) I say no. It's strength. It's true strength. Truly. The hard thing is not to do, but to see. It's seeing that's hard. You get strength from looking things full in the face. Seeing everything, missing nothing, and not being frightened. (*As he speaks, he turns and looks Janetta in the face from across the room.*) And now I'll read. (52)

The action cuts to another scene so we do not hear him read, yet the context (and the significant look he gives Janetta) indicates the kind of "things" Leonard sees full in the face. The next morning he leaves Janetta forever with no explanation, because he senses from her restlessness that one day she would leave him because what they shared was not enough.

However, there is no further direct evidence of what Leonard sees. He is loquacious about his extraordinary capacity to see, yet tongue-tied about the nature of what he sees. At the reading he explicitly draws attention to his capacity for "seeing everything, missing nothing," and earlier with Janetta he says that the war opened up a world beyond the "real world," yet he firmly retreats behind the silence of his poetry (which we are never privy to) when she tries to draw him out on the subject of the war. "You don't talk about it much," she says, to which he replies, "No. That's what poetry is for. To say what can't be said" (25).

Ian Tyson (Gary Oldman), the man who lures Janetta away from Leonard for three days, is cut from the same mold as Marion, the materialistic Thatcher-like character in *The Secret Rapture*. After serving in the war, Ian returned to England and began buying property in London with a single-minded passion. He used his demobilization money to buy his first house. He is in every way the antithesis of Leonard. With the simplicity of a morality play, Ian, like Marion, is a "doer" and represents matter; while Leonard, like Isobel, possesses an aptitude for "being" a certain way and represents spirit. For Ian the material world is real. He attends to surfaces rather than depths. His passion is for money and property rather than for writing poetry. When Janetta defends Leonard's effort "to work out what he believes" in poetry (35), Ian tells her bluntly that what one believes doesn't matter. For Ian dabbling in feelings is a useless luxury. He admires those who just do it:

You can waste your life sitting there with your poet. I've met these kind of people. "Oh, I think this; oh, I think that . . . " (*He spreads his arms, dramatizing.*) "Oh, I feel; oh, I don't feel . . . " Of course it's fine. It's a great game. Especially for two players. (*He is suddenly serious.*) But don't ever kid yourself it's anything else. (*Ian suddenly seems almost angry.*) You're lucky, you're privileged. Spend your life asking, "What do I feel about this? Do I feel I'm doing the right thing . . . " (*He pauses.*) Or else you can just do it. I know which kind of person I like. (*There are tears in Janetta's eyes now.*) (36)

After Leonard disappears, a female friend of his tells Janetta to give up looking for him: "You never get it back. If it's perfect" (57). In the next scene a friend of Ian's explains to Janetta why Ian likes her: "He always says 'That woman will be really useful.' He always wanted you should run the whole thing. Or rather, at least be the front for it" (59). In the move from Leonard to Ian, Janetta falls from being perfectly loved to being "useful" as a charming and effective rent collector and front for Ian's business. She spends the rest of her life regretting that she momentarily left Leonard for Ian. Their perfect contentment proved to be irretrievable.

In this revisitation of the Second World War and its aftermath, as filtered through the memories of a 63-year-old woman, Hare's attitudes of the 1980s and 1990s replace those of the 1970s. The war is recast as the incubator of a certain indescribable way of being rather than a belief in national ideals. A well-bred contemplative poet replaces an angry self-righteous young woman (Susan Traherne in *Plenty*) as the representative of that which is under assault from centrifugal materialistic forces in postwar Britain.

As I discussed in Chapters 10 and 11, morality in all Hare's works, whether it appears to be public like Susan's or private like Isobel's, ultimately rests on the attitudes of those in control of Britain's cultural, educational, and political institutions; or, to put it simply, it rests on middle- and upper-class manners and pedigree. *Heading Home* fits into the trajectory of Hare's writing career as the second work after *Racing Demon* (written the year before) that begins to reveal a connection between morality and the ruling classes, in the very process of trying to mystify the connection as a perfectly natural phenomenon. On the one hand, there is an effort to keep the nature of Leonard's spiritual prowess shrouded in silence. He tells Janetta that he writes poetry "to say what can't be said." Leonard's conviction that the truly important and meaningful things cannot be talked about carries over into his relationships. After Leonard disappears without a word of explanation the day after Janetta returns from being with Ian, she painfully learns what a female friend of his told her earlier, that "things don't need saying" when they are perfect (15). However, the ideological significance of these important meanings that cannot be articulated can be teased out as they acquire a clearer social pedigree. While Leonard's superior social class must be present and visible, it must also remain unnamable and invisible if it is to retain its power. Thus the curious contradiction between stressing that Leonard possesses extraordinary spiritual powers, while at the same time stressing that such powers cannot be identified and discussed.

As in the contrast between Lionel and Tony in *Racing Demon*, class differences play a visible yet seemingly inconsequential role in the characterization of Leonard and Ian. Ian is a ruffian from an indeterminate lower class, while Leonard freely talks about his upper-class background when he tells Janetta that the war had a profound impact on him: "Like the rest of my family. I played cricket, I would have a proper career. Running the country. It was simple, I was English" (25). Although Leonard rejected a career "running the country," the privileged background that would have allowed him to do so is the only distinguishing feature that can explain why he and not Ian is the vehicle of moral and spiritual authority in the film.

Like most of Hare's leading characters who carry the moral charge, Leonard is not articulate about the nature of his beliefs, yet he is different from such previous characters in two crucial ways that have a direct bearing on the political climate of the late 1980s and the early 1990s in Britain. First, he explicitly says that he has devoted his life to beliefs that cannot be talked about openly and rationally, whereas the inarticulacy of earlier characters such as Susan Traherne and Isobel Glass is simply assumed and not explicitly asserted. Second, like Lionel Espy, Leonard is specifically placed at the upper end of the class structure that is more muted in earlier works. What social and political realities of recent years might account for these two changes?

As discontent with the highly centralized and elitist power structures grows in Britain, the mandarin classes find themselves in the delicate position of possessing only one defense that is increasingly indefensible. Their problem is how to defend their authority that flows to them primarily as a result of superior social position without explicitly endorsing the hierarchical class structure which is precisely the focus of escalating criticism. Through the figure of

Leonard, *Heading Home* presents a solution to this problem by reaffirming the traditional power structure while seeming not to. Although Leonard's upper-class background and gentlemanly integrity and refinement are on full display, they appear to represent nothing because class is never openly contested as an issue in the film, and because he refuses to talk about what he believes. The highly visible indices of real power and authority strive to appear natural and therefore invisible as they remain locked in the pre-rational, non-intellectual, instinctual level of experience.

David Hare's recent play *Skylight* (1995) is his *The Bay at Nice/Wrecked Eggs* (1986) of the 1990s. Like these two companion pieces of the mid-1980s, *Skylight* is a discussion play with a small cast confined to a single setting in which Hare tests and reaffirms ideas that are more implicitly worked out in earlier plays and films. In *The Bay at Nice and Wrecked Eggs* Hare sets out to prove to his satisfaction that morality is private rather than public, that what people are like (their character and personality) is a truer indicator of moral value than what they do or believe. Just as these two plays explicitly confirm what earlier works (*Dreams of Leaving,* 1979, *A Map of the World,* 1982, and *Wetherby,* 1984) tentatively and implicitly embrace, *Skylight* explicitly defends, in the course of intense discussion between its two main characters, what is enacted in key scenes of the plays of the trilogy: the idea that professionals in British institutions (such as Irina the young Black female lawyer in *Murmuring Judges,* and the Reverend Lionel Espy in *Racing Demon*) perform their public service to the poor as a heartfelt duty and therefore should be defended against charges that they are serving their personal and aggregate interests in the process.

In Britain, as in Canada, the United States, and every Western European country, politics in the 1990s and the early 21st century will be dominated by protracted battles between those trying to reduce government spending and high debt loads and those whose interests would be hurt by cuts in social services, welfare provisions, and military spending. Yet the battle is considerably more intense in Britain, where any scheme to reduce or redefine the role of state institutions threatens to erode not only the paychecks of politicians, professionals, and civil servants but, much more important, their cultural authority. What is really at stake in Britain is a deeply entrenched system of rulership by caste. Like the plays of the trilogy, *Skylight* is Hare's response to mounting pressure to allow the more democratic and competitive rules of the marketplace (rather than government institutions) to determine how cultural as well as financial wealth is distributed. As discussed in Chapter 11 on the trilogy, through the efforts of republicans, members of Charter 88, and constitutional reformers in the three major political parties, there has been a growing awareness since the late 1980s that Britain's economic prosperity ultimately depends on fundamental reforms in the cultural sphere.

The great contradiction in Britain in the mid-1990s is that while restrictive practices are no longer allowed in many financial institutions, government

utilities, businesses, and corporations, they continue to operate in every significant cultural and political institution. That is, for the most part, the same sort of
people with the right social pedigree and/or educational background still
"serve" the same sort of people. The debilitating consequence is that an
intelligent and talented young person from the wrong class or region has little
reason to believe they can succeed if so many professions are effectively closed
off to them.

In their efforts to dismantle the system of rulership by caste, first Tory
politicians and then constitutional reformers began to identify and criticize the
interests served in the so-called disinterested "service" of professionals. It is
this more than anything else that disturbed Hare in the late 1980s and
prompted him to write the trilogy as he indicates in this passage from the
Introduction to *Asking Around:*

I realized the country was passing through a distinctive period in its history in which a
government hell-bent on action was determined to suspect the motives of anyone who
brought news of what life was actually like on the street. It had become an article of
faith among the ideologues at Number Ten that professionals were incapable of
representing anything but their own interests. What was under attack from above was
not just the prosperity of all those whose job it was to help other people, but the idea of
professionalism itself.[2]

This passage about the Trilogy even more obviously addresses Hare's concerns
in *Skylight* which defends the idea of pure disinterested professional service
through the arguments and experience of the central character, Kyra Hollis, a
slightly-over-30 white female primary school teacher.

It is true, as Hare says, that in recent years both the "prosperity" of
professionals and "the idea of professionalism" have come under "attack" as
people have grown skeptical about the "interests" served; however, *Skylight* is
vocal about what doesn't matter, and silent about what does. It explicitly denies
that money is an "interest," while it avoids contesting the charge that "the idea
of professionalism" is an "interest" in terms of cultural power. That is, the play
deflects attention from the primary reason professional "interests" became an
issue in Britain and in the process tries to remystify (as does the trilogy) the
ethos of disinterested public service which the general public must believe in if
those doing the "serving" are to hold onto their power. Furthermore, the way
Kyra Hollis serves her students is so personalized, depoliticized, and free of
monetary rewards that there appears to be no reason why anyone would
"attack" it. No professional in Britain would be accused of serving private
interests of any kind if they were like Kyra. Which is to say that Hare defends
professionals "serving" people on the only ground those criticizing them in the
1990s would find irrelevant. He enters into a polemic with reformers and the
new right without addressing their real concern which is should the
educational, cultural, religious, judicial, and political institutions continue to

employ the same sort of people to do the "serving" and is the resultant social rigidity good for Britain?

No one would accuse Kyra Hollis of prospering financially as a mathematics teacher in a primary school located in a poor district of northwest London. She would be earning about £10,000 to £11,000 a year and it shows. She lives in a cold shabby apartment with threadbare carpets. The entire action of the play takes place in her apartment within about 18 hours and consists of her conversations with her ex-lover Tom Sergeant, who is about 50, and his 18-year-old son Edward. Unbeknownst to each other, both visit her on the same evening after four years of no contact. Edward visits to ask Kyra to "help" his father, whose pain over the loss of Kyra followed by the death of his wife to cancer is so great that he is impossible to live with. Hours later Tom shows up and in the course of the evening reveals that beneath his good humor and apparent confidence he misses Kyra profoundly and wants to reestablish a relationship. Four years before, Kyra had abruptly ended their six-year affair when, through Tom's intentional carelessness, his wife Alice discovered one of Kyra's love letters to him. Like Janetta in *Heading Home*, Tom destroyed the perfection he had because he restlessly wanted more.

Although Tom and Kyra were lovers for six years and still have great affection for each other, they are opposites in nearly every way. And it is the fundamental differences between them that emerge as the central focus of the play. Like the marriage dilemma in *Wrecked Eggs*, their unsuccessful attempt to renegotiate a relationship provides the dramatic occasion Hare uses to explore other ideas—in this case, the contrast between Kyra's life of self-sacrifice and service and Tom's restless pursuit of wealth.

Skylight is really a parable about the struggle for the soul of England: will value and identity be governed by the marketplace or by a certain manner and attitude that inheres as the result of the right breeding? What makes this parable so English is that the struggle is defined as a case of either/or. Tom and Kyra exist in different worlds and go their separate ways at the end because authority cannot be shared or divided in England, where for centuries culture has tolerated commerce rather than cooperated with it as a necessary and equal partner.

Tom is a working-class boy who made good. Starting with several restaurants in Chelsea, he built up a chain of restaurants and hotels that turned him into a very wealthy man. When he floated his company on the stockmarket its value rose to 30 times its initial value. He cannot understand why Kyra refused to accept shares from him. "You could have moved up in the world" he tells her.[3] Astonished at the squalor of her apartment, he repeatedly criticizes her lifestyle and choice of career. His criticism becomes more aggressive as he grows increasingly exasperated with the quiet certainty of her manner and resolute detachment from his neediness. The big blowup occurs when he demands to know why someone with a "first class degree" who "came out top" of their year and could teach at any university in the country would throw their life away teaching kids in one of the worst schools in London: "I can't see anything more tragic, more stupid than you sitting here and throwing your talents away. . . . Kyra, you're teaching kids at the bottom of the heap" (78). His provocation elicits the key speech of the play in which she says she helps poor children because they need to be helped:

It's only happened of late. That people should need to ask why I'm helping these children. I'm helping them because they need to be helped. . . . Everyone makes merry, discussing motive. . . . Well I say, what the hell does it matter why I'm doing it? Why anyone goes out and helps? The reason is hardly of primary importance. If I didn't do it, it wouldn't get done. (*She is now suddenly so passionate, so forceful that Tom is silenced.*) I'm tired of these sophistries. I'm tired of these right-wing fuckers. They wouldn't left a finger themselves. They work contentedly in offices and banks. Yet now they sit pontificating in parliament, in papers, impugning our motives, questioning our judgments. (79-80)

What is significant about this speech in defense of helping is that there is no institutional or structural dimension to it. Krya reduces helping children to the apolitical simplicity of a personal preference with which no one would have any reason to disagree, except a disgruntled ex-lover with personal motives for provoking her. In reality, helping people has recently become an issue for "right-wing fuckers," as Kyra calls them, insofar as it appears to be a disinterested public service within powerful institutions that actually help a relatively small group of people exercise an effective monopoly in the cultural and political arena.

The play concludes with a description of an even purer and more disinterested helping. After an emotionally exhausting night with Tom, Kyra sleeps a few hours and is awakened at dawn by Edward, who appears with a complete breakfast from the Ritz—one of the things she said she missed from Tom's world. They sit down to eat and her mood transforms into "a purposeful high humour" as she tells Edward that she has to hurry to meet a student she tutors for free: "I have to eat quickly. There's a boy I'm late for. I'm teaching him off my own bat. Extra lessons. Early, so early! I sometimes think I must be going insane . . . there's only one thing that makes the whole thing make sense, and that is finding one really good pupil. . . . You set yourself some personal target, a private target only you know it—no one else—that's where you find satisfaction." (101) Hare is so eager to defend helping people as a disinterested vocation that he does so on the only ground no one would contest. Kyra's giving free math lessons to a student at 7:30 in the morning is obviously an admirable act of personal charity, yet it is irrelevant to the debate about the nature of the cultural "interest" that accrues to professionals in British institutions.

Nevertheless, *Skylight* has a great deal to "say" about the cultural "interest" that accrues to professionals, and the seemingly incidental way such "interest" is conveyed makes the play an even more telling parable about Britain in the

1990s. Like the undemocratic viruses that infect the intestinal workings of the British state and society, the true basis of power and value in *Skylight* is manifest everywhere, yet it aspires to appear natural, uncontested, and inevitable. Material wealth, which is ultimately not important to the professional "serving" classes, is openly debated and willingly relinquished, while cultural power, which is of utmost importance, appears in *Skylight* as it has for centuries—as the natural dispensation of certain people with the right background. The only thing Tom and Kyra should be arguing about (for it is the real issue in Britain today) is the only thing they cannot argue about because to be explicit about the basis of Kyra's superior sense of self-worth, which is breeding, would destroy the magic of social pedigree upon which her sense of worth depends.

In sharp contrast to Tom, Kyra is portrayed as holding all the cards worth holding in life. He is poor in spirit and rich in money; she is rich in spirit and poor in money. Although she earns very little money and lives in a shabby apartment, Kyra brims over with confidence, happiness, vocational purpose, and a sense of personal worth. In response to Tom's skepticism about her future, she says "I have an idea of the future as well. . . . A future doing a job I believe in" (68). She is filled with "purposeful high humour" as she "happily" tells Edward over breakfast about the special boy with a "spark" that she is about to rush off to tutor (101). Whereas Tom, despite all his immense success building a business empire, is running on empty. He is a hollow man plagued with guilt and low self-esteem. He tells Kyra that no amount of work fills up the void in his life. After a long day at the restaurants, he says he usually goes out for a walk, sometimes at around three in the morning: "Always the same thought. I find myself thinking: something must come of this. . . . My foot's on the floor, I'm pumping, I'm flooring that fucking pedal, and nothing's moving. I'm getting no fucking pleasure at all" (70). He needs Kyra to extend the forgiveness to him that his wife wouldn't, and he needs Kyra in his life to feel whole and fulfilled.

Although Kyra is the one who declares that she no longer reads newspapers or watches TV and prefers classic novels and old films, Tom is the one who is exiled from the only world that really matters (27). Like many of Hare's previous emotionally challenged characters, Tom by himself is not equipped to enter into the spiritual and emotional world that he feels cut off from. This is evident in his every reflex. At one point he recoils from a moment of intimacy with Kyra and begins talking, the stage directions say, *"as if the next thought were completely logical"* (36). At another point Kyra asks him how he now feels after his description of how it was to live with his dying wife who withdrew to punish him for the affair. According to the stage directions, he *"looks at her blankly for a moment"* before he tries to "hide his distress" (47).

There are questions that remain to be asked, variations on questions that I have asked of every Hare play and film. Why is Kyra full and Tom empty? What is the basis of her confidence and self worth and his abject neediness and feelings of unworthiness? Where does Kyra's deeply rooted instinct to serve come from? What prevents Tom from having this instinct? Would he become a happy, fulfilled person if he became an underpaid schoolteacher in a bleak suburb of London?

Through the on-going contrast between Kyra and Tom, *Skylight* vigorously reasserts the old truth in England that with few exceptions there is no such thing as "moving up in the world" by making money. Early in the play Tom tells Kyra that she "could have moved up in the world" had she accepted shares from him (22). However, as the rest of the play demonstrates, people can only be born and bred "up in the world." The essential operative difference between them is that Kyra is the daughter of a seaside solicitor and Tom is from the working class, "bog-ordinary people" he says of his family (74). Her background was sufficiently genteel for her to imbibe the instinct to serve; and his background was sufficiently ordinary that no amount of money could instill in him the confidence and feelings of self-worth that she possesses in abundance. (To clear Kyra of the suspicion that she is merely slumming for a few years, we are informed that she inherited almost no money from her father, whom everyone, including herself, believed was fairly wealthy [66]). Somehow he spent it all before he died the year before. Note how it is important that we know she grew up in a fairly wealthy family, and also that such wealth has disappeared to preserve her disinterest in the present.)

For the coalition of reformers who are convinced that Britain will continue to stagnate as a society unless it learns how to better harness the energies of a wider spectrum of its people, Tom's experience goes to the heart of what is wrong with British society. As long as people are valued for who they are and not for what they do, businessmen like Tom will continue to derive very little psychological and emotional sustenance from their work. The fact that Kyra and others like her maintain a monopoly on cultural "interest" is the fundamental issue in Britain (nobody accuses schoolteachers of making too much money), and yet Tom is not prepared to question her effortless sense of worthiness and the class system that undergirds it because he is an eager and willing hostage of her mandarin value system from the start. He is acutely aware of his lack of self-worth, and yet such awareness propels him to visit her with the hope that she will fill him up rather than to ask what is it about his society that makes him feel so empty and Kyra feel so full.

NOTES

CHAPTER 1

1. Quoted in Kathleen Tynan, "Dramatically Speaking," *Interview*, March 1989, 128.

2. David Hare, Introduction to *The History Plays* (London: Faber and Faber, 1984), 11-12.

3. John Bull, *New British Political Dramatists* (New York: Grove Press, 1983), 60.

4. David Hare, A Lecture in *Licking Hitler* (London: Faber and Faber, 1978, 67.

5. Quoted in Gerard Raymond, "*The Secret Rapture*: David Hare's X-Ray of the Soul," *TheatreWeek* 30 (October 1989), 16.

6. Mel Gussow, "Ideas and Ideals Populate the World of David Hare," *New York Times*, 13 October 1985, H3.

7. Quoted in Tynan, "Dramatically Speaking," 80.

8. David Hare, Introduction to *Writing Left-Handed* (London: Faber and Faber, 1991), xi-xii.

9. Carol Homden, "A Dramatist of Surprise," *Plays and Players* (September 1988), 6.

10. Jim Hiley, "The Wetherby Report," *The Observer*, 11 March 1985, 64.

11. Michael Billington, Review of *The Secret Rapture*, in *London Theatre Record*, 23 September to 6 October 1988.

12. Sheridan Morley, Review of *The Secret Rapture*, in *London Theatre Record*, 23 September to 6 October 1988.

13. Tynan, "Dramatically Speaking," 80.

14. Bull, *Political Dramatists*, 82.

15. Ibid., 85.

16. C.W.E. Bigsby, ed. *Contemporary English Drama* (New York: Holmes & Meier, 1981), 43.

17. Ibid., 45.

18. Quoted in ibid., 44.

19. Quoted in Tynan, "Dramatically Speaking," 80.

20. Hare, A Lecture, 57-58.

21. Quoted in Bigsby, *Contemporary English Drama*, 44.

22. Tom Nairn, *The Enchanted Glass: Britain and Its Monarchy* (London: Hutchinson Radius, 1988), 274.

23. Ibid.

24. Ibid.

25. Raymond Williams, *The Long Revolution* (London: Chatto & Windus, 1961), 46-47.

26. Raymond Williams, *Marxism and Literature* (Oxford: Oxford University Press, 1977), 132.

27. John Osborne, "They Call It Cricket," in *Declaration*, ed. Tom Maschler (New York: E. P. Dutton, 1958), 47.

28. David Hare, *Licking Hitler* (London: Faber & Faber, 1978), 54. All subsequent citations are from this source.

29. David Hare, *Knuckle* (London: Faber & Faber, 1974), 36. All subsequent citations are from this source.

30. David Marquand, *The Unprincipled Society* (London: Fontana Press, 1988), 211.

31. Ibid., 242.

32. See Nairn, *The Enchanted Glass* esp. Ch. 4 about how republican forces have been marginalized in England since the Glorious Revolution in 1688; Frank Vibert, ed., *Britain's Constitutional Future* (London: Institute for Economic Affairs, 1991), esp. Ch. 3 by Stephen Haseler, 37-43, Ch. 5 by Graham Mather, 73-93, and Ch. 9 by Richard Holme, 137-144; Stephen Haseler, *The Battle for Britain Thatcher and the New Liberals* (London: I. B. Tauris, 1989; Tony Benn and Andrew Hood, *Common Sense: A New Constitution for Britain*, ed. Ruth Winstone (London: Hutchinson, 1993); Neal Ascherson, *Games with Shadows* (London: Radius, 1988), esp. Part 2 "Druids: The Politics of Unreformed Britain," 81-158; and a collection of essays from a conference in 1993 organized by Charter 88 and *The Times* to debate the role of the monarchy in Anthony Barnett, ed., *Power and the Throne* (London: Vintage, 1994).

33. Tom Nairn, *The Break-up of Britain* (London: NLB, 1977), 50.

34. Peter Ansorge, "Current Concerns," *Plays and Players*, July 1989, 22.

35. Trevor Griffiths, *The Party* (London: Faber & Faber, 1974), 67.

36. Lindesay Irvine, "Howard Barker," *Plays and Players*, April 1994, 46.

37. Ronald Bryden, *"Teeth'n'Smiles,"* *Plays and Players*, November 1975, 21-22.

38. Rhoda Koenig, Review of *Racing Demon*, in *London Theatre Record*, 29 January to 11 February 1990.

39. Graham Hassell, "Hare Racing," *Plays and Players*, February 1990, 10.

40. Williams, *The Long Revolution*, 260.

CHAPTER 2

1. David Hare, "Commanding the Style of Presentation," interview by Simon Trussler and Catherine Itzin, *New Theatre Voices of the Seventies*, ed. Simon Trussler (London: Methuen, 1981), 115.

2. Robert Hewison, *Too Much: Art and Society in the Sixties 1960-75* (London: Methuen, 1986).

3. Howard Brenton, "Petrol Bombs through the Proscenium Arch," interview by Trussler and Itzin, *New Theatre Voices*, 97.

4. Hare, "Commanding the Style," 115.

5. Georg Gaston, "Interview: David Hare," *Theatre Journal* 45 (1993), 215.

6. Howard Barker, *Arguments for a Theatre*, (London: Calder, 1989), 16.

7. Gaston, "Interview: David Hare," 215.

8. David Hare, How *Brophy Made Good*, in *Gambit* 17 (1971), 106. All subsequent citations are from this source.

9. David Hare, *Slag* (London: Faber & Faber, 1971), 19. All subsequent citations are from this source.

10. David Hare, *The Great Exhibition* (in *The Early Plays*) (London: Faber & Faber, 1992), 126. All subsequent citations are from this source.

11. Quoted in Peter Ansorge, "Underground Explorations," *Plays and Players*, February 1972, 72.

12. Quoted in Carol Homden, "A Dramatist of Surprise," 6.

13. Herbert Marcuse, *One-Dimentional Man* (Boston: Beacon Press, 1969). All subsequent citations are from this source.

14. Herbert Marcuse, *An Essay on Liberation* (Boston: Beacon Press, 1969), 34.

15. See the excellent discussion about the "turn to Gramsci" in British cultural studies in the introduction and first two chapters in Tony Bennett, Colin Mercer, and Janet Woollacott, eds., *Popular Culture and Social Relations* (Milton Keynes: Open University Press, 1986); see also Alan Sinfield, *Literature, Politics, and Culture in Postwar Britain* (Los Angeles: University of California Press, 1989), 178, 179, 242; Stuart Hall, "Notes on Deconstructing 'the Popular,'" in *People's History and Socialist Theory*, ed. Raphael Samuel (London: Routledge and Kegan Paul, 1981), 227-240.

16. Hall, "Notes on Deconstructing," 223.

17. David Hare, "Cycles of Hope: A Memoir of Raymond Williams," in *Writing Left-Handed* (London: Faber & Faber, 1991), 8.

18. Quoted in Ansorge, "Underground Explorations," 18.

19. David Hare, "Time of Unease," in *At the Royal Court*, ed. Richard Findlater (Derbyshire: Amber Lane Press, 1981), 139-142.

20. Hare, "Commanding the Style," 118-119.

21. Ibid., 113-114.

22. Ruby Cohn, "Rare Hare, Licking Women," in *David Hare: A Casebook*, ed. Hersh Zeifman (New: York: Garland, 1994), 24.

23. Hare, A Lecture, 66.

24. Angus Calder, *The People's War* (London: Jonathan Cape, 1969).

25. Hare, "Commanding the Style," 118.

26. Quoted in Peter Ansorge, "Current Concerns," *Plays and Players*, July 1974, 20.

27. Sinfield, *Postwar Britain*, 274.

28. Raymond Williams, *Culture and Society 1780-1950* (New York: Columbia University Press, 1958), 291-292.

CHAPTER 3

1. Sinfield, *Postwar Britain*, 156.

2. Raymond Williams, "Raymond Williams: Building a Socialist Culture," interviewed by Dave Taylor, *The Leveller*, March 1979, 26.

3. Ibid.

4. Marquand, *The Unprincipled Society*, 48.

5. Hewison, *Too Much*, 157.

6. Hare, Introduction to *The History Plays*, 13-14.

7. Dennis Kavanagh, *Thatcherism and British Politics: The End of Consensus* (Oxford: Oxford University Press, 1987), 151.

8. Hare, "Commanding the Style," 118.

9. Ibid.

10. Sinfield, *Postwar Britain*, 282.

11. Hare, "Commanding the Style," 118.

12. David Hare, *Teeth'n'Smiles* (London: Faber & Faber, 1976), 86. All subsequent citations are from this source.

13. Quoted in Ann McFerran, "End of the Acid Era," *Time Out* 29 (August 1975), 15.

14. See Michael Brake, *The Sociology of Youth Culture and Youth Subcultures: Sex and Drugs and Rock'n'Roll?* (London: Routledge & Kegan Paul, 1980); Dick Hebdige, *Subculture: The Meaning of Style* (London: Methuen, 1979); Hewison, *Too Much*; Charles Reich, *The Greening of America* (New York: Random House, 1970); Paul E. Willis, *Profane Culture* (London: Routledge & Kegan Paul, 1978).

15. Michel Foucault, "Truth and Power," in *Critical Theory Since Plato*, ed. Hazard Adams (Orlando: Harcourt, Brace, Jovanovich, 1992), 1142.

16. Nairn, *The Breakup of Britain*, 262.

CHAPTER 4

1. Hare, "Commanding the Style," 119.

2. David Hare, Preface to *Fanshen* (London: Faber & Faber, 1976), 7.

3. Quoted in Michael Coveney, "Turning over a New Life," *Plays and Players*, June 1975, 10.

4. Hare, Preface to *Fanshen*, 9.

5. William Hinton, *Fanshen: A Documentary of Revolution in a Chinese Village* (New York: Monthly Review Press, 1966), 26.

6. Ibid., 46.

7. Hare, *Fanshen*, 13.

8. Ibid., 16.

9. Hinton, *Fanshen: A Documentary*, 113-117.

10. See Gaston, "Interview: David Hare," 219; Janelle Reinalt, "Fanshen: Hare and Brecht," in *David Hare: A Casebook*, 127-140.

11. John Willett, ed. and trans., *Brecht on Theatre* (London: Methuen, 1957), 37.

12. Hare, "Commanding the Style," 119.

13. Hare, Preface to *Fanshen*, 8.

14. Hinton, Preface to *Fanshen: A Documentary*, ix.

15. Ibid., xii-xiii.

16. Yung Ping Chen, *Chinese Political Thought: Mao Tse-tung and Liu Shao-chi* (The Hague: Martinus Nijhoff, 1966), 100.

17. Richard Walker, "Peking's Approach to the Outside World," in *Communist China, 1949-1969: A Twenty-Year Appraisal*, eds. Frank N. Trager and William Henderson (New York: New York University Press, 1970), 296.

18. William Hinton, *Turning Point in China* (New York: Monthly Review Press, 1972), 10.

19. David Hare, introduction to *The Asian Plays* (London: Faber & Faber, 1982), ix.

CHAPTER 5

1. Hare, Introduction to *The History Plays*, 12.

2. Sefton Delmer, *Black Boomerang* (New York: Viking Press, 1962).

3. Calder, *The People's War*, 18.

4. Delmer, Publisher's Foreword to *Black Boomerang*, xi.

5. Delmer, *Black Boomerang*, 259.

6. Ibid., 81.

7. Ibid., 38.

8. Robert Hewison, *In Anger: Culture in the Cold War 1954-60* (London: Weidenfeld and Nicolson, 1981), 64.

9. Hare, Introduction to *The History Plays*, 14.

10. David Hare, "Ah Mischief," in Ah Mischief: *The Writer and Television*, ed. Frank Pike (London: Faber & Faber, 1982), 48.

11. Quoted in James Park, *Learning to Dream: The New British Cinema* (London: Faber & Faber, 1984), 98.

12. Hare, Introduction to *The History Plays*, 13.

13. Ibid.

CHAPTER 6

1. Peter Ansorge, "A War on Two Fronts," *Plays and Players*, April 1978, 13.

2. Quoted in Gaston, "Interview: David Hare," 221.

3. David Hare, *A Map of the World* (London: Faber & Faber, 1982), 23. All subsequent citations are from this source.

4. Hare, Introduction to *The History Plays*, 14.

5. David Hare, *Dreams of Leaving* (London: Faber & Faber, 1980), 41. All subsequent citations are from this source.

6. David Hare, *Wetherby* (London: Faber & Faber, 1985), 92. All subsequent citations are from this source.

7. Quoted in Homden, "A Dramatist of Surprise," 6.

8. Quoted in Benedict Nightingale, "An Angry Young Briton of the 80s Brings His Play to New York," *New York Times*, 17 October 1982, sec. 2, 6.

9. Hare, Introduction to *The History Plays*, 15.

10. Hare, A Lecture, 66.

11. Mel Gussow, "A British Hedda," *New York Times*, 20 April 1980.

12. David Hare, *Plenty* (London: Faber & Faber, 1978), 82, 83. All subsequent citations are from this source.

13. T. J. Thompson and E. P. Thompson, eds., *There is a Spirit in Europe. . . : A Memoir of Frank Thompson* (London: Victor Gollancz, 1947), 169.

14. David Piper, *The Companion Guide to London* (London: Prentice-Hall, 1983), 164.

15. Michael Frayn, "Festival," in *Age of Austerity 1945-1951*, eds. Michael Sissons and Philip French (London: Hodder and Stoughton, 1963), 337.

16. Ibid., 336.

17. Richard Hoggart, *The Uses of Literacy* (London: Chatto and Windus, 1957), 157- 158.

18. A.C.H. Smith, *Paper Voices and the Popular Press and Social Change* (New Jersey: Rowman and Littlefield, 1975), 150.

19. Quoted in ibid., 152.

20. Hoggart, *Uses of Literacy*, 160.

21. David Hughs, "The Spivs," in Sissons and French, *Age of Austerity*, 95.

22. Hoggart, *Uses of Literacy*, 225, 230, 231.

23. David Widgery, *The Left in Britain 1956-68* (Middlesex: Penquin, 1976), 49.

24. P. J. Madgwick, D. Steeds, and L. J. Williams, *Britain Since 1945* (London: Hutchinson, 1982), 358.

25. Quoted in Alan Sked and Chris Cook, *Post-War Britain: A Political History* (Middlesex: Penquin, 1979), 153.

26. Widgery, *The Left*, 49.

27. Christopher Hollis, "Parliament and the Establishment," in *The Establishment*, ed. Hugh Thomas (London: Anthony Blond, 1959), 184.

28. Ibid., 185.

29. Ibid.

30. J. B. Priestley, *Topside or the Future of England: A Dialogue* (London: Heinemann, 1958), 7.

31. Ibid., 27.

32. Widgery, *The Left*, 49.

33. David Edgar, *Maydays* (London: Methuen, 1983).

34. Quoted in Julien Petley, *"Wetherby," Monthly Film Bulletin*, March 1985.

35. Quoted in Mel Gussow, "Playwright as Provacateur," *New York Times*, 29 September 1985, 47.

36. Raymond Williams, *Modern Tragedy* (Stanford, CA: Stanford University Press, 1966), 121.

CHAPTER 7

1. Peter Fiddick, *"Dreams of Leaving," The Guardian*, 18 January 1980.

2. Michael Ratcliffe, "Capturing the Music of the Sphinx," *The Times*, 17 January 1980, 25.

3. David Hare, *Dreams of Leaving* (London: Faber & Faber, 1980), 39. All subsequent citations are from this source.

4. Ratcliffe, "Capturing the Music," 25.

5. Hoggart, *Uses of Literacy*, 141.

CHAPTER 8

1. Crispen Audrey, "The Making of *1984*," in *Nineteen Eighty-four in 1984*, eds. Paul Chilton and Crispen Aubrey (London: Comedia Publishing, 1983), 2.

2. George Orwell, *1984* (New York: Harcourt Brace, 1949), 90. All subsequent citations are from this source.

3. Arthur L. Morton, *The English Utopia* (Berlin: Seven Seas Publishers, 1968), 268.

4. Hiley, "The Wetherby Report," 64.

5. Stuart Hall, "The Crisis of Labourism," in *The Future of the Left*, ed. James Curran (London: Polity Press and New Socialist, 1984), 31.

6. Hiley, "The Wetherby Report," 64.

7. Nightingale, "An Angry Young Briton," 1, 6.

8. Quoted in Petley, *"Wetherby,"* 70.

CHAPTER 9

1. Tynan, "Dramatically Speaking," 80.

2. Ibid., 130.

3. David Hare, *The Secret Rapture* (London: Faber & Faber, 1988), 78. All subsequent citations are from this source.

4. Tynan, "Dramatically Speaking," 128.

5. Ibid.

6. I am indebted to Ann Douglas's discussion of the rise of sentimental literature in America in the early 19th century in *The Feminization of America* (New York: Doubleday, 1977).

7. Suzanne Clark, *Sentimental Modernism* (Bloomington: Indiana University Press, 1991).

8. Benedict Nightingale, "David Hare Captures His Muse on Stage," *New York Times*, 22 October 1989, 25.

9. Quoted in Raymond, "Hare's X-Ray of the Soul," 16.

10. Quoted in Homden, "A Dramatist of Surprise," 6.

11. The strapless dress is one of several fetishistic images that arguably entrap Lillian as an object of male fantasies and thus undermines her ostensible movement toward spiritual self-sufficiency and independence.

12. John Dugdale, "Love, Death and Edwina," *Listener Arts*, 15 September 1988, 38, 39.

13. Homden, "A Dramatist of Surprise," 5-8.

14. Tynan, "Dramatically Speaking," 130.

15. Marquand, *The Unprincipled Society*, 216.

16. Ibid., 215.

17. John Peter, "How to Make a Play for Failure," *The Sunday Times*, 15 May 1988, C8.

18. Although Hare borrowed many atmospheric details from Frank Snepp, *Decent Interval* (New York: Random House, 1977), he departs from Snepp's focus on the

institutional causes for the U.S. failure in Vietnam, which, as the CIA's chief strategy analyst, he was well positioned to expose; see also Stuart Herrington, *Peace with Honor?* (San Francisco: Presidio Press, 1983); George Herring, *America's Longest War* (New York: Knopf, 1979).

19. Hare, Introduction to *The Asian Plays*, x.

20. Tom Stoppard, *The Real Thing* (London: Faber & Faber, 1982), 33.

21. David Hare, Introduction to *Paris by Night* (London: Faber & Faber, 1988), v.

22. Margaret Thatcher, *The Revival of Britain* (London: Aurum Press, 1989), 53.

23. Marquand, *The Unprincipled Society*, 217.

24. For reviews of the National Theatre production of *Pravda,* see reviews in *London Theatre Record,* 24 April to 7 May 1985: Lyn Gardner of *City Limits* calls Pravda a "cartoon look" at Fleet Street; for Kenneth Hurren of the *Mail on Sunday* it is "a crude and bilious burlesque"; and for Jim Hiley of *Listener* an "unapologetic piece of agitprop."

25. Stuart Hall, *The Hard Road to Renewal* (London: Verso, 1988), 192.

26. Andrew Gamble, *The Free Economy and the Strong State: The Politics of Thatcherism* (Durham: Duke University Press, 1988), 21.

27. Howard Brenton and David Hare, *Pravda: A Fleet Street Comedy* (London: Methuen, 1985), 102. All subsequent citations are from this source.

28. Howard Brenton, "Writing for Democratic Laughter," *Drama* 3 (1985), 11.

29. Howard Brenton, Translator's note in *The Life of Galileo* (London: Methuen, 1980).

30. Howard Brenton, *Greenland* (London: Methuen, 1988), 51.

31. Hall, *Hard Road*, 11.

32. Howard Brenton, "A Crazy Optimism," *New Statesman*, 30 July 1982, 27.

33. Brenton, *Greenland*, 54.

34. Tynan, "Dramatically Speaking," 128.

35. Raymond, "Hare's X-Ray of the Soul," 18.

36. David Hare, *The Bay at Nice and Wrecked Eggs* (London: Faber & Faber, 1986), 43. All subsequent citations are from this source.

37. Tynan, "Dramatically Speaking," 128.

CHAPTER 10

1. Julian Barnes, "The Modernizer," *The New Yorker*, 29 August 1994, 66-71.

2. Hare, "Commanding the Style," 118.

3. Nightingale, "An Angry Young Briton," 6.

4. Michael Bloom, "A Kinder, Gentler David Hare," *American Theatre*, November 1989, 32.

5. Quoted in Tynan, "Dramatically Speaking," 128.

6. Ibid., 80.

7. Quoted in Jack Kroll, "Women of Thatcherland," *Newsweek*, 13 November 1989, 89.

8. Quoted in Nightingale, "David Hare Captures his Muse," 24.

9. Ibid.

10. See Williams, "Raymond Williams: Building a Socialist Culture," 25-27; Haseler, *The Battle for Britain*, 22-25, 33-36, 39-42; Richard Heffernan and Mike

Marqusee, *Defeat from the Jaws of Victory* (London: Verso, 1992); Nigel Young, *An Infantile Disorder? The Crisis and Decline of the New Left* (Boulder: Westview Press, 1977), 70-78; Hall, *The Hard Road to Renewal*, 196-210.

11. Howard Brenton, *Magnificence* (London: Methuen, 1973), 17.

12. Frayn, "Festival."

13. Brenton, *Magnificence*, 17.

14. Howard Brenton, *Weapons of Happiness* (London: Methuen, 1976), 40.

15. Kenneth O. Morgan, *The People's Peace: British History 1945-1989* (Oxford: Oxford University Press, 1990), 490-491.

16. David Owen, *A United Kingdom* (Middlesex: Penquin, 1986), 11.

17. Alan Watkins, "The Chattering Classes—Who Are They?" *Manchester Guardian Weekly*, 3 December 1989, 25.

18. Ibid.

19. Geoff Mulgen, "Outside Establishment," *Marxism Today*, March 1990, 5.

20. Roger Scruton, "The Left Establishment," *The Salisbury Review*, December 1988, 36.

21. Quoted in Mulgen, "Outside Establishment," 4.

22. Ibid.

23. Scruton, "The Left Establishment," 36.

24. Quoted in Nightingale, "David Hare Captures His Muse," 24-25.

25. Quoted in Bloom, "A Kinder, Gentler David Hare," 33.

26. Quoted in Nightingale, "David Hare Captures His Muse," 25.

27. Tony Manwaring and Nick Sigler, eds., *Breaking the Nation* (London: Pluto Press, 1985), 77.

CHAPTER 11

1. Ascherson, *Games,* 92.

2. Robert Chesshyre, *The Return of the Native Reporter* (London: Viking, 1987), 25.

3. Ascherson, *Games*, 105.

4. Stuart Weir, "Talking Liberties," *New Statesman & Society*, 3 December 1993, 15.

5. Charter 88, "Charter 88," *New Statesman & Society*, 2 December 1988, 10-12.

6. Stuart Weir, "A Child of its Times," *New Statesman & Society*, 3 December 1993, 16.

7. Eddie Goncalves, "Make a Date with Democracy," *New Statesman & Society*, 22 June 1990, 31.

8. Weir, "A Child of Its Times," 17.

9. Anthony Barnett, "The E-Word," *New Statesman & Society*, 21 September 1990, 6.

10. Robert Maclennan, "Levers of Power," *New Statesman & Society*, 6 July 1990, 6.

11. Vibert, ed., *Britain's Constitutional Future*.

12. Weir, "A Child of its Times," 17.

13. Paul Johnson, *Wake Up Britain: A Latter-Day Pamphlet* (London: Weidenfeld and Nicolson, 1994); Benn and Hood, *Common Sense: A New Constitution for Britain.*

14. David Hare, Introduction to *Asking Around: Background to the David Hare Trilogy*, ed. Lyn Hall (London: Faber & Faber, 1993), 5.

15. Hollis, "Parliament and the Establishment," 182-183.

16. Weir, "A Child of It's Times," 17.

17. Anthony Barnett, "A Claim of Right for Britain," *New Statesman & Society*, 2 December 1988, 15.

18. Vibert, *Britain's Constitutional Future*, 15.

19. Heffernan and Marqusee, *Defeat from the Jaws of Victory*, 93-202.

20. Gamble, *The Free Economy and the Strong State*, 52.

21. Haseler, *The Battle for Britain*, 97.

22. L. A. Siedentop, "Viewpoint: The Strange Life of Liberal England," *Times Literary Supplement*, 16 August 1995, 900. All subsequent citations are from this source.

23. Nairn, *The Enchanted Glass*, 302.

24. Christopher Hitchins, "The People and the Monarchy," in *Power and the Throne*, 72.

25. Sue Townsend, "Do You Believe in Fairies?" in *Power and the Throne*, 84-85.

26. Billy Bragg, "England Made Me Too," in *Power and the Throne*, 138-139.

27. Caroline Ellis, "A Right Little Royalist," in *Power and the Throne*, 140.

28. Ibid., 141.

29. Ibid., 143.

30. Ibid., 144.

31. Hilary Wainwright, "Across to London," in *Power and the Throne*, 148.

32. Richard Holme, "Not in Front of the Children," *New Statesman & Society*, 9 December 1988, 12.

33. David Marquand, "Rule Britannia," *New Statesman & Society*, 22 June 1990, 10.

34. Rosalind Brunt, "Right Royal Opposition," *Marxism Today*, September 1988, 20-25.

35. Andrew Morton, "Prospects for the Family," in *Power and the Throne*, 108.

36. Quoted in Jolyon Jenkins, "Wrongs of a Bill of Rights," *New Statesman & Society,* 20 July 1990, 12.

37. Quoted in Ascherson, *Games*, 105-106.

38. Asherson, *Games*, 149.

39. Nairn, *The Enchanted Glass*, 9.

40. Ibid., 97.

41. Hare, *Asking Around*, 5.

42. Ibid., 7-8.

43. Ibid., 8.

44. David Hare, "Looking Foolish," in *Writing Left-Handed* (London: Faber & Faber, 1991), 45-46.

45. Ibid., 52.

46. Ibid., 54.

47. Ibid., 55.

48. Hare, *Asking Around*, 94.

49. David Hare, *Murmuring Judges* (London: Faber & Faber, 1991), 49. All subsequent citations are from this source.

50. James Fenton, "Who Are They to Judge the Prince," in *Power and the Throne*, 100.

51. David Hare, *Racing Demon* (London: Faber & Faber, 1990), 12. All subsequent citations are from this source.

52. David Hare, *The Absence of War* (London: Faber & Faber, 1993), 4. All subsequent citations are from this text.

53. Kenneth Leech, "Turbulent Priest," *Marxism Today*, February 1986, 13.

54. Haseler, *The Battle for Britain*, 129.

55. Ibid., 135.

56. See Anne Nothof, "Virtuous Women: Portraits of Goodness in *The Secret Rapture, Racing Demon,* and *Strapless,*" in Zeifman, *David Hare: A Casebook*, 194; Ann Wilson, "'Our Father': The Profession of Faith in *Racing Demon*," in ibid., 215.

57. Hare, *Asking Around*, 228.

58. Fay Weldon, "On Having a Queen and a State Religion Both," in *Power and the Throne*, 88.

CHAPTER 12

1. David Hare, *Heading Home* (with *Wetherby* and *Dreams of Leaving*) (London: Faber & Faber, 1991), 26. All subsequent citations are from this source.

2. Hare, Introduction to *Asking Around*, 7.

3. David Hare, *Skylight* (London: Faber & Faber, 1995), 22. All subsequent citations are from this source.

SELECT BIBLIOGRAPHY

PRIMARY WORKS BY DAVID HARE

Individual Plays and Films

The Absence of War. London: Faber & Faber, *1993.*
The Bay at Nice and Wrecked Eggs. London: Faber & Faber, 1986.
Dreams of Leaving. London: Faber & Faber, 1980.
Fanshen. London: Faber & Faber, 1976.
The Great Exhibition. Plays and Players, May 1972, 63-81.
How Brophy Made Good. Gambit, 17 (1971), 84-125.
Knuckle. London: Faber & Faber, 1974.
Licking Hitler. London: Faber & Faber, 1978.
A Map of the World. London: Faber & Faber, 1982.
Murmuring Judges. London: Faber & Faber, 1991.
Paris by Night. London: Faber & Faber, 1988.
Plenty. London: Faber & Faber, 1978.
Racing Demon. London: Faber & Faber, 1990.
Saigon: Year of the Cat. London: Faber & Faber, 1983.
The Secret Rapture. London: Faber & Faber, 1988.
Skylight. London: Faber & Faber, 1995.
Slag. London: Faber & Faber, 1971.
Strapless. London: Faber & Faber, 1989.
Teeth'n'Smiles. London: Faber & Faber, 1976.
Wetherby. London: Faber & Faber, 1985.

Collected Plays and Films

The Asian Plays. London: Faber & Faber, 1986. *Fanshen, Saigon: Year of the Cat, A Map of the World,* and an Introduction by the author.

The Early Plays. London: Faber & Faber, 1992. *Slag, The Great Exhibition, Teeth'n'Smiles*, with "A Lecture" by the author (originally published with *Licking Hitler* in 1978) presented as the Introduction.

Heading Home (with *Wetherby* and *Dreams of Leaving*). London: Faber & Faber, 1991.

The History Plays. London: Faber & Faber, 1984. *Knuckle, Licking Hitler, Plenty*, and an Introduction by the author.

Collaborations

Brassneck. Written with Howard Brenton. London, Methuen, 1974.

Lay By. Written with Howard Brenton, Brian Clark, Trevor Griffiths, Steven Poliakoff, Hugh Stoddard, and Snoo Wilson. *Plays and Players*, November 1971, 65-75, and as *Playscript 66*. London: Calder & Boyars, 1972.

Pravda: A Fleet Street Comedy. Written with Howard Brenton. London: Methuen, 1985.

BOOKS ON HISTORY, SOCIAL THEORY, AND THEATRE CRITICISM

Ansorge, Peter. *Disrupting the Spectacle*. London: Pitman, 1975.

Ascherson, Neal. *Games with Shadows*. London: Century Hutchison, 1988.

Barnett, Anthony, ed. *Power and the Throne*. London: Vintage, 1994.

Bennett, Tony, Graham Marin, Colin Mercer, and Janet Woollacott, eds. *Culture, Ideology and Social Process*. London: The Open University Press, 1981.

Bennett, Tony, Colin Mercer, and Janet Woollacott, eds. *Popular Culture and Social Relations*. Milton Keynes: Open University Press, 1986.

Bigsby, C.W.E., ed. *Contemporary English Drama*. London: Holmes & Meier, 1981.

Bock, Hedwig and Albert Wetheim, eds. *Essays on Contemporary British Drama*. Munich: Max Hueber Verlag, 1981.

Brown, Terry. *Playwright's Theatre: The English Stage Company at the Royal Court*. London Jonathan Cape, 1968

Bull, John. *New British Political Dramatists*. New York: Grove Press, 1983.

———. *Stage Right: Crisis and Recovery in British Contemporary Mainstream Theatre*. New York: St. Martin's Press, 1994.

Calder, Angus. *The People's War*. London: Jonathan Cape, 1969.

Chamber, Colin. *Other Spaces*. London: Methuen, 1980.

Chesshyre, Robert. *The Return of a Native Reporter*. London: Viking, 1987.

Coates, David, Gordon Johnston, and Ray Bush, eds. *A Socialist Anatomy of Britain*. London: Polity Press, 1985.

Corner, John and Sylvia Harvey, eds. *Enterprise and Heritage: Crosscurrents of National Culture*. London: Routledge, 1991.

Craig, Sandy, ed. *Dreams and Deconstructions*. Derbyshire: Amber Lane Press, 1980.

Curran, James and Jean Seaton. *Power without Responsibility*. Glasgow: Fontana Paperbacks, 1981.

debord, Guy. *Society of the Spectacle*. Detroit: Black and Red, 1983.

Eagleton, Terence. *Criticism and Ideology*. London: Verso, 1976.

Elsom, John, *Post-war British Theatre*. London: Routledge & Kegan Paul, 1976.

Elsom, John and Nicholas Tomalin. *The History of the National Theatre*. London: Cape, 1978.

Ewing, K. D. and C. A. Gearty. *Freedom Under Thatcher: Civil Liberties in Modern Britain*. Oxford: Clarendon Press, 1990.

Featherstone, Mike. *Global Culture: Nationalism, Globalization and Modernity*. London: Sage Publications, 1990.

Findlater, Richard, ed. *At the Royal Court: 25 Years of the English Stage Company*. Derbyshire: Amber Lane Press, 1981.

Friedman, Lester, ed. *Fires Were Started: British Cinema and Thatcherism*. Minneapolis: University. of Minnesota Press, 1993.

Gamble, Andrew. *Britain in Decline*. London: Redwood Burn, 1981.

———. *The Free Ecomony and the Strong State: The Politics of Thacherism*. Durham: Duke University Press, 1988.

Hall, Peter. *Diaries*. New York: Harper & Row, 1984.

Hall, Stuart. *The Hard Road to Renewal*. London: Verso, 1988.

Hall, Stuart and Martin Jacques, eds. *New Times: The Changing Face of Politics in the 1990s*. London: Lawrence & Wishart, 1989.

Harrington, William and Peter Young. *The 1945 Revolution*. London: Davis-Poynter, 1978.

Haseler, Stephen. *The Battle for Britain: Thatcher and the New Liberals*. London: I. B. Tauris, 1989.

Heffernan, Richard and Mike Marqusee. *Defeat from the Jaws of Victory: Inside Kinnock's Labour Party*. London: Verso, 1992.

Hewison, Robert. *In Anger: Culture in the Cold War 1945-60*. London: Weidenfeld & Nicolson. 1981.

Hoggart, Richard. *The Uses of Literacy*. London: Chatto & Windus, 1957.

Kavanagh, Dennis. *Thatcherism and British Politics: The End of Consensus?* Oxford: Oxford University Press, 1987.

Kureishi, Hanif. *London Kills Me: Three Screenplays and Four Essays*. London: Penguin Books, 1992.

Mander, John. *The Writer and Commitment*. London: Secker & Warburg, 1961.

Marwick, Arthur. *British Society Since 1945*. London: Penguin, 1982.

———. *Culture in Britain since 1945*. Oxford: Blackwell, 1991.

Maschler, Tom. *Declaration*. London: MacGibbon & Kee, 1957.

McGrath, John. *A Good Night Out*. London: Methuen, 1981.

Nairn, Tom. *The Break-up of Britain*. London: NLB, 1977.

———. *The Enchanted Glass: Britain and Its Monarchy*. London: Hutchinson Radius, 1988.

Riddell, Peter. *The Thatcher Government*. Oxford: Basil Blackwell, 1985.

Samuel, Raphael, ed. *Patriotism: The Making and Unmaking of British National Identity*. Volume Three: *National Fictions*. New York: Routledge, 1989.

Scruton, Roger. *The Meaning of Conservatism*, 2nd ed. London: Macmillan, 1984.

Sinfield, Alan. *Literature, Politics, and Culture in Postwar Britain*. Los Angeles: University of California Press, 1989.

Sissons, Michael and Philip French, eds. *Age of Austerity 1945-1951*. London: Hodder and Stoughton, 1963.

Thatcher, Margaret. *The Downing Street Years*. New York: HarperCollins, 1993.

Thomas, Hugh, ed. *The Establishment*. London: Anthony Blond, 1959.

Thornton, Peter. *Decade of Decline: Civil Liberties in the Thatcher Years.* London: National Council for Civil Liberties, 1989.

Trussler, Simon, ed. *New Theatre Voices of the Seventies.* London: Methuen, 1981.

Widgery, David. *The Left in Britain 1956-68.* Middlesex: Penguin Books, 1976.

Wiener, Martin J. *English Culture and the Decline of the Industrial Spirit 1850-1980.* New York: Cambridge University Press, 1981.

Williams, Raymond. *Culture and Society 1780-1950.* New York: Columbia University Press, 1958.

——————————. *Politics and Letters.* London: *New Left Review,* 1979.

Wright, Patrick. *On Living in an Old Country: The National Past in Contemporary Britain.* London: Verso, 1985.

Zeifman, Hersh, ed. *David Hare: A Casebook.* New York: Garland, 1994.

INDEX

About the Author

FINLAY DONESKY is Assistant Professor of English at the University of Kentucky. He has published articles on contemporary British and American drama.

ISBN 0-313-29734-7

EAN

9 780313 297342

90000>

HARDCOVER BAR CODE

DATE DUE

GAYLORD   PRINTED IN U.S.A.